THE
TALES OF TRIUMPH & DISASTER
CAPE HORNERS' CLUB
AT THE WORLD'S MOST FEARED CAPE

ADLARD COLES NAUTICAL

B L O O M S B U R Y
LONDON · OXFORD · NEW YORK · NEW DELHI · SYDNEY

Adlard Coles Nautical
An imprint of Bloomsbury Publishing Plc

50 Bedford Square
London
WC1B 3DP
UK

1385 Broadway
New York
NY 10018
USA

www.bloomsbury.com
www.adlardcoles.com

ADLARD COLES, ADLARD COLES NAUTICAL and the Buoy logo are
trademarks of Bloomsbury Publishing Plc

First published 2017

British Library Cataloguing-in-Publication Data
A catalogue record for this book is available from the British Library.

Library of Congress Cataloguing-in-Publication data has been applied for.

ISBN: HB: 978-1-4729-1252-7
ePDF: 978-1-4729-1254-1
ePub: 978-1-4729-1253-4

2 4 6 8 10 9 7 5 3 1

Typeset in Berling LT Std by Deanta Global Publishing Services, Chennai, India
Printed and bound in Great Britain by CPI Group (UK) Ltd, Croydon CR0 4YY

To find out more about our authors and books visit www.bloomsbury.com.
Here you will find extracts, author interviews, details of forthcoming events and
the option to sign up for our newsletters.

CONTENTS

Rounding The Horn
(From *Dauber*)

Then came the cry of 'Call all hands on deck!'
The Dauber knew its meaning; it was come:
Cape Horn, that tramples beauty into wreck,
And crumples steel and smites the strong man dumb.
Down clattered flying kites and staysails; some
Sang out in quick, high calls: the fair-leads skirled,
And from the south-west came the end of the world.
John Masefield (1878–1967)

It is there, fragile and yet mighty, as ambivalent as all the objects of our dreams, delicate in the lacy clouds crowning its summit, solid in its massive virility among the waves. It is there, the hotly contested prize in a battle of Titans between the sea and the rock, craggy as though hewn by strokes of some unimaginable axe, furrowed by wrinkles, striped by crevasses.
Alain Colas (1943–1978)

Cape Horn stands sentinel to the most feared seaway in the world

AUTHOR'S NOTE

I based the selection of individual sailors' stories and experiences at Cape Horn on some loose criteria of my own devising, centred on variety of endeavour, of personality, of vessel, of chronology and of precedent – had they achieved some wider acclaim of which rounding Cape Horn formed a part? That is not to say that those selected ticked every box, nor does it mean that those omitted – there is a fuller list of non-racing singlehanded Cape Horners given in the Appendix – are not equally varied and interesting. They undoubtedly are, but to include more than 20 entries would have necessitated too much of a compromise on detail or rendered the book too weighty a tome. Inclusion does not infer any kind of seniority in terms of achievement or status. Indeed, history has largely forgotten some, while others, not included, enjoy world renown.

The publisher persuaded me to include my own story as reassurance to readers that I had actually been to Cape Horn and sailed the hard (nautical) miles and so confer at least a degree of authenticity when writing about others who had embarked on similar adventures. I reluctantly acquiesced – reluctant because it meant deselecting another previously included sailor, and so, to him, I apologise.

On another note (and the reason why the word *nautical* above is in parentheses), distances at sea are given in miles – by which I mean nautical miles, but for readability I have omitted the qualifier *nautical*. In the interest of clarity, however, 1 nautical mile is equivalent to 1.15 statute or land miles and 1.85 kilometres.

CAPE HORN

ape Horn, the coccyx at the base of the Andean spine, stands at longitude 67°17'21" west, latitude 55°58'48" south. A forbidding buttress of naked, black rock, it rises 424 metres (1,391 feet) above the sea at the southern tip of *Isla Hornos* or Horn Island, the southernmost of the Hermite Islands, which cluster at the southern end of the Tierra del Fuego archipelago. It is just about as southerly as one can go on any continental landmass without actually setting foot in Antarctica.

Cape Horn is a gateway, both literally and symbolically, forming the northern boundary of the 800-kilometre-wide (500-mile-wide) Drake Passage that separates South America from the Antarctic Peninsula. It is the

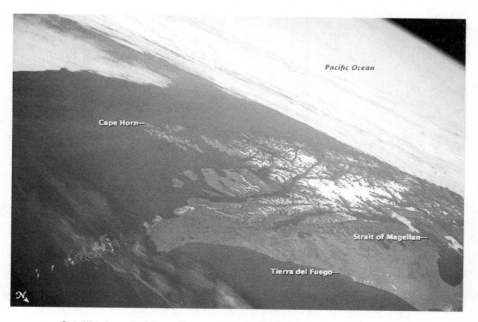

Satellite image of Cape Horn and the Drake Passage seen from the east

only choke point in the Southern Ocean where winds, waves and currents – unfettered for thousands of miles – are impeded and, like wild animals cornered and trapped, become frenzied in their zeal to regain freedom.

There is no land to the west, none to the east, all the way around the world. This is a savage place. The Southern Ocean rolls ceaselessly around the planet goaded by westerly winds that, without land to decay them, regularly build to hurricane strength. The 3,220-kilometre-wide (2,000-mile-wide) ocean piles through the narrow gap of the Drake Passage, sucking water in from the Pacific side and spilling out on the Atlantic one. Currents rip around the headlands. The sea maddens. Winds funnelled by the high mountains of the Andes and the Antarctic Peninsula collide over the water. On the South American side of the passage, depths are relatively shallow. The seabed on the Antarctic side is more than 9.6 kilometres (6 miles) deep. This dramatically sloping bed has the effect of spinning the water channelling through, adding to turbulence.

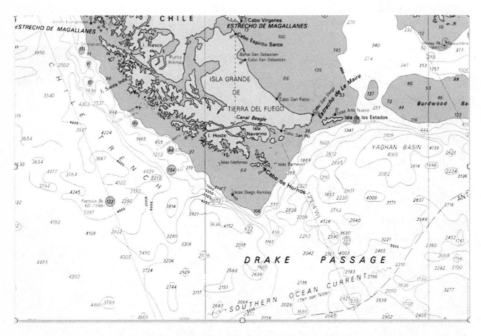

Cape Horn lies at the southern extreme of the South American continent

In round numbers, the surface of the earth extends to 317 million square kilometres (197 million square miles). Of this, 71 per cent – or 225 million square kilometres (140 million square miles) – is water. Amid this vast area, the relatively tiny stretch around Cape Horn has earned the reputation as the most treacherous of all the seaways.

For mariners, Cape Horn was once a necessary trial, lying as it does on the shortest and therefore most profitable commercial shipping route between Europe and the Far East. For yachtsmen, though, Cape Horn represents the ultimate challenge. Storm-lashed for 300 days of the year, it is a place of unremitting fury, a place that tests seamanship in the hardest school of all. Thus has it been ever since the supercontinent of Pangaea broke up some 200 million years ago – long before men took to the water in boats.

Then, when the earth's landmass was a single block surrounded by a gigantic sea, what is now Antarctica was tucked up on the south-east side of Africa, butting up against modern-day Mozambique. The South American continent cuddled Africa's western seaboard, its eastward-curving southern

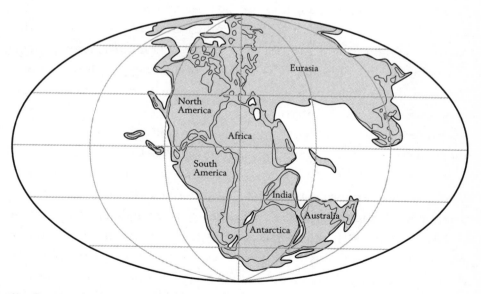

How Pangaea might have looked some 200 million years ago, before it started to break apart

tip – Tierra del Fuego – caressing Africa's southern flank and extending sufficiently far to overlap with Antarctica's westward-jutting peninsula. Today, that peninsula is called Grahamland, named after Sir James Graham, First Lord of the Admiralty, by the English explorer John Briscoe, at the time of his Antarctic expedition in 1832.

As the earth's guts convulsed, spewing magma and ash, its crust fractured. Tectonic plates shuddered and slid, tearing and grinding, ripping the land apart, dividing the one sea into a series of smaller oceans. Despite this, even as they travelled thousands of miles over millennia, the South American and Antarctic landmasses maintained their clinging, desperate union, until their touching fingers were finally prised apart to be separated by a mere 800 kilometres (500 miles). Today, that gap is filled with the ever-shifting waters of the Southern Ocean and named after the foppish, ginger-haired Elizabethan buccaneer, Sir Francis Drake, who found it. Here, between the reaching tips of two continents, geography has conspired to create interminable fury as if in retribution for the separation of erstwhile lovers.

Air, made frigid by the Antarctic ice sheet, spills outwards from the South Pole to engage with warmer, moisture-laden equatorial air. As they collide – the cold, denser air falling and the warm, tropical air rising – the earth's eastward spin flips them into clockwise-rotating depressions, setting a train of destructive force marauding westwards, driving the relentless westward march of the Southern Ocean below. And nowhere on the track of these depressions is there any interruption by energy-sapping land. It is, in short, a hurricane factory dumping its product onto a conveyor belt that launches them on their trajectory around the base of the planet.

Whipped by the winds, the sea's surface absorbs colossal quantities of kinetic energy, expressing its presence in wave formation. Without the rude imposition of land to get in their way, these waves build into mountainous seas. However, all of this, to a degree, is mitigated by the width of the Southern Ocean; the energies of wind and wave can dissipate northwards into the South Pacific, the South Atlantic and the Indian Oceans – everywhere, that is, except at the Drake Passage. Here sits Cape Horn, smack in the storm track. There is nowhere to run – neither for the wind, nor for the waves – and nowhere to hide – not for anyone on a boat.

Only New Zealand's South Island, Tasmania and a scattering of islands (the Falklands among them) lie south of the 40th parallel, but all of these are way to the north relative to Cape Horn and the Drake Passage. As the westward-migrating mass of the Southern Ocean hits this roadblock, it fuels the northward-running Humboldt Current racing up Chile's eastern seaboard. Water driven through the Drake Passage creates the treacherous Cape Horn Current, which close inshore can run at speeds sufficient to overpower the engines of most small craft. For any engineless vessel struggling under shredded sails or worse, getting caught in the Cape Horn Current is tantamount to a death ride.

All the ingredients required for a recipe for disaster are gathered in this place: the short, choppy seas generated by the shoaling effects of the continental shelves; the bitter cold; icebergs calved from the Antarctic ice sheet; the dense air, which packs a much greater punch than the warmer, lighter air found further north; and the heaving, mountainous seas that regularly spawn monstrous rogue waves.

That these are treacherous conditions has been acknowledged time and again by sea-goers. For instance, Jean-Michel Barrault – a naval writer, circumnavigator and journalist born in 1927 in Nantes – wrote in the foreword of *The Logical Route*, a book by his friend the legendary French sailor Bernard Moitessier (logical because the quickest way back from Tahiti to France was via Cape Horn): 'There isn't a sailor who doesn't shudder at the thought of Cape Horn.'

So the question is: why would anyone wish to go there, least of all in a boat? The answer is they don't, not any more, bar a few hardy or perhaps foolhardy souls. Cape Horn stands as a mighty challenge to those who venture to sea by sail, a silent beckoning against which to test their seamanship, their courage and their spirit. Perhaps these adventurers see a contest against the elements as a means to plumb the hidden depths of their characters or to attempt to exorcise their demons or, worse, to win bragging rights.

In 1936, Captain Warwick M Tompkins sailed his 85-foot schooner, *Wander Bird*, with a crew of 10, including his wife and two children, from Gloucester, Massachusetts to San Francisco. The track of the *Wander Bird* took her westwards around Cape Horn, and of that challenge, he wrote:

> A man who loves the sea and ships can aspire to no more searching
> test than a Horn passage. It is the last word in the lexicon of sailormen.
> There nature has arranged trials and tribulations so ingeniously that in
> the van of all synonyms for sea cruelty and hardship is the ironbound
> name of Cape Horn. Winds blow elsewhere at times as strongly as they
> do south of fifty. Seas elsewhere may pyramid as high, break as heavily.
> There may be places equally remote and as bleakly lonely. Currents
> in other regions may be as adverse. These foes the sailorman may
> encounter separately or in pairs here and there, aye, encounter and best,
> but always in his heart he will wonder if he could face all combined. If
> he glories in the unequal contest of human muscles and artifices with
> the ocean, if the sea shouts an insistent challenge, he can never be truly
> content until he has voyaged from Fifty South in the Atlantic to Fifty
> South in the Pacific in his own command. This is the ultimate test, given
> to very few to know.

Captain Tompkins was alluding here to the commonly accepted definition of a true rounding of Cape Horn, passing from a latitude of 50° south in one ocean to 50° south in the other, leaving Horn Island itself to the north.

No one comes to Cape Horn in a small boat without trepidation in their hearts because they know that here, at the edge of the world, they face the greatest risk. If they have vulnerabilities – and everybody does – Cape Horn will find them and crack them open. If the boats in which sailors place their faith and hope have a weakness, Cape Horn will expose it. And if a mariner can pass through the Cape Horn region unmolested, whether by dint of good fortune, clever tactics or advance information, then he or she will breathe the greatest sigh of relief of their life.

ADRIAN FLANAGAN

'If you are afraid to do something, then you must do it or remain forever afraid.'

Born .... 1 October 1960
Nationality .... British
Date of Cape Horn rounding .... February 2006
Boat name .... *Barrabas*
Designer .... François Charpentier
Year of build 1991
LOA .... 38 feet
Material .... Stainless steel
Rig .... Cutter

My first encounter with Cape Horn occurred via words when, as a 15-year-old schoolboy, I read Sir Francis Chichester's account of his 1966–1967 round-the-world voyage. The legend of Cape Horn has beguiled me ever since. Years later, in February 2006, I found myself at its threshold.

My rugged boat – *Barrabas*, a 38-foot cutter – had been built by a Frenchman, Bernard de Castro, a former special forces soldier who had fought in the Algerian war before going to work for the state-owned French stainless steel fabricator Ugine as a master welder. He had lovingly constructed *Barrabas* by hand over a six-year period, acquiring the titanium-enriched

Barrabas

316L stainless steel for the boat at cost. I wanted to attempt a singlehanded circumnavigation following a 'vertical' route westwards around Cape Horn and the Russian Arctic – a route that no one had tried before, perhaps for good reason – and being both beautifully engineered and immensely strong, *Barrabas* had all the design characteristics I was looking for: flush decks, low coach-house profile, deep fin keel, skeg-hung rudder, solar- and wind-power generation, centre cockpit, and that indefinable quality that instils confidence.

Barrabas and I set sail from Southampton on 28 October 2005, with my ex-wife Louise working as expedition manager. By 5 February 2006, Staten Island (*Isla de los Estardos*) was just 119 kilometres (74 miles) south of my position. Past the island, the Cape Horn current ripped along, sometimes reaching 9 knots close inshore. Only by venturing deep into the Southern Ocean could we avoid it and create a better angle to climb north towards the Pacific. Winds to storm force 10 were imminent and forecast to last for three days. I decided to wait, protected by the continental landmass.

The vicious low cell tore through Cape Horn on Sunday 12 February while I held station, so, in order to ascertain the predicted future conditions, I ordered up a five-day GRIB weather file of the Cape Horn area. This GRIB file (GRIdded information in Binary) is a computer-generated forecast released for general use by the US National Weather Service, among others. GRIB data for anywhere in the world is collected remotely by weather balloons, marine weather buoys and satellites, and is then fed into the US GFS (General Forecast System), a computerised modelling program, where it is compressed into files of only a few kilobytes that can be downloaded as an email. For me, these short-term forecasts – up to 36 hours ahead – have always proved unerringly accurate and, together with GPS, this more recent technology gives latter-day sailors a huge advantage over those earlier pioneers who relied instead on a sextant and interpretation of cloud patterns. In short, I had the advantage of approaching Cape Horn with my eyes open. Many of those who had gone before went in blind.

I studied the data, then went on deck to make checks before committing *Barrabas* and myself to this most perilous stretch of water – running rigging, standing rigging, cuddy, emergency tiller, guardrail wire tension, liferaft, dinghy lashings, hatch storm covers. Other than the fact that the Hydrovane self-steering unit was vibrating – the bolts securing the gear to the transom needed tightening – all other checks were clear.

In the murky twilight, I saw the distant lights of a ship. Was it a fishing boat or a cruise liner? The relative safety of a larger vessel compared with my small yacht seemed to compound my vulnerability and, with that, my tension ratcheted up a notch at the prospect of facing Cape Horn alone.

As if to allay these fears, Louise forwarded a message from Bernard De Castro: '*Je suivais la route de Adrian jour après jour, le Cap Horne n'est pas loin! Je lui souhaite courage et determination pour la suite.*' ('I've followed Adrian's route day by day, Cape Horn is not far away! I wish him courage and determination for what lies ahead.')

It was time to go. We sailed south-east in the early morning of St Valentine's Day, on a course to clear the dangerous overfalls east of Staten Island. The sky changed quickly from light, broken cloud to a purple darkness. The log showed speed through the water of 6.2 knots. The GPS displayed speed over the ground of 3.4 knots. The Cape Horn current was running at 2.8 knots.

By 7pm, we were south of Staten Island and I was able to pick out Vancouver peak. The wind came round to the north-west. Close-hauled, *Barrabas* was on a good heading, south-west. The latest weather data, which I'd downloaded at 4pm, indicated the north-west winds holding – the perfect wind to get me to the Diego Ramírez Islands.

The wind shifted to the west during the night. I hove-to and monitored our drift. Too fast! We were moving east at 2 knots, borne along on the current that drives the Southern Ocean ever eastwards. I gybed *Barrabas* and headed south. Through the night of 15 February, the winds veered north as I slept for a few hours. I woke, sensing a difference in the attitude of the boat. Something about her motion through the water generated an excitement in me. I stumbled from my bunk and peered at the GPS. I could scarcely believe the figures on the small screen: COG 2-6-0 (Course Over Ground 260°). Perfect! Our course was now just south of west, putting us on a line directly towards the Diego Ramírez Islands.

The Cape spat squalls at me, letting me know that she could defeat me at any time, sapping my strength but, more than that, keeping me keyed up and anxious, pinning me down at the base of a psychological mountain I had to try to climb. I trimmed and re-trimmed the rig for three hours – shaking out reefs, putting in reefs and altering the sail combinations to squeeze every yard of speed out of the elements while I was still making a favourable course. If this wind did not hold, I faced the prospect of being beaten back, unable to match the onslaught of wind and current from the west.

I thought and re-thought our strategy. Stay high or go south? Meet the blows forecast for the next 24 hours or dodge them by heading south but waste valuable time? For the moment, though, we were heading west and eating up the miles.

At 9pm, a squall front came over. The north winds disappeared, replaced with headwinds from the south-west. I hove-to, drifting north and east at 3 knots. Was this a permanent wind change or a temporary situation? My euphoria morphed into despair as the precious westing slipped away.

Two hours later, another squall passed over, flipping the winds back over to the north-east. We were sailing again, due west! I tended *Barrabas* constantly, steering either side of due west to wring out every yard – it was grinding work. Every yard westward was like a small nugget of gold in the pan.

I set *Barrabas* to a close-haul with the headsail deep-reefed but the mainsail full to keep her bows pointing up on my preferred course just south of due west. As night settled in, the solitary rock of Cape Horn Island lay 80 kilometres (50 miles) north-west. I did not want to risk being caught over-canvassed in the dark so I reefed down and then went to my bunk. Sleep came easily. When I woke at 1am, we were sailing south-east on 142°. The wind had backed through the hours of darkness. I raced on deck, gybed the boat, set full sail and eased the boom wide. We were running downwind around the Horn!

I sat at the chart table. In the three days since coming round Staten Island we had sailed close-hauled, reached with the wind abeam, and run with the wind behind. On Saturday 18 February, I wrote in the log: 'The only scenario left to complete the set is a real blow...'

I would not have long to wait. To the west, a Cape Horn storm gathered its strength.

Low grey cloud, pregnant with rain, blocked us to the west. *Barrabas* was delicately poised; a soft wind from the east was pushing her gently towards the Pacific. The grey cloud, incongruous among its fluffy white neighbours, was coming towards us, propelled by an opposing wind at higher altitude. Suddenly, the air exploded. The wind-speed indicator cycled through numbers, 42 knots, 45 knots, 50 knots, 55, 58, 60, 62. I started the drill to reduce sail, hair whipping around my face. Just then, the mainsail halyard shackle failed. It was a stupid error on my part – I had not checked the shackle to make sure the pin was tight. Untethered, the sail thrashed wildly. I tore at the sailcloth, pulling it down onto the boom. The halyard had dropped down inside the mast, only stopping at the masthead because of the knot in its end.

I furled the headsail. *Barrabas* settled beam-on to the seas. I wanted to minimise drift eastwards and get some mainsail up so *Barrabas* would not be vulnerable lying a'hull. The pendulum motion of the boat was too great to climb the mast and retrieve the halyard, so I decided on a makeshift rig. I fetched a block, grabbed a spare halyard and with one end clamped between my teeth, climbed the mast steps to the level of the lower spreaders, about halfway up. *Barrabas* bucked wildly – with no mainsail up she was unstable. Wrapping one leg around the mast to hold myself, I shackled the block to a mast step, ran the halyard through the block and climbed back down to the deck. Although I'd only been aloft for a short time, the effort was akin to riding a wild horse. I felt physically drained. Quickly, I tied the halyard to the head of the mainsail then hoisted. *Barrabas* immediately settled.

The wind had shifted. It was now screaming out of the west. What were my options? Gybe and go north? Not enough sea room. Run before the storm going east towards the Atlantic and lose ground? Never. West, straight into wind, was impossible. I had to go south.

The storm raged all day and into the evening. The seas had now built to 7.5 metres (25 feet). I knew that a breaking wave half that height could easily roll *Barrabas* over if she were caught flush on her side. I set the Hydrovane self-steering and lashed the wheel hard over to windward to create an angle of attack to the oncoming waves and avoid lethal direct beam-on wave strikes.

It was then that the head blocked, regurgitating effluent into the bilges. The manual bilge pump was out of action. The outlet for the electric pumps on the port side was underwater with the heel of the boat. I stood braced below decks, clinging to the companionway. 'Great,' I thought. 'I'm in a bloody washing machine with four gallons of sewage!' I could hear the sizzling rush of breaking water, then the massive impacts of the strikes. Each time, the boat stopped dead, her rigging shaking, bulkheads groaning.

I pulled open the hatch and took two steps up the companionway, poking my head and shoulders into the maelstrom, steadying myself against the extreme heel of the boat. The storm boiled around us. Long, breaking crests raked the ocean, leaving great flattened swathes of white in their wake. The next moment, an ominous sizzling sound came from behind me, menacingly low at first, then amplifying quickly to low thunder. I spun around. Too late! All I could see was a wall of white, crushed water. The wave roared over the deck. *Barrabas* heeled, and then kept going, further and further with a heart-stopping momentum. My chest compressed against the side of the companionway hatch as *Barrabas* went over. All was still. The mast lay along the surface of the sea, the half-exposed hull acting as a windbreak. *Barrabas* was suspended sideways on the ocean, whipped by wind and spray. The instrument panel above the chart table on the ship's port side had become the new floor directly beneath my feet. Icy water cascaded off my shoulders, around my waist and between my legs, and poured onto the panel. I looked down in horror, trying desperately to block the flood of water with my body, already hearing the sizzle and pop of electrical circuits shorting out.

Barrabas's keel, filled with 4 tons of ballast, pulled her slowly upright. The wind caught the sail, smacking it taut, and creamed water gushed from her deck, running through the scuppers like a hundred open taps.

I ducked below and slammed shut the companionway hatch. The seawater inside – I estimated about 90 litres (20 gallons) – had mixed with spilled sewage and was sloshing over the cabin floor. Acrid white fumes from an electrical fire began spilling from the locker beneath the chart table. I used a cloth to douse the flames. The storm was building. I hadn't slept for 20 hours but sleep was impossible – I was too on edge, too scared.

Every bone-jarring impact seemed to sound the boat's death knell, but she kept going, kept fighting.

It was the evening of Saturday 18 February. Sunday was another country. The latest forecasts indicated conditions continuing like this for another 24 hours at least. As we sailed southwards, drifting ice became a looming danger.

Through the long, dark night I braced myself below decks, regularly going on deck to check the Hydrovane, making adjustments, seeing only blackness streaked with the dull grey spume of broken waves all around. The noise was deafening. The rolling seas groaned a deep bass. The wind shrieked a high-pitched whine. This was the sound of fury and it terrified me. Even with minimal sail, *Barrabas* heeled so far over that her port-side deck skimmed beneath the surface.

The seas continued to pummel *Barrabas*, hurling more big hits against her starboard bow. Like a sparring boxer, she ducked and weaved, presenting her side obliquely to draw power from the waves.

At dawn on Sunday, I spent hours pumping the bilges by hand – a mixture of oil, diesel, seawater and sewage. The spill had turned the cabin sole into an ice rink. In the pitching seas, every movement needed planning. The consequence of a slip or fall – a broken leg or worse – would be that my chances of getting through this would evaporate. As I pumped, I talked aloud, hour after hour, to ease the anxiety chasing around my guts like some mad, cornered animal.

With the bilges finally clear, I went on deck and clipped my lifeline to a strongpoint in the cockpit. While the wind and the spume flogged my face, I visually checked the rig, the Hydrovane, the lashing on the wheel and the liferaft. If the worst happened, I was out of rescue range. Which breaking wave might be my executioner? I felt like a man on the gallows.

When the realisation came that I was afraid of fear itself, it was startling in its clarity. I began to laugh. Maybe fear had loosened my grip on sanity. Or maybe my fear, like smoke in the wind, had been shredded and was gone. I went below, grinning like an idiot, and to my eternal surprise found I was actually enjoying the experience.

By late evening, barometric pressure began slowly creeping up. The wind still tore through the rigging, but without the intensity of earlier, as though the heart had gone from nature's fight. Even from below deck, I sensed the depletion.

Barrabas had managed to stay west of south, but only by the narrowest margin. Now, with the air pressure rising, the wind began to back from north-west to west, forcing our course off to 180°, due south and then progressively to east of south.

Wind-churned water found *Barrabas's* every weakness to penetrate the inside. Everything was wet – my bunk, my sleeping bag, my clothes – and, once wet, they stayed wet. I glanced at the glass. Barometric pressure was slowly creeping up: 1003, 1004, 1005 … 1008. The storm was dying over my small patch of sky.

Finally, at 11.30pm, I gybed round, bringing the wind over the port side, setting *Barrabas* as close to the wind as she could go. The storm had forced us 320 kilometres (200 miles) south, deep into the iceberg zone. We needed to get back north but our heading had to be the right side of north: west not east. The compass began to slide towards north – 350°, 351°. My eyes were riveted to the display: 352°, 353°. I could barely breathe. 'Please hold! Don't go any more! Stay west!' I murmured like a mantra, over and over.

The GPS compass heading stopped its slide at 354°, 6° west of north. Quite unbelievably, the instruments at the chart table were all functioning normally after their dousing with seawater during the knockdown. I stayed watching the compass and periodically checked topside until 3am on Monday 20 February. With little more to do but wait for the winds to back round more and improve our heading, I collapsed, fully clothed, into my damp sleeping bag, giddy with fatigue. I had gone without sleep for 50 hours.

At daybreak, with the storm spent, I stood on deck in the cold early light. To take advantage of the favourable weather window that had emerged in the night, *Barrabas* needed to fly full sail to make north-west and out of the path of the storm-stuffed low-pressure systems flooding in from the west. To do that, I had to go to the mast-top to retrieve the halyard. The wind was gusting to 30 knots. The sea was running with a 6-metre (20-foot) swell, the aftermath of the storm. As I stood on the pitching deck and watched the horrific pendulum motion of the mast, I realised I had another mountain to climb.

Although not particularly high as masts go, it seemed to tower above me to an impossible height. It was a psychological game. Just climb, I told myself, don't look down, don't think about the movement of the ship, just hold on, don't consider the consequences of a fall. I breathed deeply then heaved myself up, a ½ metre (1½ feet) with each step.

The physical effort of just holding on was exhausting, and the higher I climbed, the greater became the arc of the mast's swing. I was wearing half-fingered gloves, and my fingertips became numb with cold. Reaching the mast-top, I grabbed the knotted end of the halyard, clamped it between my teeth, then clung to the mast with both arms. Briefly, I surveyed the scene – an endless grey sea peppered with white, desolate and forbidding. Bruised and drenched in sweat, I clambered down and stepped back onto the deck. My knees buckled and I fell forwards among the rigging, feeling the reassuring strength of *Barrabas* waiting patiently for me to get up.

> Log: Monday 20 February 2006, 7.40am local time (1140 UTC). 57.05 south, 66.13 west, COG 344, SOG 3.2, Wind W 18, BP 1014. *Barrabas* has been utterly magnificent. She has taken the punishment. Time and again she has been dealt keel-shuddering blows. Most times they stop her dead in her tracks. But she brings her bow round and surges on. She is so brave, so courageous. She has spared nothing to keep me safe. I weep in gratitude to her as I write this. I could not have asked more of her. She has the heart of a lioness.

Through the day, the wind continued to lighten and the glass kept rising. At long, long last, *Barrabas* was flying. At 5.53pm, she crossed westwards over the longitude of Cape Horn. We were on the Pacific side. My overriding emotion was relief that we had come this far.

At dawn the following day, I sighted the Diego Ramírez Islands – black, jagged teeth in the steely maw of the ocean.

A high-pressure system had settled over Cape Horn, blocking the depressions to the west. By evening, the winds were in the east. *Barrabas* sped along at 7 knots, her boom splayed out on one side, her headsail poled out on the other. We sailed on over the following two days, the air temperature becoming noticeably warmer, my breath no longer clouding and my feet feeling less like blocks of ice. For now, Cape Horn smiled beneath blue skies. Albatrosses wheeled in fanciful free flight. On my northern horizon, sun-polished ice peaks towered heavenwards and the sea was a mauve cushion laced with white. It was a scene of staggering beauty.

I had personified some of the gear on board and the strongest character to emerge, essentially a helmsman who did not need food or sleep, was Harry (the Hydrovane). I spoke to him whenever I was on deck and occasionally yelled up from below, 'What the hell are you doing, Harry!', 'Well done, Harry!' Standing on deck, drinking in the scene, feeling the relief of this respite flooding my body and re-energising my mind, I heaped praise on Harry. The Hydrovane had held *Barrabas* to her course, all 15 tons of her, through the storm.

At first light on Saturday 25 February, *Barrabas* began turning into the wind for no reason that I could make out. I shortened the main to second reef but *Barrabas* was still turning into the wind, the sails flogging as they depowered. I put in a third reef, then a fourth, occasionally muttering under my breath at Harry for being so bloody lazy. Still *Barrabas* turned her bows into the wind.

I went to check on Harry and noticed that small changes in the attitude of the windvane were not transmitting any corresponding minor corrections to the rudder. Stepping down onto the sugar scoop among 80 litres (18 gallons) of fuel stowed in four 20-litre (4.4-gallon) cans secured within steel cages was awkward. I inspected the Hydrovane. The screw linking the vane to the pendulum that moved the rudder shaft had sheared, effectively disengaging the vane from the rudder. I apologised profusely to Harry. The boat was coming up head-to-wind because the lashed wheel had no counter-steer from the Hydrovane. I breathed a great sigh of relief. Had that pin failed during the storm, at night – making it more difficult and treacherous to replace – *Barrabas* would have been in very serious trouble. I freed the wheel so *Barrabas* could hold course on her own through the balance of the sails.

With a 9-metre (30-foot) swell and 30-knot winds, I tried to get the sheared bolt out, but it was jammed in tight. I removed the linkage piece, took it below, clamped it in the vice and drilled out the bolt. Then I put the whole thing back together with a new screw. With Harry once more operational, I shook out the reefs to get more boat speed, set Harry and re-lashed the wheel. I stayed on deck for the next 30 minutes just to ensure that we held course.

I charted our position – 450 kilometres (279 miles) south of the 50th parallel. I rewarded myself with a hot-water footbath in the cockpit. Meanwhile, my socks were drying out in the oven – baking on low heat. That worked very well and raised my morale for the rest of the day.

Cape Horn was never going to let me past without spitting in my eye, and spat she had, with ferocity and with venom, challenging *Barrabas* and me to the very limits of our endurance. Then she gave us a reprieve and showed us her kinder face, a face of startling beauty. At 3.18am local time on Tuesday 28 February (0918 UTC) *Barrabas* breached latitude 50° south in the Pacific Ocean. We had officially rounded Cape Horn westabout.

I came to Cape Horn with hope and fear. Now I was leaving exhilarated, with memories that would endure for my lifetime.

We completed our voyage in stages, arriving back in Southampton on 21 May 2008.

I bought a gold earring for *Barrabas*, her badge as a Cape Horner, as a tribute and a thank you. It is hidden somewhere on the boat, on her starboard side, the side facing Cape Horn as she sailed past.

My voyage was an attempt at a circumnavigation, but in many ways it became distilled and to an extent focused on Cape Horn. Why? A major factor was the fearsome reputation of the Cape Horn region. Riding that obstacle, that psychological hurdle became so immense that, once I was past it, the future seemed set on a downhill incline. It all seemed somehow easier even though, in the end, I was thwarted by the Arctic ice pack.

There is no doubt in my mind that getting past Cape Horn changed my attitude – to sailing, to danger, to threat, to life in general. My overriding feeling heading north-west into the wild reaches of the Pacific Ocean was one of relief and gratitude – relief at surviving and gratitude for the experience of that. I was also conscious of the very great advantages I had compared with earlier venturers – satellite communications, advanced weather forecasting, GPS, and the emergency position indicating radio beacon (EPIRB) in case the worst happened. My admiration and respect for those who had gone before without these psychological handrails escalated to new highs.

I was also fortunate in another respect: that I was not, in the end, alone. *Barrabas* was as a person to me – living and breathing, with a distinct personality and possessing all the charms, foibles, conundrums, contradictions,

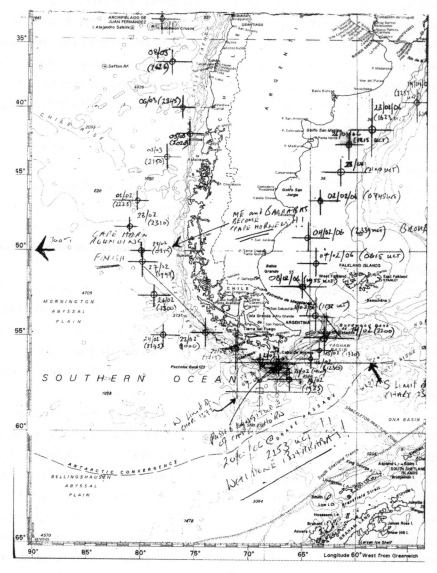

Route of *Barrabas* around Cape Horn – February 2006

strengths and weaknesses we usually associate with people. I came to love her as we battled Cape Horn together and with that love came the desire to protect her as she protected me from the wet and the cold and the tumult of wind and waves.

As *Barrabas* and I headed further north, into warmer climes and the Pacific trade winds, I wondered more about the experiences of other singlehanded sailors who had carved their way around Cape Horn. Had they been as afraid as I had been? Had the bond with their boats comforted them and strengthened their resolve? Had the aloneness of singlehanded sailing altered them? Had their experiences changed them and affected their lives?

Some of this I knew, but in the wider context of researching their stories, I imagined these people gathered in one place. Alfon Hansen, a young Norwegian with an open smile, would probably gravitate towards Vito Dumas of Argentina and Marcel Bardiaux of France, united by their love of travel and open appreciation of others. Francis Chichester, Chay Blyth and Mike Golding might chatter about speeds and records, unable to repress keen competitive instincts. Bernard Moitessier would probably look on with wry amusement, sharing a joke, an insight perhaps, but all the while wishing he could be back at sea, alone, away from life's smothering rules and regulations. Alec Rose, Alain Colas and Nigel Tetley, all generous, sociable men possessed of near-infinite patience and goodwill, might frequently divert their attention from the conversation to satisfy themselves that everyone's glasses were full. Dr David Lewis and Robin Knox-Johnston, both fervent and patriotic, would probably be engaged in a detailed discussion of the more technical aspects of navigation and sailing. Kay Cottee, Webb Chiles, Naomi James, Lisa Clayton and Jessica Watson might be more involved in wondering where their exploits could lead them later in life, to what fulfilment, to what new horizons. Minoru Saitō would probably float among them all, achieving lasting friendships with just a smile. Chichester would call everyone to supper. Knox-Johnston would propose the toast. *Bon vivant* Dumas would likely cause raucous bursts of laughter. He and Bardiaux would already have decided who among the ladies tickled their fancy. This would be an eclectic gathering – introverts, extroverts, lovers of people and lovers of solitude, those with a hunger to mine the strata of humanity for a deeper spiritual meaning and those who would not give such thoughts more than cursory attention. Competitiveness in some would meet attitudes in others that decried such a trait as vulgar. Generosity would brush up against selfishness, kindness against egocentricity, courage against fear, honesty against deception. Some might be dressed in finely tailored clothes that fortune affords and fame demands. Others might be wearing borrowed shoes. Here would be a gathering of people who, despite sharing the common denominator of being Cape Horners, would be as different from each other as it is possible to be on the spectrum of human personality.

Experiencing Cape Horn at first hand has changed my perspective from terror to fascination, perhaps because I know I will not venture there again, at least not in a small boat, and definitely not alone.

A solo sailor cannot hide from Cape Horn in ways a member of a crewed yacht might through companionship, sleep, shared work, talk, ideas and pooled thinking – be it on navigation, strategy, contingency or emergency. By sleeping, a lone sailor invites greater risk. Cooking below decks or attending to other myriad tasks means the singlehander cannot maintain a round-the-clock watch. Decisions cannot be shared, nor responsibility for the consequences. The onus is entire. But alone, a sailor's experience of Cape Horn will be absolute, raw, unabridged. Through that purity the true nature of the place reveals itself, and so too the truth of that sailor, that person.

WHERE THE WIND BLOWS

Since man first took to the seas, vessels and lives have been lost in all the oceans on earth, but nowhere have the losses been so high as at Cape Horn. When hurricanes are conceived off the west coast of Africa and develop on their westward track towards the Caribbean or are spawned in the western Pacific and slam into Japan and the east coast of China, any shipping on the storm tracks is liable for a pummelling or worse. Some of these storms are category-five monsters (wind speeds greater than 250kph (155mph). Of these, Katrina is perhaps the most infamous of recent times, when sustained wind speeds of 280kph (175mph) lashed New Orleans in August 2005 – making it every bit as severe as anything that might evolve in the Southern Ocean.

There are storm nurseries in the eastern Atlantic; the eastern, central and western Pacific; the northern Indian Ocean; and the south-west Indian Ocean. All of these are seasonal – the season running broadly from June to November, except in the south-west Indian Ocean, where it lasts from November through to April – and this confers one huge, if impractical, advantage on the mariner: he knows when to avoid an area. In the Southern Ocean, however, there is no seasonality – just a variation in storm frequency – 30 per cent during the austral winter, 20 per cent in summer. If a vessel is in the Cape Horn area in summer (December, January and February) for more than 20 days, the chances are it will have to weather a storm. In winter, it's practically guaranteed.

Hurricanes, cyclones, and typhoons are all the same weather phenomenon. In the Atlantic and north-east Pacific, the term 'hurricane' is used. The same type of disturbance in the north-west Pacific is called a 'typhoon', and 'cyclones' occur in the south Pacific and Indian oceans. All these storms are fuelled by air laden with moisture rising from the ocean surface.

January

July

Wind Speed (metres/sec)

| 0 | 7 | 14 |

Seasonal distribution of global wind speed

The depressions of the Southern Ocean are generated not from the ocean itself – the waters of the Southern Ocean are much cooler – but because of the presence of the Antarctic ice sheet.

The sheer size of the Antarctic ice sheet boggles the mind, and the term 'sheet' is something of a misnomer. The ice is 3.2 kilometres (2 miles) thick, has a volume of 27 million cubic kilometres (6.5 million cubic miles), and accounts for more than 60 per cent of all the fresh water on the planet. During

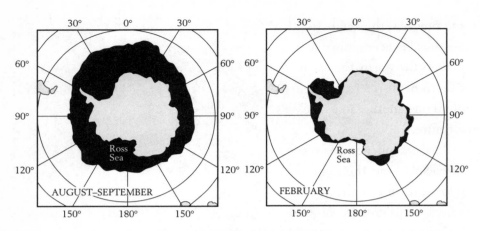

Extent of seasonal Antarctic ice, shown in black

the austral winter, freezing sea adds a further 23 million cubic kilometres (5.5 million square miles) of sea ice around the periphery of the continent that, during the summer, melts, calving massive icebergs in the process. The continental ice never melts. In recent years, it has been expanding for reasons that scientists have yet to fully understand. If the Antarctic ice were to melt completely, sea levels everywhere would rise by 62 metres (200 feet).

The effect of this ice is to render frigid the entire air mass above it, from broadly 65° south latitude to the South Pole – an area of approximately 18 million square kilometres (7 million square miles). The lower temperature of the air makes it denser. The less heat there is in the air, the less individual air molecules (oxygen, carbon dioxide and nitrogen) will oscillate and therefore the less space they will occupy. This air is heavy and its relative density means that it spills outwards, northwards, along every meridian, tumbling over the Southern Ocean that envelops the Antarctic continent. As some point, these waves of cold, dense air meet warmer air occupying the lower latitudes, air that has picked up moisture from the warmer seas to the north. Typically, this confrontation occurs anywhere between latitude 60° south and 40° south – in other words, over a distance of 1,930 kilometres (1,200 miles).

At the interface, an area of low pressure develops. Occurring in isolation of other exacerbating factors, there would be heavy cloud formation from the condensation of moisture in the warmer air mass, rain as a consequence and some breeze – the katabatic wind generated by cold air falling. But there is one crucial exacerbating factor – the eastward spin of the earth. As the cold air meets the warm, the earth's spin deflects the air masses to the left (in the southern hemisphere; to the right in the northern hemisphere) so they coil around one another in a clockwise rotation, leaving the low-pressure area at the centre.

All natural phenomena result from an insult to equilibrium, the upsetting of a balance, and the same is true for a storm system. Air rushes towards the low-pressure centre to attempt to equalise pressures across the pressure gradient – this creates wind. The greater the pressure gradient, the stronger the resulting wind. This inrushing wind does not move straight to the target and neutralise the pressure gradient and thus decay the storm system. It can't. This is because the earth is spinning, deflecting the wind to the left so that it spirals around the centre. This effect of the earth spinning – the Coriolis effect – then sends the storm system off on an eastward trajectory.

The more violent the collision between warm and cold air masses, the steeper the resultant pressure gradient will be, and the more brutal the ensuing storm. So any mariner, with a wary eye on the barometer, will watch falling mercury with alarm; the faster it falls, the more alarmed he will be.

So what? This is a regular depression, just like those found elsewhere in the world. The difference is this – trace along the line of 60°S and you will not encounter land. None. Not even an island. This 60° south latitude describes the track these depressions follow as they barge their way eastwards. Until, that is, they arrive at the Drake Passage. There is nothing to deflect them and nothing to deflate them. The northern and southern hemispheres are very different in their constituent parts. The southern hemisphere contains only two of seven continents – the smallest two – Antarctica and Australia. Around 80 per cent of its surface is covered with water. Once a system moves over land, it is deprived of its foodstuff. It cannot survive. Death by landfall does not occur in the Southern Ocean. The only thing that can kill a storm system down there is exhaustion – when the low-pressure centre gets filled with inrushing air and the pressure gradient eventually equalises.

Winds in Southern Ocean depressions can and frequently do reach hurricane force (sustained winds at or exceeding 117.3kph (72.9mph) or 64 knots) – force 12 on the Beaufort scale. The average wind speed between 40° south and 60° south is 27.4–43.5kph (17–27mph), with the strongest winds typically between 45° south and 55° south.

The belt of westerly winds surrounding Antarctica is subject to variability, a low-frequency oscillation, either expanding away from Antarctica (negative phase) on to a more northerly track or contracting towards Antarctica (positive phase). This oscillation, also called the Southern Annular Mode (SAM), has a direct bearing on the storm tracks.

In its negative phase, the Antarctic Oscillation can redirect the storm track sufficiently north that depressions pile into the jagged mountainous coast of Tierra del Fuego, dissipating some of their energy. In its positive phase, the storm track passes slap bang through the middle of the Drake Passage. Recent research to reconstruct a 1,000-year record of the Antarctic Oscillation suggests it is currently in its most positive phase, attributed to increasing levels of atmospheric greenhouse gases and ozone depletion in the stratosphere.

Some early mariners on the Cape Horn route tried to outsmart the prevailing westerlies by forging deep into the Southern Ocean – as far south as they could go, to within hailing distance of the Antarctic coast. Here, an inner band of easterly winds offered the hope of a downwind passage to get from the Atlantic to the Pacific, with the attendant benefit of a westward-moving current. But there are no shortcuts. To get to the east winds, a ship has to cross the Southern Ocean from north to south, all the while at risk from the storms rampaging westwards, and, for all of that time, the vessel will be presenting her starboard beam to weather. If the ship makes it that far and then transits the Drake Passage successfully, she has to cross the width of the Southern Ocean again to get north, this time offering her port beam to the seas. All that is supposing she can dodge the icebergs that litter the Antarctic coast and stray far beyond, north to the ice limit as far as 45° south.

Wind can be eerily disquieting, even downright terrifying. The sound of it screaming through rigging sets nerves on edge, raises doubt, breeds fear. At Cape Horn, because the air is colder – thus denser and heavier – a 50-knot wind will smack you with considerably more force than would a 50-knot wind on the equator (force = mass x acceleration, so the greater the mass, the greater the force). But wind itself is not the antagonist – wind can be easily and quickly mitigated by a vessel under sail by reducing canvas or reefing down, even to the point where the vessel is under bare poles. It is waves, bred by wind, that cause the damage.

Beaufort wind force scale

Specifications and equivalent speeds

Beaufort wind force scale	Mean wind speed		Limits of wind speed		Wind descriptive terms	Probable wave height	Probable maximum wave height	Sea-state	Sea descriptive terms
	Knots	ms-1	Knots	ms-1		in metres	in metres		
0	0	0	<1	<1	Calm	-	-	0	Calm (glassy)
1	2	1	1-3	1-2	Light air	0.1	0.1	1	Calm (rippled)
2	5	3	4-6	2-3	Light breeze	0.2	0.3	2	Smooth (wavelets)
3	9	5	7-10	4-5	Gentle breeze	0.6	1.0	3	Slight
4	13	7	11-16	6-8	Moderate breeze	1.0	1.5	3-4	Slight–moderate
5	19	10	17-21	9-11	Fresh breeze	2.0	2.5	4	Moderate
6	24	12	22-27	11-14	Strong breeze	3.0	4.0	5	Rough
7	30	15	28-33	14-17	Near gale	4.0	5.5	5-6	Rough–very rough
8	37	19	34-40	17-21	Gale	5.5	7.5	6-7	Very rough–high
9	44	23	41-47	21-24	Strong gale	7.0	10.0	7	High
10	52	27	48-55	25-28	Storm	9.0	12.5	8	Very high
11	60	31	56-63	29-32	Violent storm	11.5	16.0	8	Very high
12	-		64+	33+	Hurricane	14+	-	9	Phenomenal

To convert knots to mph, multiply by 1.15; for m/s, multiply by 0.514

ALFON HANSEN

'My voyaging is not in search of anything but contentment.'

Born	19 February 1905
Died	August/September 1934
Nationality	Norwegian
Date of Cape Horn rounding	July/August 1934
Boat name	*Mary Jane*
Designer	Colin Archer
Year of build	Unknown
LOA	36 feet
Material	Wood
Rig	Gaff rigged sloop

Alfon Möller Hansen's name is indelibly etched in the history of sailing for his irreducible accomplishment of being the first yachtsman to singlehandedly double Cape Horn. ('Doubling' is a quirky nautical term used by Cape Horners to describe bending a ship's course round a cape, peninsula or headland so that it effectively 'doubles' back on itself.)

Hansen, a Norwegian from Forvika in the remote Nordland, was a seaman from an early age. His ambition was not to carve a life for himself on land by earning his living from the sea as his forebears had done, but to actually live on the sea, at sea. He stated his ambition simply as being: 'to make the ocean and small craft voyaging my career'.

Al Hansen acquired a taste for adventure sailing while serving as crew on the luxury yacht *Zaca*, owned by Charles Templeton Crocker, an American millionaire whose grandfather, Charles Crocker, had constructed the Central Pacific Railroad. Built in 1930 at Sausalito, California to a Garland Rotch design, *Zaca* was a double topsail schooner measuring 118 feet in length that many considered to be one of the finest yachts afloat.

After an education at Yale, where he struck up a close friendship with Cole Porter, Crocker spent his time as an impresario before taking up an interest in sailing and commissioning *Zaca* at a cost of a quarter of a million dollars. Crocker decided that sailing around the world would be a reasonable way to see out the Great Depression and departed San Francisco on 7 June 1930.

Exactly when Hansen joined *Zaca* as crew is uncertain, but he was definitely aboard when the yacht arrived at Nuku Hiva in the Marquesas Islands, and it was here that Al Hansen met fellow Norwegian Erling Tambs, who was cruising aboard his cutter, *Teddy*.

Hansen returned to Norway inspired by his experiences, and worked as a commercial fisherman until he had earned enough money to purchase a Colin Archer-designed 'double-ender', a robust, seaworthy 36-foot gaff rigged sloop that had served as a *redningskjoite*, a lifeboat of the Norwegian Coast Patrol. She had no engine. He renamed her *Mary Jane* and set out from Forvika on 15 July 1932, along with his grey cat, Sailor, and Mate, his black dog.

Hansen crossed the North Sea and called in at Weymouth in Dorset on England's south coast where, to earn funds, he fitted out a yacht, the *New*

Moss Rose, for a local businessman. His wandering route then took him further south, to Portugal. In Lisbon, short of funds again, Hansen sold his sea boots to buy provisions. After a rest stop in Las Palmas, Hansen set off on his first truly long-haul sail, across the Atlantic. The voyage took 43 days, with a best day's run of 283 kilometres (176 miles). He arrived in Miami on Christmas Day 1932.

Hansen wanted to visit the Century of Progress Exposition in Chicago, so he sailed upriver along the Mississippi adhering to his philosophy, which he had once stated as being: 'not to make plans. Fate may sometimes force one to abandon them, or deviate.'

Hansen arrived back in the Atlantic by way of the Great Lakes and the Saint Lawrence River before meandering south to Buenos Aires. It was here that he met Vito Dumas, who in 1931 had made a 74-day singlehanded passage from Arcachon in France to the Argentine capital, a newsworthy feat in those days about which Hansen must surely have known. The two became close friends, bonded by their love of the sea and shared ambition (if that word can correctly be applied to Hansen) to sail around Cape Horn. The boat Dumas had under construction at the time was similar to Hansen's own, a 'Norwegian-type' ketch, designed by Manuel Campos on lines modified from the Colin Archer principle. It was another common denominator between the two men.

Hansen set off from Buenos Aires in the austral winter. His rounding of Cape Horn, from 50° south in the Atlantic to Ancud on the *Isla Grande de Chiloé*, took him a soul-sapping 110 days, averaging about 48 kilometres (30 miles) each day. It must have been brutal to stay that long in those treacherous conditions, hugging a lee shore all the while, but Hansen stayed in Ancud only a few days before he weighed anchor and stood north for Puerto Corral 240 kilometres (150 miles) distant, so perhaps he was not as exhausted as might be assumed.

Whatever Hansen's condition or the state of his boat, he was never seen again. Weeks after his departure, wreckage of the *Mary Jane* washed up on the coast of Chiloé.

Almost a decade later, on 12 June 1942, the United States Navy acquired *Zaca* from Charles Templeton Crocker to serve as a local patrol and rescue vessel around the San Francisco area during World War II. After the war, in 1946, Errol Flynn bought *Zaca* and owned the yacht until his death in 1959.

Now in private ownership, *Zaca* has her winter mooring in Monaco, haunted, so rumour goes, by the ghost of Errol Flynn. Perhaps Al Hansen stalks the decks with him.

VITO DUMAS

'It's out there at sea that you are really yourself.'

Born	26 September 1900
Died	28 March 1965
Nationality	Argentinian
Date of Cape Horn rounding	June 1943
Boat name	*LEHG II*
Designer	Manuel M Campos
Year of build	1934
LOA	31 feet
Material	Wood
Rig	Ketch

Vito Dumas was the antithesis of the stereotyped, hard-bitten loner most people have come to associate with singlehanded voyagers. Part city dandy, part tough country rancher and perpetually broke, Dumas did have a way about him, a transparent appreciation of others, that often won him favour. He was good company, a raconteur, a bon vivant and a lover of women. Hidden among his complex character traits was also an adventurous impulse, a burning need for recognition and a hunger for celebrity.

Born into straitened circumstances in Palermo, Buenos Aires on 26 September 1900, Dumas grew into an artistic child but left school early to help contribute towards the family finances – his father ran a one-man tailoring business – although he still found time to receive some formal art-school training. He also managed to supplement his income by selling seascapes, occasionally singing on Argentine radio and sometimes working as a swimming coach.

Dumas enjoyed swimming and he was good at it. He was also savvy enough to recognise that the sport might provide just the platform he was looking for to launch himself on the world. He thus set his sights on swimming across the River Plate, a feat that no one had yet accomplished, and for good reason, since the river spans 48 kilometres (30 miles) between Colonia in Uruguay and Punta Lara in Argentina. Acclaim would surely be his if he succeeded.

It was not to be, however. Dumas attempted this daunting challenge no less than five times, but failed on every occasion. Downhearted but undeterred, he then travelled to England in 1931 to have a go at swimming the shorter distance across the English Channel. Once more his efforts met with failure. Swimming, clearly, was not to be his path to glory. Instead, Dumas, still looking towards the sea, decided that sailing might offer a way forward.

To this end, he bought a boat in France, which he named *LEHG*. These are the initials of his mistress, whose identity is still a mystery, though it is widely supposed that she owned the large estate outside Buenos Aires where Dumas had worked as a farmhand when he was not otherwise engaged in painting and selling seascapes or swimming. Naming his boat thus was Dumas's way of giving private recognition to her for providing much of the funding for his various fame-seeking adventures.

From Arcachon, Dumas sailed *LEHG* to Buenos Aires in 121 days (though he spent several of these stranded on the Brazilian coast) and, finally, received a hero's welcome. Singlehanded endurance sailing was unheard of at this time and for Dumas, the unadulterated admiration he received sparked an idea. The sea offered a blank canvas on which he could paint his name into immortality by sailing alone around the world. He would not be the first – that honour had gone to American Joshua Slocum voyaging on his 37-foot gaff rigged oyster boat *Spray* from April 1895 to June 1898 – but he would be the first Argentinian.

In the intervening years, between his voyage from France and the outbreak of war in 1939, Dumas only occasionally ventured out to sea. This was not for lack of want but because of practicalities. In 1934, emboldened by his earlier success, Dumas had begun construction on a new boat, *LEHG II*, for his world-girdling attempt. However, with funds in short supply and stretched by the fact that he needed to invest in his new farming business, and specifically a tractor, just before war broke out, financial imperative forced Dumas to sell the new boat. As with many men whose dreams are robust during sleep but ethereal by day, Dumas tried to forget about the sea and concentrate instead on making a living.

As war ground on, Dumas became increasingly restless. His business was not doing well. Perhaps the deaths of so many young men in battle, all that wasted potential, brought into focus the futility of a life not lived as he meant to live his. Being in Argentina, neutral and unengaged while war raged far afield, might have weighed on his conscience. His mistress may have exerted pressure on Dumas to remain with her. Whatever its precise nature, some aspect of futility at least provided the impetus for Dumas to make the decision to sail around the world, no longer as a half-baked idea but as a concrete plan, to demonstrate, if only to himself, that dreamers fuelled by their inner visions of romantic adventure could not be thwarted.

Dumas's intention was to sail alone around the world, sticking broadly to the path of the 40th parallel and passing south of the three great capes – the Cape of Good Hope, Cape Leeuwin and the most fearsome of all, Cape Horn. It is probable that meeting Al Hansen in Buenos Aires in 1934 and Hansen's subsequent passage around Cape Horn influenced his choice of route. Hansen's death offered Dumas the further inducement of becoming the first singlehanded sailor to get around Cape Horn and live to tell the tale.

The first thing to do was find *LEHG II* and get her back. Along with his brother, Remo, they sought out Dr Raphal Gamba, who had bought the boat and still owned her. Having found her, they discovered that the boat needed repairs, equipping, a new rig and a set of sails. Once again, the problem was money, or a lack thereof, since Dumas's attempts to sell his cattle to raise sufficient funds had been unsuccessful.

Fortunately, his friends and associates came to his aid. A friend, Arnoldo Buzzi, lent him the money to buy back the boat; Dumas's Fencing and Gymnastic Club in Buenos Aires paid for new sails; and a host of others helped to make the necessary repairs to the boat, provision her for the voyage and provide clothing and a medical kit.

LEHG II was a ketch rigged Norwegian double-ender, similar to Hansen's *Mary Jane*, 31 feet 6 inches in length with a beam of 10 feet 10 inches. Fully laden, she drew 5 feet 8 inches, stabilised with a cast-iron keel weighing 3,500kg (7,700lb). Dumas cannibalised his original boat, *LEHG*, for parts, re-deploying the main mast made in France in 1913.

As for *LEHG II*, she was the only boat Dumas would contemplate as a partner for his quest. He knew her well enough and she had earned his confidence with her ability to cope in heavy weather. An example of this had occurred during a trip to Rio de Janeiro in 1937, before he had sold her to Dr Gamba, when a sudden squall, a *pampero*, had blasted the boat with 70-knot winds. A wave had caught *LEHG II* broadside and rolled her over. Dumas, who had been making hot chocolate below, had suddenly found himself sitting on the cabin ceiling. He knew it was pointless struggling and conceded later that he had felt a calm acceptance of death, followed, as the boat righted herself, by a feeling of deep gratitude. Dumas *knew* the boat had saved his life, as though her actions were somehow deliberate. He could have bought or built another yacht, but it was that conviction, that belief in *LEHG II*, that compelled him to seek her out for this perilous undertaking.

Dumas departed Buenos Aires on 27 June 1942, a cold but sunny day, on the first stage of his voyage to Cape Town. He began the day, dressed in a lounge suit, with a visit to the barber at the Fencing and Gymnastics Club – a trim followed by a hot shave, manicure and shoe polish. He followed this with lunch at the Argentine Yacht Club before finally heading for *LEHG II* just before 1pm. On the way, Arnoldo Buzzi enquired how much money he had. Quickly inspecting his wallet, Dumas pulled out a 10-peso note. Buzzi responded by taking out his own wallet and handing Dumas 10 British 1-pound notes.

From there, Dumas and *LEHG II* proceeded to sail 6,760 kilometres (4,200 miles) in 55 days. The passage was not without serious incident. Within a few days of departure, the boat sprang a leak, and Dumas awoke on the morning of 4 July to find the floorboards awash. He bailed desperately to get the water level down before he could start moving provisions stored beneath the cabin sole and try to isolate the leak. For reasons known only to himself, Dumas never sailed with a bilge pump and his tool chest was rudimentary, comprising a screwdriver, a hammer, some nails and screws. Upon investigation, he discovered that a hull plank had split in the rough conditions offshore from Montevideo so, using a strip of canvas, some red lead, putty, hammer, nails and a bit of wood, he secured the leak as best he could. His best was not, however, good enough, and the boat would continue to bleed water for the remainder of the voyage to Cape Town.

Worse, Dumas had been tossed about below decks as he made the repair and had cut his hands badly in the process. Within two days, infection had set in, affecting his right arm. Despite administering a series of antibiotic injections, the infection spread. By 10 July, his arm had swollen to grotesque proportions and he had developed a high fever. Any movement was agony. He mulled over his options through the long, painful night that followed. The choice was stark. If the situation did not improve, he would have to run for land or amputate his arm. Calculating distance and time, he realised he would never make it to land in time to save his arm. Girding himself for the agony of cutting off his own limb, Dumas fell into a feverish sleep, awaking at 2am on 12 July to find a 7.5-cm (3-in) hole in his arm gushing pus. He dug out as much of the rot as he could manage with a marlinspike, bandaged his arm, gave himself an injection of antibiotics – the fourth one – and returned to the helm. Fortunately, the infection responded to the drugs, the immediate danger seemed to have passed, and with that the grim prospect of amputation receded.

LEHG II arrived in Cape Town six weeks later, on 25 August 1942.

In contrast to his solitary sailing ambitions, Dumas was an extrovert who enjoyed people enormously and missed the company of others, particularly women. His easy charm, debonair affectation and wry good humour had proved a winning combination, and so it did again in South Africa. During the three-week stay in Cape Town, Dumas managed to conduct an affair with a wealthy younger woman. Indeed, so smitten was his latest conquest that she tried to persuade him to join her on a more permanent basis and immigrate to the Seychelles. Dumas, however, revelling in the popular reception he had received on arrival in Cape Town (stoking his craving for publicity and fame), and with an eye ever on the prize – a circumnavigation – reluctantly declined in favour of continuing with his quest.

The next leg of the voyage was brutal: 11,900 kilometres (7,400 miles) to Wellington, New Zealand, which he covered in 104 days. The frightening reality of that passage surpassed anything he had experienced before as a sailor. This was a baptism of fire in preparation for what Dumas considered at the time to be the biggest challenge he faced – Cape Horn.

It was an uncomfortable ride in other ways, too. By modern standards, Dumas's clothing was completely inadequate. He stuffed newspaper into his underpants and around his body for warmth. When the sun shone and he was able to dry off on deck, his clothes were so impregnated with salt that as soon as he returned below, they became damp once again.

In addition to the physical discomfort, the approach to Wellington was made more difficult because Dumas could not communicate – he carried no radio aboard, worried from the outset that if he were caught at sea by the Allies with one on board he would almost certainly have been arrested and charged as a spy. Even though Argentina was neutral, her sympathies towards Germany placed any Argentines abroad under immediate suspicion, something that was demonstrated by the New Zealand port authorities in Wellington when they interrogated Dumas before allowing him to moor up and come ashore. However, they were less suspicious than he had expected, perhaps impressed by his intention to go round Cape Horn alone.

As if as a reminder both of his vulnerability as a citizen of a country sympathetic towards Germany and of his sailing ambitions, Dumas saw a ship anchored in the harbour. This was not just any ship. *Pamir*, a four-masted barque, was one of the great Cape Horners – owned by the German shipping line of F Laeisz – and had worked the Chilean nitrate trade before being switched to the Australian wheat trade, when she had been seized by the New Zealand government on 3 August 1941 while in port at Wellington. *Pamir* was destined to later become the very last commercial sailing ship to round Cape Horn, in 1949.

During his month of rest in Wellington, Dumas's sparkle and wit came to his rescue again, and he befriended the Meadows family. With mutual affection, they 'adopted' him: their home became his home – food, sleep, laundry, bathing – whatever he needed, they happily provided. His gregarious company filled the Meadows' home with colour, laughter and vicarious adventure, until he once more set sail.

The passage to Chile began from Wellington on 30 January 1943 and in comparison with the two previous legs it was uneventful. Dumas arrived in Valparaíso on 12 April, where his mood began to change in anticipation of the next and final stage, round Cape Horn and home. The prospect filled him with dread. Al Hansen had perished on the Chilean coast and now Dumas had to contemplate a voyage south along that treacherous lee shore into ever-more hostile territory and probably over the very spot where his friend had died.

As if he needed any further reminder of the looming dangers, his departure from Valparaíso took him past a Canadian ship, a five-master, which had returned to port after failing in an attempt to make an eastward rounding of Cape Horn with her cargo of timber. She had taken such a battering that hull planks had sprung, putting the ship in danger of foundering and forcing the captain to order her return to Valparaíso while the crew manned the pumps day and night.

Researching his route before setting off from Buenos Aires, Dumas had read in the Argentine Nautical Instructions that the best time to round

Cape Horn was between the beginning of June and mid-July – the middle of the southern hemisphere winter. This seems counter-intuitive because this is the season when storm frequency is at a maximum. Despite this, in Valparaíso a Chilean naval officer agreed with this plan, particularly, he emphasised, if Dumas could time his rounding of Cape Horn to coincide with a full moon, which experience suggested tended to influence calmer conditions. To accommodate these timings, Dumas duly left Valparaíso on 30 May.

Two days out, *LEHG II* sprang a leak, which – despite a thorough search – Dumas was unable to locate. He remained steadfast, however, resigned to expect the worst in light of the severe ordeals he had already experienced in previous voyages. And a few days later, more bad things did indeed come to pass. On 9 June, while he was at the helm in a rising storm, a huge wave broke over the boat, swamping the craft and Dumas, who clung desperately to the mizzen mast to prevent himself from being washed away. Afterwards, having returned to deck, Dumas's fingers became numb as the temperature began to fall, limiting the amount of time he could spend on deck. In an attempt to restore feeling and warm his hands, Dumas struck matches and cupped his fingers over the naked flames. All the while, a head wind was forcing *LEHG II* towards the coast, so Dumas tacked to win sea room.

On 18 June, *LEHG II* had reached the latitude of Cape Pilar, the western entrance to the Strait of Magellan, and by now the cold was almost paralysing. A storm had been blasting the area for six days without respite, strafing Dumas and his boat with hail. For most of the time now, Dumas waited below by the hatch and watched while *LEHG II*, tiller lashed, sailed on into the onslaught. By 20 June, 650 kilometres (400 miles) from Cape Horn, Dumas steered *LEHG II* east in a 40-knot wind, feeling more confident that if the wind and heavy seas did not get any worse, then *LEHG II* should prove equal to the task of getting round the Horn. He had, frankly, been expecting worse than this, although during a rare moment of introspection he had anticipated that Cape Horn might yet prove an insurmountable obstacle if the weather did deteriorate, causing him to wonder whether he had come here, to this graveyard, seeking death.

The wind veered to the north while the Cape Horn current bore the boat eastwards. On 24 June, only 145 kilometres (90 miles) separated Dumas from the longitude of Cape Horn. At this point, what disturbed Dumas more than the actual reality of Cape Horn – a gale, though relatively moderate, was blowing – was the legend of the place and the psychological impact that it had on him, manifesting as fear. The very name, Cape Horn, conjured a sense of menace, adding to the vicious chill in the air and Dumas's thoughts of the vast cemetery to lost men and ships lying beneath the eternally boiling sea.

Even as the longitude of Cape Horn drew ever closer, Dumas felt that some sudden turn of events, a dramatic escalation of the weather, some monstrous strike, would yet rob him of his prize and that in a matter of moments his voyage, indeed his life, could be over.

In Valparaíso, some people had suggested that he should not take his logbooks on the voyage. The message was clear: he could not survive the Horn, and it would be a shame to leave behind no record of his voyage from Buenos Aires. Such sentiments could only have exacerbated an imagination already laced with thoughts of doom.

At midnight, in the big seas, clinging to handholds below, Dumas reckoned Cape Horn should be abeam. A paraffin lamp cast a dim glow through the cabin. At this momentous point in his journey, at the very pinnacle of all that he had set out to achieve and at the precise time of passing his psychological nemesis, Vito Dumas was busy mending a telltale. Unseen, a wave crashed against the boat. The shock of the impact hurled him across the cabin, smashing his face and almost knocking him unconscious. Blood gushed from his shattered nose. Staggering with dizziness, he found some cotton wool and pressed it to his nose to staunch the flow. Still feeling faint and unable to see properly, he wedged himself into a corner and began a finger examination of his face while the boat continued to roil on the seas. As well as a broken nose, he had also sustained a deep laceration to his forehead. Mostly, he was worried about his eyes, but gradually his vision cleared. He stayed wedged for half an hour until the bleeding finally began to slow and eventually stop. For a man given to philosophical musings, he decided that Cape Horn had after all exacted its toll, though Dumas maintained that he had paid a small price against what might have been.

By daylight, Dumas was able to examine his face in a mirror. The reflection that greeted him was a hideous mess, misshapen, distorted and blood-stained.

On deck, Dumas could see no sign of land. The boat continued to leak, so Dumas busied himself with baling. Despite the leak and the pain of his broken nose, however, he was exultant – his latest sun sight confirmed that he had come full circle back into the Atlantic and, moreover, he had the dawning realisation that he was now the first man to have rounded Cape Horn singlehanded and survived. Thoughts of Al Hansen were also in his mind, as he recalled their meeting on a sunny morning in 1934, when the Norwegian had found him with *LEHG II*, then under construction, and signed his name on one of the boat's panels. Always saddened whenever he thought of the fate that had befallen Hansen, Dumas, perhaps with gratitude and relief, broke down and wept.

Vito Dumas arrived in Buenos Aires on 7 September 1943 to a tumultuous welcome.

The voyage, quite apart from the celebrity status it imparted to Dumas, was also to prove good for the sailor's bank balance, which must have been most welcome given that he had relied almost exclusively on the generosity of others to fund his adventure. One such example of this munificence is evident from a telegram Dumas – having spent most of his loyal friend's £10 in Cape Town – had received from Arnoldo Buzzi in Wellington asking if he needed more money. Dumas replied immediately. Yes, he did, and would Arnoldo mind sending it without delay? Such gestures were no longer required following his rounding of the Horn, however, because in 1946 the newly elected president, Juan Perón, awarded Dumas a naval pension.

In 1959, Vito Dumas won the inaugural Slocum Award from the Joshua Slocum Society and the Blue Water Medal, awarded annually by the Cruising Club of America.

Dumas died on 28 March 1965 and was buried at Cementerio de la Chacarita in Buenos Aires. He was 64.

MARCEL BARDIAUX

'Nature is well worth some of our attention. Why live like a machine tool built for the high-speed production of objects which are often unnecessary?'

Born	2 April 1910
Died	February 2000
Nationality	French
Date of Cape Horn rounding	May 1952
Boat name	*Les Quatre Vents*
Designer	Henri Dervin
Year of build	1949
LOA	30 feet
Material	Wood
Rig	Cutter

Bardiaux's tough start in life imbued within him a tenacity that would serve him well for the rest of his days. He set himself difficult goals and then, with unshakeable self-belief, pursued them relentlessly. His ambition always focused on physical challenge rather than monetary gain, but if he could make money from his sporting challenges as well, that was all to the good.

Marcel Bardiaux was born on 2 April 1910 in Clermont-Ferrand. Ironically for a man destined for sailing greatness, Clermont-Ferrand in central France is about as far from the sea as it is possible to be in that country. Raised in austere circumstances, at the age of eight, Bardiaux lost his father to World War I only days before the Armistice. Failing to make ends meet on the meagre war widow's pension she received, his mother was forced to sell the family's possessions and move to Paris.

Bardiaux was sickly as a child, and his future in Paris looked every bit as bleak as it had in the countryside, so his mother, desperate and near destitute, placed the young Marcel in a religious orphanage for five years. Here, he thrived and was one of the best pupils, and by the age of 11 he had also toughened up and developed an insatiable appetite for the outdoors and adventure. Things weren't so good for Madame Bardiaux, though, and despite being such a promising pupil, the young Bardiaux was forced at the age of 13 to go to work to help support his mother. Jobs included plumbing, joinery and some sewing, skills that must have been useful when he somehow managed to build his first boat despite his straitened circumstances. This craft consisted of a rough wooden box made from planks, which he launched in the Seine, only to watch in horror and disappointment as it sank. Despite this setback, however, by the time he turned 14 the idea of travelling the world had become so firmly rooted that he ran away to Le Havre to join a ship. This attempt was not to be successful, since the police intercepted him and returned him to his mother in Paris.

Trapped in the capital, Bardiaux first looked to camping and canoeing as his escape, designing a lightweight tent and then a collapsible kayak, which he began to sell very successfully, leading him to establish the Kayak Club de France. By the age of 19, now fit and lean, Bardiaux had become the French kayak champion – an achievement that was an early expression of the defining qualities that would eventually lead him to greatness within sailing circles in France: self-reliance, an ability to focus on a goal, and the tenacity to pursue his objectives relentlessly.

In the same year, 1929, a meeting with Alain Gerbault altered the course of his life. Here was a man whose achievements had won him renown in France but, more than that, a man whose adventurous life pretty much reflected Bardiaux's own aspirations. Gerbault was seven years older and had been born into wealth and privilege but, like Bardiaux, was a champion sportsman, having won the French national tennis title. What really enthused Bardiaux, though, was hearing about Gerbault's crowning achievement – his singlehanded circumnavigation via the Panama Canal in his 39-foot boat *Firecrest*. He had set off from Gibraltar six years previously on 6 June 1923, and the first stage – across the Atlantic to Fort Totten on Long Island – had taken exactly 100 days. For that feat the Cruising Club of America had awarded Gerbault its inaugural Blue Water Medal. He completed his circumnavigation in Cherbourg on 21 July 1929, becoming only the third man to do so, behind Joshua Slocum in 1898 and Harry Pidgeon in 1925. In response, France bestowed on him its highest civilian accolade, the *Légion d'Honneur*.

Invigorated by Gerbault, the following year, in 1930, Bardiaux embarked on his first truly ambitious adventure. In a self-built kayak named *Belle Étoile*, Bardiaux paddled the Danube to the Black Sea, then went on to Istanbul before crossing the Aegean and Mediterranean to Marseille, and finally, via a network of inland waterways, headed back to Paris. This adventure was to prove a template for more expansive wandering, and sparked a new ambition: to circle the world in a boat made with his own hands. With his confidence burgeoning, Bardiaux never forgot Gerbault nor the debt he owed him for the seed that had now taken root.

Having performed his national service in the Navy, Bardiaux was a naval reservist when war broke out in 1939. Interned by the Germans after the occupation, he managed to escape, evading his pursuers by submerging himself in a river and breathing through a metal tube. Following this audacious getaway, he returned to Paris, where, while war raged all around, browsing in a bookshop he stumbled upon plans for a 30-foot boat designed by

Henri Dervin. Bardiaux's idea of building his own boat, made dormant by the privations of war, reawakened as he scanned the drawings. The anticipation was thrilling. Bardiaux fumbled in his pocket for coins to purchase the plans and, with them, his hopes for the future.

Eagerly, he set about the construction in a shed. He had to scavenge for every scrap of material – wood, nails, canvas, lead for the keel from old battery plates. Dervin's design was for an inshore day-sailer, a boat in which to potter about in calm weather in protected waters close to land and which was hardly suitable for long-distance, blue-water passage-making. Ever resourceful, however, Bardiaux merely modified the plans. He had no sailing experience, but gleaned information about the design requirements for an offshore sailer by studying books by Joshua Slocum, Harry Pidgeon, Alain Gerbault and Conor O'Brien.

Years would pass and so did the war in Europe before Bardiaux eventually launched *Les Quatre Vents*. This he did on 29 July 1949 by characteristically inventive methods that saw him using a cradle he had built from reclaimed material – including two tractor axles – and by means of manpower alone, to roll the boat from his workshop along the cobbled streets of Le Perreux-sur-Marne in the eastern suburbs of Paris to the River Marne.

Here she remained while Bardiaux fitted out the interior, supporting himself by writing articles for *Le Yacht* magazine, which also provided opportunities to publicise his proposed circumnavigation.

When the day came to get underway to his start point at Ouistreham, the engine failed to start. Jeers erupted from the large crowd that had come to watch on the quayside while the press scribbled and TV cameras rolled. Among those gathered was the legendary nautical artist and 1936 winner of the Blue Water Medal, Marin Marie, who looked on with curiosity and no little admiration and called to Bardiaux to ignore the taunts.

Bardiaux sculled his boat away from the dock and, once out of sight of the crowd, accepted a tow. It had not been a good day – on his way to the boat that morning the police had arrested him for speeding.

Like Vito Dumas, Bardiaux was never short of female company, and on board with him was his companion of the moment, whom he referred to only as *marraine* (godmother). Also on board was long-time friend Maurice Naslet who, usually talkative, was silent. After Bardiaux's unfortunate getaway, tension was high. Bardiaux wanted to be on his own and Naslet knew this, but the girl was reluctant to leave. Bardiaux lost his temper. Naslet escorted the girl off the boat.

Bardiaux sailed to Ouistreham and, after several months of final preparations and victualling, began his circumnavigation on 24 May 1950. After his difficult early years, the constraints of war and the long gestation of his boat, Bardiaux thrilled to the wanderlust that drove his imagination. He wanted, simply, to be free. He harboured no ambition to set records for speed or distance, but just wanted to wander around the world with the intention of stopping wherever and whenever he liked. There was one exception to this guiding principle, however, which assumed an increasingly pivotal focus – one place he had to go, a place he felt would challenge him to the utmost of his physical limits: Cape Horn.

By late June, he reached La Rochelle on the Atlantic coast. Here he met another French sailing legend, Captain Louis Bernicot, who, inspired by Joshua Slocum's book *Sailing Alone Around the World*, had completed a solo circumnavigation on his 41-foot boat *Anahita* (modelled on Slocum's *Spray*), by way of the Strait of Magellan, between August 1936 and May 1938. He was the fifth singlehanded sailor to do so. Bardiaux, an avid student of the adventurer sailors, got Bernicot to sign his copy of *The Cruise of the Anahita*. The two men spoke at length about Cape Horn. Bernicot told Bardiaux to avoid imprudence, warning that any accident would likely prove fatal. As for Cape Horn, Bernicot advised that only patience would offer any hope of victory: patience to wait for a rare lull and then capitalise on it.

Bardiaux had the distinct impression that the older man did not believe he had sufficient experience to get round Cape Horn as he suggested that once he got near the Strait of Magellan, any test of endurance would, by then, have been sufficient for him. To underline his point, Bernicot pulled out his own charts of the strait and gave them to Bardiaux.

Bardiaux did not entertain compromise. It was to be Cape Horn or nothing. From La Rochelle, *Les Quatre Vents* made a short trip to Arcachon, from where Dumas had set off on his first long voyage across the Atlantic. Bardiaux left France on 21 October 1950 and set course for Vigo, Spain. After Vigo, he sailed to Lisbon and stopped at various small ports in the south of Portugal before arriving in Casablanca.

Casablanca was a magnet for wanderers and sea vagabonds, infused with an air of excitement and camaraderie, the boat community knitted together by stories of voyages made and plans for future travels. Here, Bardiaux met Englishman Edward Allcard, an Eton-educated naval architect, who was planning a singlehanded circumnavigation after making two transatlantic crossings. With him was a beautiful 23-year-old woman called Ortilia Frayao, whom Allcard had met towards the end of the second crossing – back to Europe from the USA – during an emergency stopover in the Azores to repair storm damage. While he was stationary, Ortilia had insisted on cleaning out the forward part of the boat for him and, two days after he left Horta, she'd emerged on deck through the forward hatch like an apparition – her plan having been all along to stow away. He could not return to the Azores against headwinds so he continued, and now here he was with her in Casablanca.

Bardiaux did not have any rules set for himself, even whether to sail alone or with crew, thus when he met Ortilia he was sorely tempted to take the beautiful stowaway on board. After some agonising, he decided instead to continue alone. Bardiaux left Casablanca with lingering regrets about Ortilia, stopping at Las Palmas and Dakar before heading across the Atlantic for Rio de Janeiro. From there, he bounced southwards along the coast, eventually putting in to Buenos Aires.

By Wednesday 7 May 1952, Bardiaux had worked his way south, close to Cape San Diego, which marks the south-east tip of Tierra del Fuego and the northern entrance to the treacherous Le Maire Strait. His situation was not good. Battling a current he estimated at 9 knots, with the barometer falling and a head wind kicking up enormous waves, brought to his tired mind the fate that had befallen HMS *Bounty*, unable to battle westwards round the

Horn and forced instead to turn and run eastwards around the Cape of Good Hope. Exhausted by the struggle, Bardiaux put into Thetis Bay to look for a safe mooring place, but he could only find a small basin accessed by a rocky channel, the navigation of which in the gathering gloom was too great a risk; *Les Quatre Vents* might well end up smashed to driftwood. Near the channel, Bardiaux instead put out three anchors and a warp to shore, but even then, tossed about on the strong current, he could not sleep and returned constantly topside to check the anchor chains.

By daylight the following morning, the channel seemed less threatening. A hailstorm followed by heavy snow and freezing temperatures only added to his anxiety, but Bardiaux nevertheless braved the channel and made it into the basin, touching bottom as he went. The result of heading for the calmer refuge was that, at low tide, *Les Quatre Vents* grounded, at which point he deliberately ran the boat onto a sandbank so that at least he would be able to get some sleep without worrying about drifting onto rocks. As he lay down, Bardiaux appreciated that he was now less than 100 miles from Cape Horn, a destination that was the goal of his dreams.

He had arranged the mattress so that he was lying flat as the boat rested on her side in the mud, calculating that as the tide flooded, the boat would gradually right herself, waking him gently as she did so. He had not thought the weight of the boat pressing into the mud would create a vacuum and that instead of the boat rising slowly, the mud would hold it fast until her buoyancy overcame the suction and that *Les Quatre Vents*, suddenly released from the grip of the mud, would spring upright, hurling him to the floor.

Despite this rude awakening, rejuvenated by sleep and encouraged by the moderated winds and a rising barometer, Bardiaux unfroze his sails by dipping them in the sea, navigated out of the basin taking advantage of an ebb tide to speed progress, and was ready to take on Le Maire Strait. Again, he found a strong current running, which, against the wind, was kicking up big breakers.

Bardiaux's alterations to Dervin's original design were paying off. There were no gunwales to slow the run of water off the deck and the steep cant of the decks meant any shipped water dispersed rapidly. In the conditions he found in the Le Maire Strait, with tons of water washing over the deck, it came as a relief to see the green water spilling back into the sea.

The west wind backed to the south-west, effectively becoming a head wind that Bardiaux – in the absence of an anemometer – reckoned at force 11 (60 knots). Unable to make any meaningful progress, he decided to heave-to and arrest sternway by deploying a sea anchor. When he left the helm to go below and retrieve his equipment, *Les Quatre Vents* swung beam-on to the seas. A breaking wave roared up, smashing into the hull, sending a cascade of water through the companionway. In the cabin, Bardiaux was thrown to one side, then on to the cabin ceiling, which had become the floor as *Les Quatre Vents* rolled. The weight of stores stashed below the cabin sole rained down on Bardiaux. Scrambling to his feet as the boat righted herself, Bardiaux vaulted out of the cabin into the tiny cockpit and had just enough time to kick the hatch closed when the boat rolled for a second time. Bardiaux went over with his ship into the icy water, where *Les Quatre Vents* stayed inverted for longer than before because of the bellyful of water swallowed by the cabin. Bardiaux, submerged beneath the boat, unable to see or breathe, believed he had met his end. However, the boat righted herself agonisingly slowly and listing badly and Bardiaux hauled himself aboard to assess the damage. The storm trysail was gone and the canvas cockpit shelter torn away. Rather than risk going below again to get the sea anchor, Bardiaux grabbed a long warp that had become pinned below the binnacle, made one end fast to the anchor chain and hurled it overboard. The braking effect was immediate, but the steep, breaking seas continued pummelling *Les Quatre Vents*.

When he got below, the cabin was a mess. His second anchor stored below decks had dislodged and smashed the table and a small chest full of provisions. Broken glass littered the floor. Fumes from two ruptured fire extinguishers made the air barely breathable. The engine that powered two bilge pumps refused to start, so Bardiaux set about pumping by hand. Taking advantage of slack water as the tide turned, he raised a small sail to get the bow pointing upwind, making the boat better able to ride the oncoming waves at an oblique angle, and moved out of the strongest current by making his way closer to shore. Soaked and freezing, Bardiaux knew he had to get to Aguirre Bay or risk hypothermia. He made it after dark, changed into dry clothes kept in a waterproof kitbag and grabbed a few hours of fitful sleep on the bare boards of the bunk – his mattress soaked and useless.

In La Rochelle the previous June, Bardiaux had accepted the charts of the Strait of Magellan from Louise Bernicot as a souvenir with no intention of using them. Now, relatively safe, his mattress, clothing and kit festooning the decks and shrouds to dry in watery sunshine, Bardiaux had time to reflect. He was lucky to be alive. He wondered again at the advice of the older and more experienced Bernicot about imprudence likely proving fatal. Bardiaux had long since learned the best way to deal with any adverse situation was to take action, so, moored in Aguirre Bay, he got on with various jobs – clearing away broken glass, reinforcing the chocks that held down the floorboards and re-stowing gear. He also consulted his charts, which told him that there was really no safe anchorage except at Ushuaia.

Bardiaux set off again on 11 May straight into a huge swell. If the seas started to break, he doubted he would survive. Deceit Island lay 145 kilometres (90 miles) distant, just north-east of Cape Horn. *Les Quatre Vents* made good headway – 130 kilometres (80 miles) in 16 hours. He dropped anchor in darkness, guessing that Deceit Island was 3.2 kilometres (2 miles) away. His plan was not to rest – he felt this spot was too exposed, the swell curling round the island from the west adding to the dangers of reefs and rocks to the north and south – but to wait for dawn. With daylight he could sail round Cape Horn and record the moment with photographs or, better still, land on Horn Island and leave a sealed bottle containing a message as proof of his rounding.

Physically, Bardiaux was not in great shape. The combination of cold and salt had split the skin of his hands, causing him to flinch every time he had to haul a rope, and he had not slept for over 24 hours and could not see any opportunity to get rest for the next three or four days. He was suffering from chilblains on his face and his entire right side had become painful. Despite this, his thoughts surprised him; until now, he had never believed he would say to himself that if he got away with it this time, he'd never set foot on a boat again.

During that night, Bardiaux prepared a vacuum flask of coffee and enough food for the next few days. Throughout 12 May, a storm raged through the

Drake Passage, spilling snow and hail. The swell had become enormous. The rocks and reefs south of Deceit Island protected *Les Quatre Vents* to a degree, but as soon as he ventured into open water, the wave heights became monstrous. One small mercy – and Bardiaux would take anything he could get – was that the wave crests were not breaking close to Deceit Island. Visibility was close to nil so sun sights were impossible. He could only estimate his position.

At 12.30pm, a rent in the clouds gave him what he had been searching for – a view of Cape Horn. Unfortunately for Bardiaux, he could not record the moment with a photograph as he'd hoped. A sudden blast of hail obliterated the black pyramid of rock. Unable to discern how far he was from the Cape – one mile or five – Bardiaux tacked onto a heading south-west. To celebrate breaching the longitude of Cape Horn, and to warm himself, Bardiaux ducked into the cabin and allowed himself a tot of rum. There he saw the sealed bottle containing his message but immediately abandoned the idea of making a landfall on Horn Island, instead scanning his charts for a refuge in which he might escape the battering.

By 11pm, Bardiaux had reached 56°20' south latitude. The danger of icebergs now loomed – he had already passed outriders. Tacking again, to the north-west, he decided to reduce sail, but the canvas was frozen. Worried about cracking the canvas if he wound it round the boom, he boiled water and poured it over the foot of the sail before winding in.

Nearing the western end of Hermite Island, Bardiaux encountered a new threat – a williwaw. These katabactic-type winds result from cold high-density air accumulating at altitude on mountain peaks before falling under the influence of gravity, much like an avalanche. In extreme cases, wind speeds can reach hurricane strength. The event is explosive rather than sustained and can last many seconds, and the consequences for a boat caught beneath such a falling wind can be devastating, like a nut suffering a hammer blow. The williwaw that hit *Les Quatre Vents* knocked the boat flat. When he had recovered from the shock, Bardiaux took in some of the main, noticing that one of the seams had started to part. In darkness, freezing winds and breaking waves drove over the bow, but he had to mend the sail before it split. In order to do so, Bardiaux first deployed a sea anchor – his long warp attached to the anchor chain. Then, lashing himself to the boom and with hands so chapped and numb he could barely hold the needle, he set to work. Under normal conditions, the job might have taken 20 minutes. Bardiaux was still at it two hours later. *Les Quatre Vents* had gone past Hermite Island northwards, but the wind veered to the north-west and began forcing the boat irresistibly towards the north of the island.

The Argentine Navy was expecting Bardiaux in Ushuaia, an arrangement cemented during Bardiaux's stopover earlier at Rio Grande, and he wanted to explore the Patagonian channels. At the same time, he thought about continuing on westwards and making landfall on Chiloé Island. Eventually, though, moving past Hermite Island, he decided on Ushuaia. Aside from the social commitments, *Les Quatre Vents* needed repairs after the punishment meted out by Cape Horn.

Despite having already experienced the devastating effects of williwaws, Bardiaux thought the channels would offer him protection from raw exposure to the elements. It was, of course, a trade-off, more protection perhaps, but also a greater likelihood of a williwaw smashing down on top of him.

He thus set course for the Murray Channel. The wind veered, heading the boat and pushing him among a scattering of rocks, forcing a change of course across Nassau Bay. The night was dark as pitch. A sudden splintering impact shook the boat. Bardiaux was immediately confused. This was deep water? Maybe his charts were inaccurate. A tearing sound rent along the side of the boat and a white mass slipped past. *Les Quatre Vents* had struck an iceberg. Bardiaux searched ahead with the benefit of weak moonlight. Other icebergs dotted the view, one just ahead. He hove-to and waited for morning.

With daylight came another williwaw, a downward rush of icy wind which, had Bardiaux been showing any sail, might have caused significant damage. He cast out the warp and an anchor to stabilise the boat while he had something to eat and grabbed some sleep as the boat drifted eastwards before resuming his tortuous passage towards Ushuaia, tacking through the strait dividing Lennox Island and Navarino Island (the same route followed by Al Hansen almost 20 years previously) and into the Beagle Channel. Seeing a light ahead, he correctly assumed it was the *estancia* (hostelry) at

Port Haberton, which he had heard about in Rio Grande. Snow was falling heavily as Bardiaux manoeuvred into a small, protected bay just before dawn. No sooner had he dropped anchor and changed into less wet clothing than the owner of the *estancia* came alongside to invite him up to the house. Here, his host plied him with food and Chilean *aguardiente* (schnapps), the local firewater, which Bardiaux, maintaining his machismo, managed to swallow without blinking.

Bardiaux's craving for sleep then overcame his inclination towards sociability and he returned to his boat for the night, fitting a tarpaulin over the cabin roof for extra insulation. This was augmented by the 20cm (8in) of snow that fell during the night and froze, meaning that come daybreak, he had to chip the ice away with a hammer. Before leaving, the *estancia*'s chef gave him a leg of lamb for breakfast, and by way of departure gifts, the *estancia* workers gave him a cooked half lamb and a sheepskin as a foot warmer.

Bardiaux arrived in Ushuaia on the evening of 16 June, to be greeted by the government's deputy sub-prefect who, in his boss's absence, was under instruction to fetch the lone navigator, feed him and put him in the VIP suite. However, Bardiaux preferred to sleep on board *Les Quatre Vents*, not for any reason of comfort, but so that he would be present if any emergency threatened her safety.

During the few weeks Bardiaux stayed in Ushuaia to make repairs to *Les Quatre Vents* he made many friends. The more he was at sea, the more he enjoyed the company of women on land, and women seemed to enjoy his company equally in return. On 9 June, the eve of his departure, his friends threw a touching farewell dinner. Each guest wrote a few words in their native language. Only later, when Bardiaux had the messages translated, did he realise that some had been declarations which – had he known about them at the time – might have compelled him to linger a while longer in Ushaia.

Bardiaux had injured his back during the two capsizes in Le Maire Strait, though the symptoms had yet to manifest fully. Early signs showed as pain in his right side. He struggled on, ignoring the pain, arriving in Ancud on Chiloé by August, again tracing Al Hansen's route. By then the pain had become severe, and his right leg numb and practically paralysed. The Chilean Navy thus organised air transport for him from its base at Quintero to Santiago so he could receive treatment, but almost a year later in Tahiti, there had been little improvement. Bardiaux would spend almost 12 months in hospital recuperating from what he felt was the cruel vengeance of Cape Horn.

From Tahiti to Durban, then to Cape Town and New York and eastwards across the Atlantic, with hundreds of stopovers en route, Bardiaux finally arrived back at Arcachon on 25 July 1958, more than eight years after he left. In recognition of his accomplishment, he received that year's Blue Water Medal for sailing the first westabout circumnavigation, emulating his hero Alain Gerbault.

Les Quatre Vents had served him well but she was not a dry boat. For this reason, Bardiaux eventually built another yacht, drier and stronger, constructed of stainless steel. He was nothing if not direct, and it showed in his choice of name for the new boat – *Inox*, French for 'stainless steel'. He subsequently voyaged many tens of thousands of miles aboard *Inox* and lived on her until his death in February 2000. He was 89.

FROM RIPPLES TO ROGUES

Wind blowing over a flat surface of water encounters resistance. Resistance creates friction and friction is energy. Through friction, the wind's energy transfers to the water, corrugating the surface into tiny capillary waves. Within a given area – a square metre or a square mile – this corrugation effect massively increases the surface area of the water, providing the wind with increasing purchase, leading to an inexorable rise in energy transfer. Waves get bigger, and so the process continues – depending, of course, on whether or not the wind continues to blow.

Wind duration is not the only factor involved with wave formation, however – there are four others. The more sustained each of these factors is, the more severe the sea-state will become. The most obvious of these is wind speed. The greater the velocity of the wind, the greater the rate of energy transfer to the water. Not so obvious but equally critical is the length of uninterrupted open water over which the wind blows in a given direction – what oceanographers call the *fetch*. The greater the fetch, the greater the energy transfer. So how big is this fetch down by Cape Horn? The answer is pretty much the entire Southern Ocean area, a region that occupies about 4 per cent of the Earth's surface – 12,626,913 square kilometres (7,846,000 square miles). The third factor is the width of the area affected by the fetch. The wider the area of the fetch, the greater is the surface area of sea for wind to act upon. Finally, depth of water affects wave speed. Deeper water offers less friction to a wave travelling at its surface: the deeper the water, the greater the wave velocity. The Southern Ocean is deep, ranging from 4,000 to 5,000 metres (13,125 to 16,400 feet) below sea level over most of the area it occupies.

In the high southern latitudes, the machinery of storm genesis never stops – somewhere over the reaches of the Southern Ocean encircling the

Antarctic continent there will always be wind – lots of it. The depressions – feeding off an inexhaustible supply of warmer, wetter air and cold, heavy air thanks to the Antarctic ice sheet – deliver strong winds of long duration – and this strong, durable wind can run uninterrupted because there is no land to get in the way. The fetch is in effect endless. Scientists reckon that, theoretically at least, a single storm system can circumnavigate Antarctica, arriving back at the place it was born fully matured and still raging.

This is not so elsewhere on the planet. The northern hemisphere has a land-to-sea ratio of 1:1.5 – so, 40 per cent land, 60 per cent water. However, the landmasses divide the water into strips, limiting fetch. A hurricane-making landfall is thus deprived of its fuel source, warm moisture-laden air. Without its feed, the storm dies.

The margins of the Southern Ocean are not universally accepted – some suggest its northern boundary lies along the 60th parallel; others prefer the Antarctic Convergence Zone further north, where the water circulating eastwards around Antarctica meets the southern reaches of the Atlantic, Pacific and Indian oceans. The exact location of the boundary does not matter, however, at least not as far as weather phenomena are concerned. The width of the fetch that has a direct impact at Cape Horn extends from 45° south to the Antarctic coast or, in winter, the ice edge – a width of 1,600 kilometres (1,000 miles) or more in places. And this water is deep, so there is no shoaling to suck the energy from the waves, slow them and suffocate them. Thus, here is a geographical factory mass-producing storm systems capable of generating strong winds of long duration howling over a wide and limitless fetch of deep water. There is literally nothing to stop abominable sea-states developing constantly.

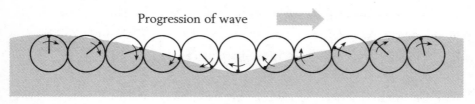

Direction of rotation of water particles at different points along a wave

There is also, however, a complicating factor – the movement of individual water particles. A wave at sea is not quite the reflection of a smooth sine wave. At the surface, water particles move in a circular motion as the wave energy passes, rotating forwards as the peak moves through and backwards as the trough passes. The net effect is a slight forward progression of surface water particles as they complete each orbit. The result is a steeper wave. As a wave steepens it loses stability. As the wave amplitude (height) increases, this narrowing or steepening of the peak becomes more pronounced.

There is a direct relationship between wave height and wavelength. The greater the amount of energy invested in a wave sequence, the longer the wavelength (the distance between like points on two adjacent waves, peak to peak or trough to trough, for example), and the longer the wavelength, the higher the potential wave height.

Wind and waves in themselves pose no danger to a vessel at sea, other than making for an uncomfortable ride; a vessel will ride over the waves like a cork. The danger comes when waves break.

In deep water, as wave height increases, the peak becomes narrower and steeper, to the point when stability is lost and the wave breaks. This happens when the ratio of wave height to wavelength reaches approximately one in seven. So, for a sea running with a wavelength of 42.5 metres (140 feet), wave heights will reach 6 metres (20 feet) before they become unstable and break.

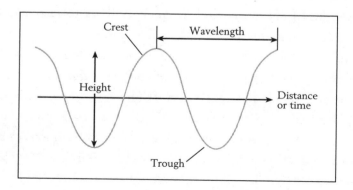

Phases of a wave

Why exactly is it breaking waves that do the real damage? Answer: because a wave that is not breaking will simply transfer kinetic energy to a boat floating on its surface – the boat moves up with the peak and down in a trough. A breaking wave, however, transfers both energy and mass. The mass translated into force can produce awesome destructive power.

An easier way to explain the transfer of power from wave to boat is to use a simple rule of thumb: a breaking wave with a height equivalent to the beam (width) of a vessel has the power to roll that vessel over if the impact is taken on the beam. So, for a sailing boat of say 33 feet loa (length overall), a beam measurement might reasonably be about 3 metres (10 feet). It won't take much of a wave to catch that boat beam-on and flip her over, keel pointing skywards and masthead light aiming at the sea floor.

Wind never blows evenly for very long – it is blustery. The resultant sea-state is, likewise, not constant with wave trains of a given wavelength and uniform wave heights; wave heights in a wave train vary, with the significant wave height defined as the average height of the highest third of the waves. It follows, then, that most waves in a wave train measure less than the significant height. However, statistically, much higher waves will also constitute part of a wave train, with approximately one wave in a hundred being one and a half times the significant wave height and one in a thousand being twice the significant wave height. At some point within a finite number of waves in a sea running with a significant wave height of 6 metres (20 feet), a monster of 12 metres (40 feet) or more is going to emerge.

In conditions of changing wind speed, several wave trains can be set in motion, each of unique wavelength and significant wave height. When these trains converge and move into 'phase' – when the wave peaks of one train join exactly with the wave peaks of another – the resultant waves are cumulative. A 9-metre (30-foot) wave falling into phase with a 6-metre (20-foot) one will result in a 15-metre (50-foot) wave. Similarly, when 'out of phase' – the peaks of one train combining with the troughs of another – the opposite effect results, a cancelling-out. A 9-metre (30-foot) wave combining with a 6-metre (20-foot) one out of phase results in a 3-metre (10-foot) wave.

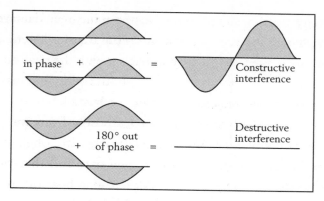

Interference patterns of colliding wave trains

For a long time, rogue waves were thought to be the stuff of tall tales from those who had spent too much time at sea, yarns to keep company with the stories of fishermen who contrived magically to transform minnows into monsters. In the days of the Cape Horn trade, when many ships disappeared, science was not equipped to investigate fluid dynamics. Even until relatively recently, rogue waves were disputed on the premise that the conditions needed to produce them were vanishingly rare.

Captain James Barker's account of the *British Isles'* encounter with a rogue wave does not now seem as far-fetched as perhaps it did when he published *Log of a Limejuicer* years later in 1936.

And Captain Barker was not alone. During his third foray to Antarctica in 1915, Ernest Shackleton met with two disasters from which he was lucky to escape with his life. The first occurred when his ship, *Endurance*, was crushed in pack ice. The crew managed to escape in lifeboats and made Elephant Island, from where, on 24 April 1916, Shackleton and four crewmen set out for South Georgia in one of the lifeboats, a distance of 1,160 kilometres (720 miles). At some point while crossing the Southern Ocean, Shackleton later recorded that he thought he was witnessing a peculiar movement among the clouds:

I realised that what I had seen was not a rift in the clouds, but the white crest of an enormous wave. During 26 years' experience of the ocean in all its moods I had not encountered a wave so gigantic. It was a mighty upheaval of the ocean, a thing quite apart from the big white-capped seas that had been our tireless enemies for many days ... Earnestly we hoped that never again would we encounter such a wave.

Shackleton seems an unlikely candidate for hysterical exaggeration, and as if to confirm this, scientists have now acknowledged that the area west of the Horn is particularly notorious for rogue waves.

The waters of the Southern Ocean driven eastwards by the prevailing westerlies generate the largest ocean current in the world, the unending Antarctic Circumpolar Current (ACC). This is not a unified body of water moving consistently – it is a collection of water currents at different latitudes, each moving at varying speeds separated by areas of slower-moving water. In places, the currents divide into many fast and narrow streams. The three major flows comprising the ACC through the Drake Passage are: from the north, the Sub-Antarctic Front (SAF) and the Polar Front (PF); and further

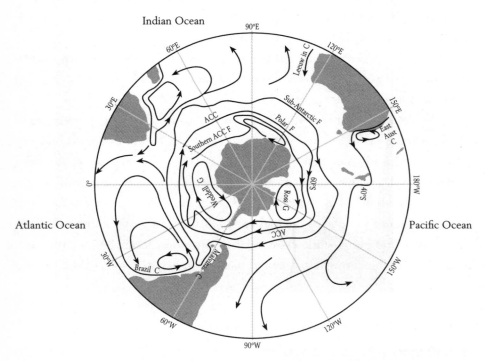

Antarctic currents and gyres (large systems of rotating ocean currents)

south, closest to Antarctica, the Southern ACC Front (SACCF), which flows along the western side of the Antarctic Peninsula before ripping through the passage.

It is the SAF that runs the fastest, its northern part streaming past Cape Horn to create the Cape Horn current that, in places, the British Admiralty Sailing Directions warn can tear along at 10 knots.

Although the speed of the current averaged out is unremarkable at about 2 knots because of the great depth of water, the sheer volume moving through

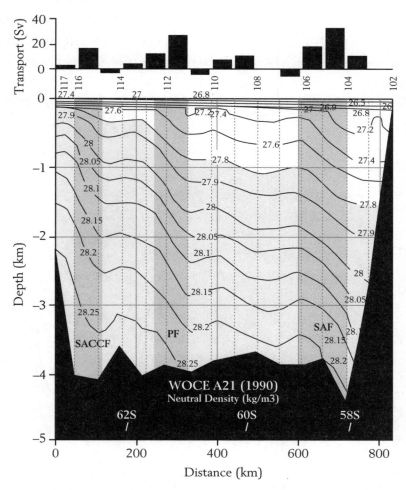

Water transported by circumpolar Antarctic currents through the Drake Passage (measured in Sverdrup units [Sv]: 1Sv = 1 million cubic metres of water per second)

the Drake Passage is staggering. It dwarfs the Gulf Stream and at 140 million tonnes per second is well over one hundred times greater than the total flow of all the rivers of the world combined.

For vessels making a westward rounding of Cape Horn, a more southerly route that steers well clear of the SAF will speed progress and avoid the steep, short seas created by the shoaling continental shelf. For those heading eastwards and downwind, an inshore path will harness the power of the Cape Horn current.

BERNARD MOITESSIER

'I am a citizen of the most beautiful nation on earth, a nation whose laws are harsh yet simple, a nation that never cheats, which is immense and without borders, where life is lived in the present. In this limitless nation, this nation of wind, light, and peace, there is no other ruler besides the sea.'

Born	10 April 1925
Died	16 June 1994
Nationality	French
Date of Cape Horn rounding	June 1966
Boat name	*Joshua*
Designer	Jean Knocker
Year of build	1962
LOA	39 feet 6 inches
Material	Steel
Rig	Ketch

Bernard Moitessier was not only a sailor, he was also a writer, thinker and philosopher. He achieved a unity with the sea that provided him with purpose and meaning, where he could exist on a plain that simply did not offer itself in any land-bound life, a location where he governed himself, where his survival depended absolutely on his own abilities and self-reliance, where the only laws were nature's laws. He yearned for a space of such immense power and humbling beauty, of such tranquillity and isolation, as to be the only place where he could fully understand all that he had been, all that he was, and all that he might become.

Bernard Moitessier was born in Hanoi in what was then French Indochina, modern-day Vietnam, on 10 April 1925 into a moderately affluent family. His childhood was privileged – home was a colonial mansion and holidays were spent on the Gulf of Siam. He was a talented linguist, becoming fluent in Vietnamese and Thai, and learned to sail with local fishermen. The cultural influence of the Orient, with its emphasis on holism and a reverence for nature, made a deep and abiding impression on Moitessier, and set up an inner conflict with the rigidity and bureaucracy of French colonialism.

The family ran an import company and his father, Robert, harboured ambitions for Moitessier – as the oldest son – to join and eventually take over the business. To this end, at 18, fresh out of agricultural school, Moitessier went to work at the Indochinese Rubber Plantation Company, supervising 300 workers on the Long Than plantation and overseeing every aspect of the operation, from the planting to the harvesting of the latex. It was during this period that Moitessier came across a giant tree that radiated a message to him that would change the direction of his life: 'The tree that climbed to the sky as I looked at it … and which became planks … which became a junk … was telling me that the world is limitless.'

World War II was raging. The Japanese had overrun Vietnam and, towards war's end, were arming the communist Viet Minh. The end of the Pacific war in August 1945 did not bring peace to the only place Moitessier had ever known; the Viet Minh continued its brutality in its war for independence, seeking unification of the area. Anti-French demonstrations became commonplace. In September and October 1945 alone, rebels killed 300 French nationals. The French government thus mobilised forces to the area to stem the threat. To aid the effort, Moitessier, now aged 20, and his two younger brothers, Jacky and François (nicknamed Françou), joined the Volunteer Liberation Group (VLG), a resistance unit made up of French and Eurasian soldiers. Hearing of his fluency in the local languages, the commander of a French gunboat, the 600-ton *Gazelle*, took Moitessier on as an interpreter while Jacky and Françou continued serving with the VLG.

After a year of military service, Moitessier joined his father's business, but the attractions of the Orient, the peacefulness of his childhood and the gentle countenance of the people had palled in the aftermath of war. Moreover, he found the job in the family business suffocating. Moitessier longed to strike out on his own, to take to the seas in his own boat and in his own command. His chance came in 1952 with the purchase of *Marie-Therese I*, a native junk so dilapidated that he often had to dive over the side to bung up leaks, and which was wrecked on Diego Garcia. A British Corvette then took Moitessier to Mauritius where, for three years, he laboured in a variety of jobs while at the same time building a new boat, *Marie-Therese II*. In 1955, Moitessier set off from Mauritius bound for the Caribbean via Durban, where he met his compatriot, Marcel Bardiaux, by then a Cape Horn veteran.

Unfortunately for Moitessier, he suffered a second shipwreck in the West Indies, so, bereft and broke, he returned to France in 1958. A student of the solo sailing pioneers who had read accounts by Slocum, Pidgeon, Bernicot, Gerbault and Dumas, Moitessier wrote the first of his five books, *Vagabond Des Mers du Sud* (published in English as *Sailing to the Reefs*), in France. The book was an instant success, feeding the French appetite for marine adventure, and it caught the attention of a well-known naval architect, Jean Knocker, who subsequently approached Moitessier with an offer to design a new boat for him gratis. Hearing of the plan, Jean Fricaud, owner of a metal-working firm and a sailor himself, offered to build the boat for just the cost of the materials. The result was a 39-foot ketch with a Norwegian stern, which Moitessier named *Joshua* in honour of Joshua Slocum.

It was during the period of the boat's construction and while he was living in Marseille that Moitessier met Françoise, herself the daughter of French colonialists. By a strange twist of fate, their parents knew one another well and had often holidayed together in Corsica; Moitessier remembered seeing photographs of Françoise as a girl in the family photo albums. How fate had contrived to bring them together so many years later was always a marvel to Moitessier and, as an added bonus, she had three children from a previous marriage, thus presenting him with a ready-made family. As a wedding gift and honeymoon, Moitessier promised Françoise a transatlantic crossing along the trade-wind route and a transit of the Panama Canal followed by a leisurely sail to the Galápagos Islands and on to the South Pacific and Tahiti. They duly set off from Marseille on 20 October 1963.

By the time Moitessier and Françoise were ready to return home more than two years had passed. The children, who had joined their parents for a holiday in the Canaries more than a year before, were in France. Françoise was eager to get back to them. From Tahiti, there were three possible routes back to France: two westward and one eastward. They could sail west either by way of the Suez Canal or round the Cape of Good Hope or take the third option – east, by way of Cape Horn. This latter choice had not been immediately appealing, but it was the shortest or, as Moitessier would later describe it, the most logical route home so, after much deliberation, they decided to take it. It is likely that any eagerness to get back to France by the quickest route was more than matched by Moitessier's desire to add that particular feather to his cap.

Joshua left Moorea, north-west of Tahiti, on 23 November 1965. Moitessier had a copy of Miles Smeeton's *Once is Enough* on board, which he read and re-read. As *Joshua* headed for Cape Horn, Moitessier prepared warps to stream from the stern to act as sea anchors, weighting their ends with 18-kg (40-lb) pigs of iron to keep them from trailing on the surface. These he stowed in readiness beneath the aft cabin sole at the foot of the mizzen mast. He also had a cargo net, lashed to the roof of the aft cabin, again ready to be deployed at the end of a warp if necessary. The lesson he had taken from Miles Smeeton's account was that *Tzu Hang* had been travelling too fast downwind, which had allowed the crests of breaking waves following up her stern to propel her down the wave face and flip her over, stern over stem. Had *Tzu Hang* been slowed with a sea anchor, white water would have travelled beneath the hull or even over the hull, but the sea anchors would have held her stern down, counteracting the boat's tendency to bury her nose and preventing the pitchpole.

Joshua picked up the westerlies in mid-December and continued to drive south-east towards the Horn. Caught in a ferocious gale, Moitessier handed all sail and, running under bare poles, streamed the warps – five of them, three with pig iron weights, one trailing the cargo net, and one trailing freely.

The seas were huge, demanding that Moitessier and Françoise spelled each other at the helm, careful to take each approaching roller from dead astern. Then, while Moitessier was at the helm watching an approaching wave roll up behind, uncertain whether it was going to break or not, the stern began to lift. As the wave passed, *Joshua* buried her nose. The front part of the boat dug in until the forward half of the boat was under water before she rose and burst free of the sea's grip. The wave had not been unduly large.

Moitessier was shocked. *Joshua* had come close to being pitchpoled despite the sea anchors. The disappointing realisation dawned with shattering effect that *Joshua* was not capable of handling these big seas. She was a trade-wind boat. But how had Vito Dumas done it? Had he not experienced seas like this in *LEHG II*? In comparison with *Joshua*'s robust steel construction and extra 8 feet of length, *LEHG II* had been undersized and rickety at best.

As the storm eased, Moitessier thought seriously of turning north and heading for the Panama Canal, but he recalled that Dumas must have faced seas as big and had claimed he had sailed downwind with as much sail as he could carry. To Moitessier, this was madness. So how had Dumas done what he did?

He called down to Françoise to dig out a book by Jean Merrien with an abridged account of Vito Dumas's circumnavigation. 'Look up "Vito Dumas" and start reading the italicised passages,' he said to Françoise.

Dumas had adopted a strategy of sailing fast downwind, angling the stern 15–20 degrees to the oncoming waves, on the basis that if the boat were moving as fast as the wave, then the danger posed by the wave was neutralised. Instinctively, Moitessier did not believe that. He reckoned that *Joshua*, deploying that strategy, would have done 'Catherine-wheels by now'.

Dumas's strategy, however, seemed to be confirmed by an earlier sailor, Captain Tommie Bohlin, who, on a transatlantic race in 1905, wrote: 'With a following sea and a gale like this the waves lifted up our stern and then … we simply slid away from them, we escaped them.'

Moitessier, still sceptical, thought that strategy might work on bigger boats (Bohlin's was a 92-ton schooner), yet *LEHG II* was a small boat, much smaller than *Joshua*.

Moitessier watched another dangerous wave approaching and yelled to Françoise to brace herself as he angled *Joshua* 10 degrees to the wave. The stern lifted then, despite the trailing warps, and *Joshua* sped down the face of the wave, heeled over so that her leeward bow was sliding on the water like a ski. Her nose did not dig in. The wave passed and Moitessier knew he had found the answer.

He shouted to Françoise above the howl of the wind to take the helm. He took up a razor-sharp knife, clipped to a pre-rigged safety line and cut through the five trailing warps, leaving them to the sea. The boat's attitude altered immediately. Moitessier took the helm, angled the stern 15 degrees to the waves and waited. She planed down the wave faces without burying her nose, even though she was still under bare poles, and responded instantly to the helm as Moitessier lined her up for the next wave. The sea, which had appeared so threatening only a moment before, now seemed relatively tame, provided that they maintained a constant vigil at the wheel while the big waves were running.

Later, Moitessier wrote: 'I thought of Vito Dumas sailing three oceans singlehanded, without an inside steering position … Compared with a man like him I was just a miserable landlubber, a shocking amateur with no guts…' As the storm died away, the legacy of huge seas continued. After 26 hours at the helm, Moitessier sat on deck with Françoise and watched 'this sea from which radiated a colossal power, a complete, absolute beauty'.

Joshua was still 4,830 kilometres (3,000 miles) from Cape Horn. What Moitessier could not then know was that he had seen nothing yet.

After three hours' sleep, Moitessier took over the helm as another depression began to envelop *Joshua*, and patiently coached Françoise on their newly discovered sailing strategy and steering technique.

The storm escalated and the sea-state worsened, generating rollers, some with breaking crests 150 metres (490 feet) long. These were the most stupendous seas Moitessier had ever seen. Often, *Joshua* was completely submerged. The force of the wind also created a phenomenon he had not witnessed before. Usually, when a wave breaks in deep water, the breaker loses energy, becomes detached from the wave crest and is left behind – white, streaming foam on the back of the wave. Here, the breaking tops of the waves, pushed by the following winds, were keeping pace with the wave crests, thus achieving a state of constantly breaking.

By 4 January, *Joshua* was 1,600 kilometres (1,000 miles) from Cape Horn. Moitessier divided his chart into squares, each of 5° longitude by 5° latitude, and noted in each square the storm frequency (percentage) for that time of year. As *Joshua* bore further south-east, the numbers rose. Despite having mastered the downwind steering technique that suited the boat, Moitessier and Françoise were tense as they approached Cape Horn, which to Moitessier's mind was 'the greatest adventure a seaman can dream of'.

Careful to steer a course that kept *Joshua* away from the Chilean coast, Moitessier ensured the boat was never in danger from a lee shore. The southern hemisphere depressions, revolving clockwise, meant an approaching storm announced itself with north-westerly winds – fine for following the coastline southwards – backing to westerly. In a west wind, the coast posed a real danger if a boat were too close inshore. As the depression passed, the wind backed further to south-west.

After the massive storm that had forced Moitessier to re-think his sailing strategy, the weather had remained relatively moderate. By 9 January, *Joshua* had travelled far enough south to 56°23' to be clear of the Chilean mainland. Cape Horn lay due west 480 kilometres (300 miles) distant.

The barometer began a slow rise, heralding a respite. On 10 January, making speed over the ground of 10 knots, Moitessier sighted the Diego Ramírez Islands. *Joshua* passed over the continental shelf edge and into shallower water – 90 metres (300 feet). A strengthening wind kicked up a vicious sea, but Moitessier did not worry. The barometer was holding steady. The wind was a lash from the tail of a passing depression, not a new storm. *Joshua* passed eastwards across the longitude of Cape Horn that evening, the sea running high but not dangerously so because the boat was again in deep water. What occupied Moitessier's mind more than the weather were thoughts of Marcel Bardiaux and Al Hansen, whose 'benevolent presence was almost tangible'.

At the earliest opportunity, dawn on 11 January, Moitessier gybed *Joshua* onto a north-easterly heading to make north. By the afternoon, she was sailing along in a light breeze.

Joshua made it back to Europe, mooring up in Alicante on 29 March 1966, a concession which, because of light winds, meant it would be faster for Françoise to travel by train to see her children than to sail on to Marseille.

SIR FRANCIS CHICHESTER

'If anything terrifies me, I must try to conquer it.'

Born .... 17 September 1901

Died .... 26 August 1972

Nationality .... British

Date of Cape Horn rounding ...... March 1967

Boat name .... *Gipsy Moth IV*

Designers .... John Illingworth, Angus Primrose

Year of build 1966

LOA .... 53 feet

Material .... Wood

Rig .... Ketch

rancis Chichester demonstrated his innate passion for adventure early when he left his boarding school, Marlborough College, aged 17 to emigrate to New Zealand without any prior discussion with his father, Charles, a Church of England clergyman and seventh son of the 8th Baronet Chichester of Raleigh.

Born on 17 September 1901 in Devon, England, Chichester began at boarding school aged six, an experience that influenced his later competitiveness, self-reliance and preference for doing things on his own. These traits showed when he arrived in New Zealand, where his resourcefulness earned him a small fortune with burgeoning businesses in forestry, mining and property. However, given the vagaries of the time, Chichester lost most of his money in the Great Depression, whereupon he returned to England in 1929 to visit family and, still sufficiently flush, gained a pilot's licence and took delivery of a de Havilland Gipsy Moth plane. That same year, he flew his new aircraft from London to Sydney with an ambition to better the record of 15½ days for a solo flight from England to Australia, a pace that had been set by Bert Hinkler, an Australian aviator, in February 1928. The record ultimately proved elusive; Chichester's de Havilland incurred a series of mechanical problems, but he did make it to Australia in 41 days.

Not satisfied – he wanted to circle the globe – he rigged the Gipsy Moth as a seaplane. Flying, it seemed, was not going to be the proving ground he had hoped it would be. As if to ram home this point, at Katsuura in Japan he flew into telephone cables that catapulted the plane into the harbour. He was lucky to walk away.

Chichester, by dint of age and poor eyesight, was considered unfit for a military commission at the outbreak of war in 1939. Instead, he joined the Royal Air Force Volunteer Reserve as a navigation instructor and penned the manual that allowed fighter pilots to navigate across Europe using kneeboard navigation techniques he had developed.

Chichester's time in the Royal Air Force combined with a keen commercial sense led him into his next business venture. At the war's end, he bought 15,000 surplus maps, pasted them onto board and cut them up to create jigsaw puzzles. This scheme led to the next project, a cartography company, which proved a success and provided the funds, years later, when he decided to revisit his original ambition to circumnavigate the globe, though this time the undertaking would be done by sea. The advent of commercial aircraft had degraded the pioneering spirit of flying, as far as he was concerned.

Chichester thus threw himself into his sailing and in 1960 won the first transatlantic yacht race, beating, among others in a small field of five, Dr David Lewis, who would later go on to circumnavigate Antarctica. Chichester had inspired the race, placing a bet with friends to race across the Atlantic westwards from Plymouth's Eddystone Lighthouse to the Ambrose lightship off New York Harbor. The prize was to be half a crown.

Four years later, in the second running of the race – this time with 15 starters – he finished second behind Frenchman Éric Tabarly. Also taking part in that race was Alec Rose, who finished fourth, and who would later go on to circumnavigate via Cape Horn.

Chichester began thinking about a circumnavigation in 1962. He researched the subject of small-boat voyages around the world and discovered that very few followed a route round Cape Horn. Moreover, the idea of rounding Cape Horn had been fermenting in his mind for years. Chichester thus determined that a circumnavigation, if it was to have any teeth, had to include a Cape Horn passage, despite admitting later to being terrified at the prospect:

> I told myself that anyone who tried to round the Horn in a small yacht had to be crazy. Of the eight yachts I knew to have attempted it, six had been capsized or somersaulted, before, during or after the passage.

His misgivings led to a deeper truth: fear had to be overcome, and fear, like a siren call, compelled him to examine his real motivations.

> I hate being frightened, but, even more, I detest being prevented by fright. At the same time, the Horn had a fearsome fascination, and it offered one of the greatest challenges left in the world.

Chichester's natural inclination as a loner, augmented by a tendency towards impatience bordering on abrasiveness and supported by rigid self-discipline, might have suited long-distance solo sailing, but he was vulnerable in his moods, prone to periods of despondency, even depression. For this reason he needed a handle, a way to project a reason for the voyage, to instil a sense of urgency and as a means of competing with himself. So he devised a kind of race: could he achieve the fastest time around the world in a small boat following the route of the clipper ships, from England to Australia? The average of the fastest runs achieved by the clipper ships was 100 days, so he set this as his target for the outward leg.

Despite his admiration for Vito Dumas, Chichester discounted the voyage of *LEHG II* as a circumnavigation since Dumas had stayed within the southern hemisphere (Dumas had had no choice, because of the war). He believed that to qualify as a true circumnavigation, the route had to contain at least one pair of antipodal points (two points diametrically opposed on the earth's surface) to shape a route as close as possible to a Great Circle – all lines of longitude and the equator being Great Circles. This inevitably necessitated crossing the equator twice, in opposite directions, and covering a distance at least equivalent to the earth's circumference.

At the launch of his new boat, *Gipsy Moth IV* – a 54-foot ketch of ply sandwich construction, purpose built for his round-the-world attempt – Chichester was concerned to see her rocking badly when a series of wavelets from a passing ferry came up her stern. That concern transmuted to alarm during sea trials, when *Gipsy Moth IV* heeled over to near 80 degrees in light winds. With thoughts of Cape Horn invading his mind, Chichester later wrote: 'Here was a boat which would lay over on her beam ends on the flat surface of the Solent; the thought of what she would do in the huge Southern Ocean seas put ice in my blood.'

It was far too late to make significant alterations to improve the boat's poor sailing characteristics. Piqued but stoic, Chichester crossed the start line off Plymouth Hoe on 27 August 1966. He sailed *Gipsy Moth IV* hard all the way to Australia, suffering frequent bouts of depression. One such incidence happened on 2 November, when the self-steering system broke – leaving the boat vulnerable in big seas when he could not be at the helm. A black wave of despondency consumed Chichester. Only one sensible option presented itself: he had to go into port, and accordingly changed course for

Fremantle to make repairs, which put paid to his self-imposed challenge of reaching Sydney within 100 days.

The failure of his mission became unbearable. On 17 November, unable to stomach it any longer and with characteristic bloody-mindedness, he altered course once more towards Sydney. It was a decision that was to prove almost fatal. He knew the 100-day target was now unlikely since he was using a smaller sail to help steer the boat in lieu of the self-steering gear, which meant he could not deploy one of the bigger driving sails. By 25 November, a huge swell was sweeping up behind the boat – Chichester reckoned the wave heights at 15 metres (50 feet) – but he had rigged lines from the tiller into the cabin to help control steering without having to kit-up in waterproofs each time he wanted to adjust his course.

The storm continued to rage. The following day, while Chichester was standing near the companionway watching the log, the needle suddenly sped round to its limit – 10 knots – and stayed there. A breaking wave had rolled up behind *Gipsy Moth IV*, gripped the canted hull and slewed the boat beam-on to the seas. The boat was knocked flat, racing forwards in the boiling water with the tips of her masts touching the surface. Chichester knew instantly that if the main mast dug in, the broach would evolve instantly into a capsize, a complete rollover. However, the seething foam raced beneath the hull, the masts began to lift clear of the surface, and Chichester could breathe once again.

Gipsy Moth IV arrived in Sydney at 4.30pm on 12 December 1966, having taken 106 days and 20½ hours (on corrected time) from England.

With Chichester moored at the Royal Sydney Yacht Squadron, Alan Payne and Warwick Hood (both naval architects who had designed Australian boats to challenge for the America's Cup) tried to persuade him that *Gipsy Moth IV* was not up to the job, design-wise, to take on Cape Horn. They were concerned that if she rolled, she would not right herself, given the contours of her hull. Surmising that the reason the boat was so tender – heeling far over at the slightest provocation – was down to the shape of the keel, they advised a keel extension to fill the area between the keel's aft margin and the heel of the rudder.

Chichester wanted to reach Cape Horn by the end of February – late in the austral summer, when storm frequency is at its lowest – which meant leaving

Sydney by mid-January at the latest. Urgency descended on the schedule of repairs to *Gipsy Moth IV.*

While Chichester waited impatiently, Captain Alan Villiers, a mariner of vast experience as a master on Cape Horners, tried to dissuade him. He said in an interview to the *Sun* newspaper: 'I beg Chichester not to attempt it (Cape Horn). The outward trip he has made is simple compared to this one ... The winds shift as if they are being controlled by some demon. I would not attempt it single-handed and I don't know any professional seaman who would. The risks are too great.'

Undeterred and relieved to be off, Chichester sailed from Sydney on Sunday 29 January, almost two weeks later than he intended, despite forecasts that a tropical cyclone was approaching from the east. After the dire warnings about Cape Horn, Chichester wondered, as he said goodbye to his wife Sheila, whether he would ever see her again.

Less than 24 hours after departure, Chichester found himself in the teeth of the cyclone, writing in his log: 'The white breakers showed in the blackness like monstrous beasts charging down on the yacht.' At this point, Chichester took to his bunk, exhausted by a combination of deck-work in the treacherous conditions, anxiety at what he might face at Cape Horn, and nausea (which he blamed on drinking Australian champagne). Chichester was also 65 years of age, and while he would probably have baulked at any suggestion that this might have been a hindrance, the physical demands of the challenge undoubt-edly exacted a heavier toll on him than they might have on a younger man.

He was woken from a fitful sleep as *Gipsy Moth IV* tipped over onto her side in the maelstrom beyond the cabin and kept going into a capsize. In the darkness, crockery, food tins, equipment and everything else not lashed or securely stowed rained down, adding to the cacophony of wind and maddened sea. *Gipsy Moth IV* did not roll through 360 degrees, but inverted, then righted herself on the same side. It was a close shave on two accounts: not only had the boat nearly capsized, but, in the light of day, Chichester found a serrated-edged knife in his bunk, embedded close to where his head had been. He crashed to a new psychological low, longing to be back in Sydney. If this could happen in 40–55 knots of wind, how, he wondered, could the boat survive the 100-knot conditions he might meet down at the Horn? Chichester was 'frightened and had a sick feeling of fear gnawing inside'.

One of the losses during the capsize was of a drogue, together with its 215-metre (700-foot) warp, which had been left unsecured on deck. Chichester would need it if he had to slow the boat and keep her stern to the seas in the Cape Horn storms. The loss added to his melancholy.

On 10 March, Chichester worked out his position – he was only 280 kilometres (175 miles) west of the spot where Miles and Beryl Smeeton's boat, *Tzu Hang*, had pitchpoled on 14 February 1957 with 2,213 kilometres (1,375 miles) still to go to Cape Horn. By 15 March, *Gipsy Moth IV* had made decent ground – 1,125 kilometres (700 miles) – and Chichester found himself in benign conditions, hoping against hope the fair weather would last long enough to see him round the Horn.

Chichester was under no illusions about the potential ferocity of the place, and in his book *Along The Clipper Way*, he had written:

> The normal westerlies pouring through this gap [The Drake Passage] are
> interfered with by the turbulent, vicious little cyclones rolling off the
> Andes... The bottom of the ocean shelves between the Horn and the
> [South] Shetland Islands and this induces the huge seas to break...

Chichester did not rely on his own interpretation. He was a voracious researcher, and among his findings, one merited particular mention:

> The Institute of Oceanography says that, according to Statistics of a
> Stationary Random Process, if a sea of average height 30 feet is running,
> then one wave out of every 300,000 can be expected to be four times
> that height i.e. 120 feet.

Chichester planned to pass between the Diego Ramírez Islands and the Ildefonso Islands to the north, giving Cape Horn itself a wide berth of 65–80 kilometres (40–50 miles). This way, he would avoid the shallows closer inshore where the current can race and ferocious winds pitch the seas into 15-metre (50-foot) breakers.

By 19 March, Chichester was 134 miles west of the Ildefonso Islands, 215 kilometres (157 miles) from Diego Ramírez. As *Gipsy Moth IV* drew closer, the wind backed from north-west to south and increased to force 9. He quickly reduced sail, hoping the wind would not continue to back to the south-east, effectively heading the boat close to a lee shore. Miraculously, the wind moderated through the night to 15 knots with occasional gusts to 36 knots. Williwaws were still a threat, however, and Chichester worried that if he strayed too close to land he was vulnerable to these potentially devastating katabatic bombs.

At dawn he expected to see land, but the horizon was empty, other than the grey sweep of the sea. Assuming his navigation was accurate, he concluded that *Gipsy Moth IV* must have already passed the Diego Ramírez Islands. Chichester accordingly decided on a new heading, east-north-east, straight for the Horn. In the moderate conditions the sea-state he had feared

Gipsy Moth IV at Cape Horn

in big winds no longer applied. Coming on deck, Chichester was startled to see a ship, HMS *Proctor*, maybe half a mile away. He immediately ducked into the cabin to call her on the radio. He learned that his voyage was gathering an ever-increasing following back in England. The Royal Navy vessel was on station to view the feat he was about to attempt. Journalists on board would report the trials of this latest national hero. HMS *Proctor* was also there to offer assistance if it became necessary.

The wind began to accelerate, to 40 knots. With Chichester on deck again to take in sail, *Gipsy Moth IV* took a wave on her quarter. The boat slewed round, beam-on to the seas. Quickly, Chichester corrected the helm and at that moment turned to see a black, forbidding fortress of rock towering from the waves – Cape Horn. *Gipsy Moth IV* sailed eastwards across the Cape's longitude at 11.15am on 21 March.

The wind continued to strengthen, kicking the sea into a vicious chop, exacerbated, Chichester thought, by the shallower water over the continental shelf. HMS *Proctor* stayed close. The presence of the ship irritated Chichester. He felt it was, in this supreme moment of accomplishment, an invasion of his privacy. He also felt seasick and overcome by a peculiar lethargy.

On board HMS *Proctor*, a Reuters journalist later wrote: 'The translucent bottle-green seas were moving mountains and valleys of water, rearing, rolling and subsiding with a fearful brute force.'

Chichester tried coaxing *Gipsy Moth IV* northwards to get into the lee of Horn Island, sailing diagonally across the breaking seas. The change in direction allowed the seas to board the boat, repeatedly swamping the cockpit and soaking Chichester. Then, the wind backed to south-west. Any protection from land was now lost and Chichester set a course straight for Staten Island at the eastern approaches to the Cape Horn area. This was dangerous – the seas were huge, and if the wind backed to the south, *Gipsy Moth IV* would find herself close to a lethal lee shore. Soon, the seas built to become some of the most vicious Chichester had experienced on the entire voyage, but, as he later wrote, 'that sea was kid's stuff compared to what was running three hours later'.

Chichester's anemometer registered the wind at 55 knots although he believed the instrument was unreliable in strong winds and estimated that the actual wind speed was higher. The seas became frightening, which Chichester put down to the seabed contours. *Gipsy Moth IV* was sailing over the cusp of shallow and deep water. Only a few miles off the starboard side, the water was 2,300 fathoms (4,206 metres (13,800 feet)), yet on the port side it was only about 200 fathoms. Chichester continued to head north-east, making for the eastern end of Staten Island, his navigation perhaps fooled by the occasional lulls in the wind. By his dead reckoning, Staten Island lay 137 kilometres (85 miles) ahead. The wind continued to back, forcing the boat onto a more northerly heading. Chichester had to get away from land, so he gybed *Gipsy Moth IV*. The boat was rolling – Chichester later described the motion as 'frightful – making it difficult to stand in the cabin'. He felt tense, 'tight as a coot' (although he admitted he had no idea how a coot could be tight), and fortified himself with a shot of hot rum.

During the storm, the self-steering gear seemed incapable of holding *Gipsy Moth IV* on the desired heading, so Chichester rigged lines to control the tiller from the companionway as a precaution. He also had a look at the windvane and found it catching in the mizzen backstay, a problem that he easily rectified by tying a preventer line to the backstay.

The following dawn, 22 March, Chichester expected to be in clear water; his navigation suggested that Staten Island should be 56 kilometres (35 miles) ahead. Preparing breakfast, he glanced out of the doghouse window to port. Panic seized him. A jagged landmass pierced the still-raging sea less than 16 kilometres (10 miles) away. He later said: 'I felt as if the roots of my hair all over my body had turned red. I was startled to the bone.'

The potential calamity registered immediately. The treacherous current must have pushed *Gipsy Moth IV* inshore during the night, meaning the boat was bearing down on Staten Island, a lee shore, in 40-knot winds. All thoughts of breakfast vanished. Chichester took three bearings of a cape *Gipsy Moth IV* was passing in order to get a position, then grabbed the sextant, took a sight and calculated, as quickly as he could, a position line. The boat's speed over the ground registered 8.8 knots. The land was closing, mountainous terrain soaring upwards behind the serrated coast. Chichester's calculations indicated he was passing the eastern cape of

Staten Island and was much closer than he had estimated, only 8 kilometres (5 miles) distant. Later, when Chichester reviewed his navigation, he concluded that the batteries of the speedometer had run down and that the instrument was displaying a false speed-over-the-ground reading. *Gipsy Moth IV* was actually barrelling along much more quickly than the speedometer was showing. Had Chichester, exhausted by lack of sleep, anxiety and seasickness, taken to his bunk, *Gipsy Moth IV* might well have run into the inescapable clutches of the Cape Horn area and been smashed to matchwood on the iron-hard black rocks of Staten Island.

The sea-state was still rough, the wind at force 6 as *Gipsy Moth IV* managed to clear Staten Island and head north-east towards the Falkland Islands. By evening, the storm had abated. Chichester felt, at last, that he had rounded the Horn and celebrated the moment by cracking open a bottle of champagne.

By 25 March, *Gipsy Moth IV* had passed the Falkland Islands and crossed north over the 50th parallel. Chichester recognised, as the clipper captains had before him, that his Cape Horn passage was over. He felt that he had endured 'a nightmare of sailing through the Southern Ocean. There is something nightmarishly frightening about those big breaking seas and screaming wind.'

Despite his achievements, he still had to get home. Chichester, perhaps through excessive fatigue, became short, bad-tempered even, with reporters on the radio. One female correspondent from *The Sunday Times* asked: 'What did you eat on your first meal after rounding the Horn?' To which Chichester responded: 'Strongly urge you stop questioning and interviewing me which poisons the romantic attraction of this voyage. I am beginning to dread transmitting nights and I fear losing my enthusiasm for worthwhile dispatches ... Difficult radio communication is a great strain anyway. Interviewing makes it intolerable.' The eminent travel writer Jonathan Raban wrote of Chichester: '... you catch a whiff of brimstone in his makeup...'

In contrast to the amiable, extrovert Dumas and the highly sociable but less tolerant Bardiaux, Chichester perhaps summed himself up best when he said: 'I never seemed so much to enjoy doing things with other people. I know now that I don't do a thing nearly so well when with someone.'

Chichester brought *Gipsy Moth IV* home to Plymouth late on a Sunday evening, 28 May 1967. The Queen knighted him shortly after his arrival using the same sword her forebear Queen Elizabeth I had used to knight Sir Francis Drake, the first Englishman to sail a circumnavigation.

Chichester died on 26 August 1972, aged 71.

After years on permanent display in Greenwich and following a subsequent restoration by the United Kingdom Sailing Academy, *Gipsy Moth IV* is now in private ownership.

SIR ALEC ROSE

'The ultimate test of man and ship is to sail round Cape Horn.'

Born	13 July 1908
Died	11 January 1991
Nationality	British
Date of Cape Horn rounding	April 1968
Boat name	*Lively Lady*
Designer	Frederick Shepherd
Year of build	1948
LOA	36 feet
Material	Wood
Rig	Ketch

Alec Rose included the terms *dark horse, dreamer, thinker, idealist* and *individualist* among the list of character traits found among singlehanded sailors, people who were prepared to stand or fall by their decisions and actions, himself being no exception. He admitted that he was not at his best in a crowd, and that he was not suited to a regular job but much preferred the long, irregular hours of self-employment.

Rose, who served on the Atlantic convoys during World War II, had thought about entering the inaugural transatlantic race in 1960 organised by Francis Chichester but decided he was not sufficiently prepared. By the time the next race rolled round four years later, he was raring to go – despite the fact that financially the quest was a stretch and that his many friends cautioned him against entering, fearing that taking part in the race was for him foolhardy and that they would never see him again. Brushing aside these admonitions, however, Rose started the race from Plymouth on 23 May in the company of sailors such as Chichester, Hasler and Tabarly. He did not harbour any expectation of winning but instead demonstrated a steely determination to finish the course. He did, coming in a creditable fourth, one place ahead of Blondie Hasler and beating David Lewis into seventh place.

Rose was born in Canterbury, Kent on 13 July 1908, one of five children. His father was a haulage contractor, ferrying hops to breweries and fruit and vegetables to Covent Garden market. No one in his family had any connection to the sea. Like Marcel Bardiaux, one of his contemporaries, Rose was fragile, often ill as a child, and for a period had to be taken to and from school in a wheelchair. Unlike his body, though, Rose's mind was active, his imagination wide-ranging. He dreamed of grander horizons, dreams fuelled by listening to his sister read of the exploits of great adventurers who had gone before. Cape Horn captured his imagination. This obsession, combined with a developing yearning for the sea, fermented his desire to one day make a solo circumnavigation.

At 20, Rose emigrated to Canada, finding work as a ranch-hand in Alberta, ploughing, logging, road building – a tough existence that turned him from the fragile child he had been into a strong, resilient man. After one year, his farmer employer was no longer able to pay his wages, so Rose returned to England to work in the family firm. This he did, along with fulfilling wartime services in the Navy during World War II, a harrowing experience that reduced him to a shadow of his former self. On his discharge in 1945, his health had deteriorated and, dogged with anxiety, he felt like a deserter. In modern medical parlance, this was probably a case of post-traumatic stress disorder (PTSD). Rose recovered slowly by throwing himself into a market-garden business, and when financial pressures became too great in the austere environment of post-war Britain, he sold the business and bought a greengrocer shop in Herne Bay.

Rose's instinct for what he called individualism began to emerge at this stage of his life. Business was slow in wintertime, so to occupy himself and find expression for his burgeoning desire for marine adventure, he bought a ship's lifeboat and converted it to sail. But, financial and personal pressures had taken their toll. Rose's marriage of 28 years broke up and he sold the greengrocer business, thus finding himself with enough time to begin sailing in earnest, at least until the money ran out. He studied inshore navigation and took his first lessons in celestial navigation from his son, Michael, a deck officer in the Merchant Navy.

A new wife, Dorothy, rapidly diminishing financial resources and escalating ambitions to sail beyond European waters altered Rose's direction. He needed to make money. To this end, in February 1961 he bought a fruiterers' shop in Southsea.

For the 1964 transatlantic race, Rose decided that his boat, *Neptune's Daughter*, was not suitable. He thus sold it and sought out another boat. Months later Rose found *Lively Lady* in Yarmouth on the Isle of Wight – a narrow-beamed, flush-decked 36-footer built in Calcutta, its frame made of padauk, a hardwood native to Asia and Africa, and planked with 3.5-cm (1⅜-in) teak.

Rose remodelled the boat, adding a doghouse over the companionway hatch, employing John Illingworth of Illingworth and Primrose (the same firm that would later design Chichester's *Gipsy Moth IV*) to design a new cutter rig and sail plan and Blondie Hasler to make and fit the self-steering gear.

The 15 starters quickly spread out and Rose, a week into the race, had his first taste of huge, breaking Atlantic rollers. The violent motion of the boat left Rose feeling stiff and sore. He was thankful for any opportunity to lie on his bunk, at times wondering whether entering the race had been foolhardy.

At the finish, Rose spent time with Dr David Lewis and Francis Chichester before heading home across the Atlantic. During this passage, he encountered more severe weather, with screeching wind, heavy rain and waves breaking over the boat. Rose found work on the foredeck particularly dangerous. Waves lifted the bow 20 feet in the air before the boat crashed down into deep valleys of water.

Undeterred by his traumatic return from America, Rose began thinking about a longer singlehanded voyage – a circumnavigation – and an opportunity to test himself against the Horn when, in 1965, Chichester announced his bid to circumnavigate. Not competitive like Chichester, Rose was content to follow him round, and set about re-rigging *Lively Lady* as a ketch. Dorothy, meanwhile, ran their shop, leaving Rose free to get on with his preparations.

Rose felt it only courteous to let Chichester know of his intention to circumnavigate, so he duly telephoned Chichester's house in London's St James's Square, only to discover that Chichester already knew about his plans. Chichester suggested they leave from Plymouth together on 27 August. He probably liked the idea of a race, particularly given that he had the superior boat. *Lively Lady* was no match for *Gipsy Moth IV* and Rose knew it. A group of businessmen-cum-yachting-enthusiasts spotted the marketing opportunity and in order to make a race of it, they suggested Rose go on a more competitive boat, which they would sponsor. Rose was uncomfortable with the idea. He did not want to be answerable to others, nor did he have any interest in racing Chichester. Rose declined, though the group did ease his preparations by underwriting the bulk of his expedition's expenses.

Rose wanted to leave before Chichester, on 7 August, in order to give himself sufficient time to round Cape Horn during the austral summer with a stop in Australia en route. It was a hectic period for Rose and by 7 August, he was exhausted. Nevertheless, *Lively Lady* crossed the start line off the Royal Albert Yacht Club at 3.00pm on the appointed date.

When the last of the escort boats departed, Rose felt depressed. He was unprepared and he knew it. The engine was not working and below, the stores were a mess and not properly stowed away. He had succumbed to media pressure. Having announced his departure date some time previously, he felt unable to delay the start and risk disappointing his many supporters.

The following day, the self-steering broke. The weather was foul. Rose put into Plymouth to fix the self-steering, tidy the boat and get the engine working, setting off again on Monday 15 August. During a foresail change just beyond the breakwater, Rose lost his hold of the halyard and saw it run up to the masthead. As he was unable to retrieve it, *Lively Lady* returned to Plymouth once more. He set off again – hoping it would be third time lucky. Those hopes were dashed early the following morning, when a ship collided with *Lively Lady*, splintering the bowsprit and damaging her mast. Rose had no choice but to go back to Plymouth for a third time.

Rose tied *Lively Lady* against the harbour wall while he carried out repairs. At low tide she stood on her keel, but she was too upright, enabling the wash from a passing tug to lift her just as she was taking the ground on an ebb tide. The rope securing her to the quay parted under the strain and she fell away from the wall, crashing heavily onto her starboard side. The damage was extensive – split hull timbers, caulking shocked out of place and damaged deck gear. It was a catastrophe. To get at the inside of the hull, Rose would have to remove all the internal joinery. He figured there was no possibility the boat would be ready before October, far too late to make Cape Horn for the southern hemisphere summer. With a seaman's superstition, Rose blamed his bad luck on a leprechaun doll given to him as a mascot by an Irish actor, so he disposed of the thing by hurling it into the furnace at Mashfords boatyard.

Rose was still in Plymouth, clearing out *Lively Lady*, when Chichester arrived on 26 August for his start the next day. He showed Rose round *Gipsy Moth IV* and Rose saw him off, a spectator on one of the escort boats, feeling sick at what had happened to *Lively Lady*.

The second start came almost one year later, on 16 July 1967, again from the Royal Albert Yacht Club, exactly seven weeks after Chichester's triumphant return to Plymouth.

The start went without a hitch but Rose was still badly affected by the disasters and embarrassment of the previous summer. Many people freely expressed negative opinions: his trip was pointless seeing as Chichester had already done it; his boat was too slow; and, most wounding of all, his critics doubted his ability to survive the voyage. Rose spiralled into depression, burdened by the pressure of not letting his many friends and supporters down again. He felt vulnerable.

Incidents peppered the passage to Melbourne. Just south of the equator, severe storms buffeted *Lively Lady*; Rose suffered dreadfully from back pain; and just west of Cape Town, on 6 October, a fire broke out behind the switchboard. Rose finally made contact with Cape Town on 10 October to learn that his daughter Jane had got married three days previously.

Halfway between South Africa and Australia, one of the twin backstays parted in high winds and the mast began whipping violently. Anxious that he might lose the mast (and thinking he might have to try for St Paul Island, where there was supposedly a cache of supplies for marooned sailors), Rose managed to set up a jury rig using the foresail halyards. On 21 November, the other backstay failed in a force 8 gale, and again, with the mast whipping dangerously, Rose had to set up a jury rig while he fixed the backstay.

As *Lively Lady* passed through Port Phillip Heads on the way into Hobsons Bay and Melbourne on 17 December 1967, the Australian Prime Minister, Harold Holt, was watching from shore, having made the trip specially to see Rose's arrival. Holt then decided to take a swim, against the advice of several friends and his police escort, and was subsequently lost, presumed drowned, his body never found.

Like Chichester's son, George, Rose's son Michael had emigrated to Australia, and now lived in Williamstown, near Melbourne. Michael came aboard with a bottle of champagne to welcome his father and introduce Rose to two people he had never met: his grandsons, Chris and Nigel.

After a month's stay and with a heavy heart, Rose left Melbourne on 14 January 1968 for the second leg: home via Cape Horn. Yet another rigging failure soon after departure forced Rose to make an emergency stopover in Bluff, New Zealand on 1 February, and it was here that he received two surprises: so generous was the local community in helping Rose repair *Lively Lady* that he did not have to put his hand in his pocket, after which, out of the blue, the Bank of New South Wales made an offer of financial help (no strings attached) which, because of the generosity of everyone involved in fixing *Lively Lady*, was not actually needed. Then, on Tuesday 6 February, repairs made, the Mayor of Bluff organised a grand send-off that drew a crowd, many of whom brought gifts of home-made jam, whisky, beer and biscuits. This cheered Rose, who, despite being alone once again, felt greatly moved by the warmth and kindness of the people of Bluff.

During the 8,000-kilometre (5,000-mile) passage to Cape Horn, *Lively Lady* was regularly battered by foul weather, the wind sometimes getting up to force 12 – hurricane strength. Rose had never experienced such fierce wind. Big seas constantly swept the deck and cockpit. All he could do was watch apprehensively, oilskins on in readiness.

All the way to the Horn, the weather followed the classic Southern Ocean pattern of gales separated by brief respites. These took their toll, in particular during the night of 26 February when, after a brief lull, the wind escalated to storm force. The seas were massive, so Rose retreated below – but not in time: a huge wave broke over the port quarter, and a deluge poured into the cabin through the open companionway. Rose became used to hearing the hissing of white water and then bracing himself for the impact of a wave smashing the hull, one of which threw him across the cabin, which he thought may have caused him to break a rib.

Like Chichester the previous year, Rose was aiming to pass between the Ildefonso Islands and the Diego Ramírez Islands. By the evening of 30 March, as he closed with Cape Horn, the north-westerly wind kicked up again to force 10 (52 knots) gusting force 12 (64+ knots), driving big seas from the port quarter, slewing the boat and laying her over. The storm persisted through the night. On 31 March, Rose sighted land – Waterman Island. A tanker, the Royal Fleet Auxiliary Ship *Wave Chief*, with orders to look out for Rose, took up station off *Lively Lady*'s port quarter as she passed north of Diego Ramírez. Rose was lucky. After all the bad fortune he had suffered during his first attempt to leave England, no one deserved some good fortune more than him. The wind died and the sea moderated.

At dawn on 1 April, Rose sighted Cape Horn 32 kilometres (20 miles) north-east, standing majestically above the horizon. *Lively Lady* passed the longitude of Cape Horn at noon, 17.5 kilometres (11 miles) off in benign conditions. It was almost with a sense of disbelief that Rose stood on deck and spied Cape Horn. Not only had he attained this enormous milestone, but after the bashing *Lively Lady* had taken in the Southern Ocean the mild conditions seemed somehow unreal, as though the other great actor in this piece, Cape Horn itself, had managed, somehow, to fluff its lines. He stood and stared at the great rock, a moment he had dreamed about and planned for. He thought of all the others who had passed that way, lone sailors as well as the crews of the great square-riggers. He felt both small and comforted as he continued to gaze with awed respect at that most fearsome of capes.

The north-westerly wind continued light. To toast his rounding of Cape Horn (and his luck), Rose went below and made himself a hot drink of lemon and honey with a generous tot of whisky. The gift of a bottle of champagne to celebrate this momentous occasion remained in the locker; a cold drink was the last thing he wanted. As he drank his toddy, a misty rain enveloped *Lively Lady* and a black cloud settled over Cape Horn, blotting it from view.

Lively Lady passed Staten Island at dawn on 2 April, 16 kilometres (10 miles) off. *Wave Chief* called on the radio to tell Rose she was leaving the area to return to her base in the Falkland Islands. As she passed by, the crew lined the rail to give Rose three cheers.

Alec Rose and *Lively Lady* had managed to slip by Cape Horn in a lull between gales. As she made her escape north-eastwards, leaving the Falklands to port, gales returned and once again lashed *Lively Lady*.

Almost a year to the day since his departure from England, Alec Rose arrived home at Southsea on 4 July 1968 to a welcoming crowd of 250,000 people. A modest, courteous man, he was staggered by the sheer scale of the welcome. The following day he learned he was to receive a knighthood.

Sir Alec Rose continued to be involved in sailing until his death on 11 January 1991, aged 82. He bequeathed *Lively Lady* to the City of Portsmouth.

TO STRIVE, TO SEEK, TO FIND
AND NOT TO YIELD

The indigenous people of Tierra del Fuego belonged to several tribes, of which one, the Yaghan, established the most southerly settlements, including on Cape Horn 10,000 years ago. Where they came from is speculative, but theory expounds the possibility that they were driven south by enemies and may originally have come from as far north as the Arctic coasts of modern-day Canada. They made remarkable adaptations to their hostile environment, evolving higher metabolic rates that maintained core body temperature a full degree higher than that of Europeans. They wore few, if any, clothes, sheltered among rocks or slept in the open, waterproofed themselves by smothering their skins in animal grease and sustained themselves by hunting sea lions and diving for shellfish in the frigid waters.

Cape Horn was destined to remain more or less unknown to anyone else until the Dutch expedition of 1616, under the command of Captain Willem Schouten, although many other expeditions from Portugal, Spain and England had preceded the Dutch venture – all glorious failures but for two led by Magellan and Drake. Over the ensuing 200 years, the arrival of Europeans introduced disease – mumps, measles and smallpox – against which the Yaghan and other Fuegian tribes had no immunity. Communities were decimated into extinction.

As ever, the conception, planning and execution of these expeditions had but one purpose: to make money by finding a quicker, more profitable route to the riches of Asia, the alternative being a long slog around Africa.

Ferdinand Magellan, a Portuguese born into minor nobility in about 1480 (the exact date is uncertain), earned the disfavour of his king, Manuel I, after involving himself in various dubious trading practices with the Moors. He did not see it that way and felt his service to the Crown merited some reward, but the King's retort was unequivocal – if Magellan wished to take himself off to Spain and curry favour there, then good luck and good riddance. Magellan duly took himself off. He also became convinced, after studying the maps and journals of earlier pioneers, that a route to the East must exist. In Seville, he persuaded King Charles I to back him.

Magellan's expedition fleet comprised five ships, *San Antonio*, *Concepcion*, *Victoria*, *Santiago*, and his flagship, *Trinidad*, which set sail in September 1519, riven with mistrust, Magellan's subordinate officers all being Spanish noblemen. During the course of the voyage, Magellan poked and prodded the Argentine coast, nosing around every bay and river delta, all promising more than they ultimately delivered. He was heading ever southwards, dealing with mutiny, ordering summary executions and rationing his men en route. While on one scouting foray, the *Santiago* was lost in a storm.

In October 1520, more than a year after departing from Spain, Magellan finally found the entrance to a passage whose tidal flows suggested that this might just be the one. He dispatched two ships to investigate. Their men reappeared five days later, delirious. Tidal movements deep into the passage indicated that it must continue and open eventually into another sea. What Magellan did not know, and nor could he ascertain, was how long the passage might be. Not prepared to take the risk involved in finding out, one of the scout ships, *San Antonio*, deserted and returned to Spain on 20 November. The three remaining ships proceeded westwards and into the passage.

Here, at night, the hillsides bordering the channel became speckled with pinpricks of lights – the myriad fires of the indigenous tribes. The sight inspired Magellan to christen this land *Tierra del Fuego*, Land of Fire.

The small flotilla emerged on 28 November, rounding the northern end of Desolation Island, greeted by blue skies and deceptively placid waters. Magellan named the new ocean *El Mar Pacifico*.

What Magellan left undiscovered was whether an open-water passage linking the Atlantic with his newly christened Pacific Ocean might exist further south. It was to be the English who found it, by accident, during

Ferdinand Magellan, 1480–1521

an expedition commanded by Francis Drake with the singular purpose of plundering Spanish treasure ships laden with Aztec riches that were being transported back to Spain from the Caribbean. Drake, a skilled seaman and courageous buccaneer, had become the scourge of the Spanish in the Atlantic by pirating their ships. The Spanish also had a fleet operating in the Pacific but, fearful of Drake, they mounted stiffer protection on the Atlantic side, presuming their Pacific operations to be safe from attack. Drake sought to take advantage of this complacency, conceiving a plan to attack the Spanish from the rear, in the Pacific.

With the tacit approval of his queen, Elizabeth I, Drake sailed from England on 15 November 1577. Like Magellan's more than 50 years previously, Drake's expedition comprised five ships and he commanded the fastest of them, *Pelican*. He soon added a sixth ship, *Mary* (formerly *Santa Maria*), a Portuguese merchant vessel captured off the coast of Africa near the Cape Verde Islands. He also added its captain, Nuno da Silva, a man with considerable experience navigating in South American waters.

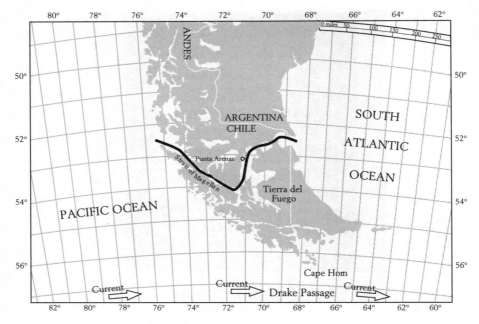

Map showing the Strait of Magellan and the Drake Passage

Despite this expertise, however, Drake lost enough men during the Atlantic crossing to justify scuttling two ships. When they made landfall in Argentina, they also discovered that *Mary* had rotting timbers, so they burned her.

The three remaining ships made it to the entrance of the Strait of Magellan, by now a known geographical landmark, where Drake renamed *Pelican* the *Golden Hind* for reasons of political expediency. He had executed Thomas Doughty – a former secretary to Sir Christopher Hatton, a privy councillor favoured by the Queen – for theft. Sir Christopher Hatton's family crest bore a golden hind.

It did not take long for Drake to navigate the 560 kilometres (350 miles) of the strait – 17 days – and he reached the Pacific on 6 September 1578. At this point, a series of vicious storms stampeding in from the west forced Drake to lead his fleet south and west for fear of being dashed on the lee shore, but nevertheless, one of the ships, *Marigold*, went down on 28 September with the loss of all hands. Unprepared to continue with the onslaught, Captain John Wynter, commanding *Elizabeth*, re-entered

Sir Francis Drake, 1540–1596

the Strait of Magellan and fled for England. Now sailing alone, *Golden Hind* continued to face a succession of storms that drove her south and west once more.

The question of whether Drake ventured sufficiently far south to assume a southern open-water route connecting the Atlantic and Pacific oceans is speculative. His journal records as much, though none of his fellow crew recalled seeing open water to the east and Drake's descriptions are more suggestive of islands to the north-west of Cape Horn. Whether he saw Cape Horn or not is moot: his name is now synonymous with it.

What is known is that the Dutch were the first to successfully navigate the open-water route and christen the rock that today is called Cape Horn. By the 17th century, the Dutch had a stranglehold on the spice trade. Many companies competed for a share of the rich pickings, and chief among these was the Dutch East India Company, one of whose founders was a trader by the name of Isaac Le Maire. To defeat the competition, the company persuaded the government to grant it sole rights to use the eastern sea route around Africa and the westabout route via the Strait of Magellan.

A dispute between Le Maire and the directors of the Dutch East India Company about the direction the company should take led Le Maire to seek a means of helping himself to the spice trade in direct competition with the Dutch East India Company. However, the only way he could achieve his goal was to avoid the trade restrictions and find another route around the South American continent, something that both he and one of the company's sea captains, Willem Schouten, believed was possible, as Drake had surmised.

Accordingly, Willem Schouten and Le Maire's son Jacob prepared to sail in two ships, *Unity* and *Hoorn*, and the small but expensively kitted-out expedition set sail in June 1615. After crossing the Atlantic, Schouten found a river on the Patagonian coast with a large tidal range in which they could beach the ships and clean the vessels' undersides using the usual method of firing the bottoms and burning off the marine growth. For the *Hoorn*, this operation went spectacularly wrong and the ship went up in smoke.

So the *Unity* continued alone. Schouten pursued the only logical option as the ship ventured further south – to follow the coastline, a decision that took a leap of faith as they altered course more and more eastwards following the eastward trend of the land. When the ship arrived at a gap in which a strong

An artist's impression of the *Unity* rounding Cape Horn in 1616

tide was running, suggestive of open water at its other end – logic similar to that earlier employed by Magellan – Schouten ordered the advance. Today this treacherous stretch of water is called the Le Maire Strait.

The problem now facing Schouten lay in determining how far west he should go before heading north. Where was the end of the continent?

He believed he had found it on 29 January 1616, recording that 'wee saw land againe lying north west and north north-west from us, which was the land that lay South from the straights of Magellan which reacheth Southward, all high hillie lande covered over with snow, ending with a sharpe point which wee called Kaap Hoorn…'

With the certain knowledge that a sea route existed that linked the Atlantic Ocean to its larger cousin, the Pacific, the story of Cape Horn could begin, a story that would change the pattern of global trade, see this place earn its brutal reputation, and move Cape Horn into legend.

BERNARD MOITESSIER AND
THE GOLDEN GLOBE

W hen Chichester returned triumphant to Plymouth on the afternoon
of 28 May 1967, his greatest achievement was the entirety of the
voyage; Chichester had raised the bar and raised it high. By completing his
circumnavigation with only one stop, the challenge became obvious. Could
one man, alone, sail around the earth without stopping? Alec Rose's near
imitation of Chichester's feat in 1968 stoked the flames.

In Britain, talk spread like wildfire at boating and yacht clubs and in the
pages of the sailing press. What a venture! Was such a feat even possible?
Who would be crazy enough to try it?

Contenders had begun emerging before Chichester had even made it
back to Britain, and included Éric Tabarly, a French naval officer who had
dominated the 1964 transatlantic singlehanded race. The race, sponsored by
the *Observer* newspaper and known internationally by the acronym OSTAR,
had the effect of hauling ocean racing into a new era of hi-tech one-design
boats funded by commercial sponsorship deals. In preparation for the 1968
OSTAR, more than 40 sailors registered interest, including Tabarly, who was
building a new boat, a monster 67-foot trimaran. Speculation was already
rife that Tabarly, a national hero and winner of the *Legion d'Honneur* for his
1964 victory, might be considering a solo non-stop circumnavigation in the
new boat following the 1968 OSTAR. Success would eclipse Chichester and
shift the widening focus on long-range sailing to France.

The Sunday Times saw the commercial possibilities of a non-stop round-the-
world challenge and stepped in as official race sponsor, appointing Sir Francis
Chichester as chairman of judges. Race rules required entrants to depart from

the UK and sail an eastward course passing south of the Cape of Good Hope, Cape Leeuwin and Cape Horn. There were no qualification requirements and no rules on boat specifications, and there was no set start date. Entrants merely had to depart between 1 June 1968 at the earliest and 31 October at the latest. *The Sunday Times* offered a Golden Globe trophy for the first to finish and, because competitors would set sail on varying dates, a £5,000 cash prize for the quickest finisher based on elapsed time, which might mean that finisher was not necessarily first past the finishing line. It was also entirely possible for the same contender to win both prizes.

The talk, the hype and the sheer audacity of the challenge became a centrifuge that gradually teased out nine men who would vie for the chance to claim an iconic place in sailing history. And so began the evolution of singlehanded racing by way of Cape Horn.

One of these nine men was Bernard Moitessier, quickly designated the race favourite given his huge experience, particularly his previous rounding of Cape Horn in January 1966. He also brought another great advantage with him – his boat. Like its owner, *Joshua* was tough, proven and – many would think the simile not overblown – made of steel.

Moitessier's entry into the Golden Globe Race was not, however, straightforward. By 1968, he was famous for his sailing exploits described in two bestselling books, though the second of these, *The Logical Route*, was causing him a problem, a mental anguish. He felt he had scratched off the book too quickly under pressure from his editor, too propelled by the attractions of commercial gain. Had he sacrificed his integrity and, worse, the purity of the marine environment he so loved and cherished on the altar of that false god, money? He felt 'sucked down by a huge inner emptiness', and wondered 'what last thoughts come to someone who has swallowed a lethal dose of poison'. What could he do to salvage himself? The idea dawned: sail around the world alone and without stopping – surely a magnificent genuflection to the sea. Moreover, he could write another book – something more considered, more thoughtful, more respectful. From the abyss, Moitessier spiralled upwards into a state of joy at the prospect, moved *Joshua* to Toulon and eagerly set about preparations for the voyage.

The Sunday Times felt it imperative that Moitessier be part of the Golden Globe Race; he was the only potential competitor who might stand a chance of actually pulling it off, and with at least one viable contender, the newspaper would reap more bang for its buck. *The Sunday Times* thus sent Murray Sayle, the reporter who had covered Chichester's voyage, to France. His mission was clear: persuade Moitessier to join the race.

Sayle found the Frenchman in a bistro in the port of Toulon. After the journalist had gone through his pitch, Moitessier was flabbergasted and appalled. This – racing around the world for cash – must surely be the ultimate prostitution of a sailor's talents. To take part, Moitessier told Sayle, would be a complete surrender of his integrity to the materialism he so abhorred. Moitessier stormed out of the bistro.

His plan, his odyssey, was to be his creation, his homage to the marine wilderness, his catharsis. He had no interest in taking part in a race.

To Murray Sayle and his superiors in London, Moitessier's reaction was – to say the least – bizarre. They had discussions, came up with a scheme, and Sayle entered the lion's den, cornering Moitessier a few days later. The new plan involved a change in race rules, which meant that competitors could start from any port north of latitude 40°N. For Moitessier, this meant a French port.

Murray Sayle needn't have worried. Moitessier, despite his apparent chagrin, had actually already changed his mind. He would join the race and, furthermore, he would sail from Plymouth.

Moitessier set sail from England on 22 August 1968, still disturbed by his internal conundrum – guilt at wilfully seeking fame and money in defiance of his self-directed mandate to reject commercialism. Once underway, he took to yoga, learning from a book given to him by a friend, on a quest to combine mind and body with the sea as he sought to find a state of harmony and balance.

Towards the end of January 1969, Moitessier was 1,600 kilometres (1,000 miles) from Cape Horn and shaping a course similar, if a little further south, to the course he had followed with Françoise three years earlier. The barometer started to drop and, fearing a storm, Moitessier reefed down as the wind reached force 7 (30 knots). Despite his fears, though, the wind did not rise further, the swell remained even and the few breaking waves posed no danger to *Joshua* as his course dropped below the 50th parallel.

Moitessier had learned the lesson from his previous excursion to these high southern latitudes about running before the wind – the importance of having a few small sails with many reefing points so he could fly exactly the right amount of sail to suit the conditions.

Forty-eight hours away from the Horn, Moitessier was on deck, grateful for the moderate wind, the sky clear and a moonbeam striking the sea 'like a huge spotlight searching among the stars'. Another moonbeam appeared, and then another before Moitessier realised it was not the moon but the aurora australis, the Southern Lights, the interplay of the sun's radiation with the earth's magnetic field. Like theatre curtains drawn across the stage, clouds moved in to obscure the moon, then the stars and finally the aurora.

By dawn, the barometer had risen, a promise of fair weather as *Joshua* barrelled towards Cape Horn 240 kilometres (150 miles) away. The wind strengthened to force 8 (37 knots). Moitessier took up station at the mast, clipped on to a lifeline in readiness to reduce sail as big seas buffeted *Joshua*. The swell increased, a portent of a storm somewhere out to the west. If there were a storm and it hit in the next 24 hours, Moitessier might find himself in shallow water with murderous seas. He therefore maintained his vigil at the mast, debating whether or not to shorten sail. An urge to go out onto the bowsprit gripped him. It would be dangerous in the extreme and he managed, with a huge effort, to resist.

Joshua surfed down the wave faces as Moitessier, spellbound, clung to the mast, the boat's nose skimming the surface, sending water cascading back along the decks. The self-steering held the boat's quarter to the approaching waves, but Moitessier knew that even one wave, mistimed, might yet result in disaster. So mesmerised was he by the experience of his boat surfing along on the very edge of sense that Moitessier later commented: '... never have I felt my boat like that; never has she given me so much.'

Memories of childhood invaded Moitessier's mind – his long walks with his brothers in search of wild honey in the woods of Vietnam, the bee stings, the Gulf of Siam – while *Joshua* rushed headlong towards Cape

Horn, dangerously fast. Snapping out of his reverie, Moitessier dropped the mainsail and checked the barometer. It was falling.

The following day, 4 February, the wind freshened, the seas marauding in great horizontal ranks. In the distance, Moitessier picked out Diego Ramírez, a tiny blue speck against the white-streaked blue of the sea. As darkness fell, the sky was clear, shimmering with brilliant stars. Moitessier went to his bunk, setting the alarm for 1am while *Joshua* held the course that would take her 32 kilometres (20 miles) south of Cape Horn. He dreamed vividly, slipping back into memories of childhood. When he woke to darkness, Moitessier lay unmoving, sensing the boat's motion, determining quickly that the wind had eased. He worked out, from the position of the moonlight striking through the portside windows, that the wind had backed to south-west. He had slept through the alarm. It was 2am. Moitessier stirred himself from his bunk. He thought *Joshua* must already have passed Cape Horn. His relief was tangible. 'I feel happy, joyful, moved; I want to laugh and joke and pray all at once.'

Moitessier estimated Cape Horn would be too far north of his position to be visible, but when he came on deck, almost disbelieving his eyes, he saw it, perhaps 16 kilometres (10 miles) distant. He had set the kettle to boil and now he heard its insistent whine. Going below, he brewed coffee, rolled a cigarette and savoured the moment for what it was – the greatest adventure a seaman could have – perhaps even more so for him on this occasion because he was alone with his boat. It was 5 February 1969.

Despite the purity Moitessier felt rounding Cape Horn for the second time, his mind was tortured: should he continue north up the Atlantic and finish the race, or abandon it altogether and carry on eastwards, around the Cape of Good Hope for a second time and on to Tahiti? He decided to quit the race. His reasons for doing this will remain forever secret. Perhaps the ignominy of coming second to Knox-Johnston was too much (Knox-Johnston was ahead in the race, but Moitessier did not know his competitor's exact position and it is a moot point whether, on his faster boat, Moitessier might have overhauled him). Perhaps the contrary pull of yin and yang that had made him restless throughout his adult life led him away from prostituting himself, as he saw it, on the altar of fame and adulation. Perhaps

Moitessier was simply uncomfortable with the idea of seeing the purity of the environment he loved reduced and diminished by a race that held at its heart, in his opinion, nothing more than the licentious greed of newspapers.

Moitessier thus sailed on to Tahiti, and spent the next two years writing *The Long Way* – a book of his spiritual journey as much as of his extended circumnavigation. He also tried his hand at farming, cultivating fruit and vegetables on the coral atoll of Ahe in French Polynesia, and spent time in the USA promoting his sailing through films. In later years, he became an environmental advocate, protesting against nuclear weapons-testing in the South Pacific.

He died in France on 16 June 1994, aged 69.

Joshua is now at the maritime museum in La Rochelle, France.

SIR ROBIN KNOX-JOHNSTON

'There's something about single-handed sailing. There is a satisfaction in doing it all yourself. Just being able to run your own life as you bloody well want.'

Born . . . . 17 March 1939
Nationality . . . . British
Date of Cape Horn rounding . . . . January 1969
Boat name . . . . *Suhaili*
Designer . . . . William Atkins
Year of build 1964
LOA . . . . 32 feet 5 inches
Material . . . . Wood
Rig . . . . Ketch

In March 1967, while Chichester was still two months from home, and the speculation about the possibility of a non-stop circumnavigation was gathering pace, a conversation took place at a house in Downe, Kent. This was the home of the Knox-Johnstons, whose son, Robin, a 28-year-old merchant seaman, was on leave before joining his new ship *Kenya* as first officer. Over breakfast one morning, Robin's father suggested that a solo, non-stop circumnavigation might be the last great sailing prize.

Knox-Johnston knew about Éric Tabarly's new boat, the 67-foot trimaran *Pen Duick IV*, and the speculation that, following the 1968 OSTAR transatlantic race, he might try for a solo non-stop circumnavigation. Knox-Johnston remembered 'the fuss in the French newspapers' when Tabarly had won the 1964 transatlantic singlehanded race, particularly the leader in *Paris Match*: 'Frenchman supreme on the Anglo-Saxon Ocean'. He was incensed.

There was no evidence that Tabarly intended to make an attempt at a non-stop circumnavigation, but he might. At breakfast that morning, Knox-Johnston, fiercely patriotic, determined that he would give it a go, not least because he felt that: 'By rights a Briton should do it first.'

His father's suggestion was not out of the blue. Knox-Johnston, like Marcel Bardiaux, was drawn early on to the idea of boats and the sea. He was born in Putney, London on 17 March 1939, the eldest of four brothers, and his family subsequently moved to Liverpool and from there, after a bombing during World War II, to Heswall on the Dee Estuary. Here, aged four, he built a raft of orange-box slats, carried it a mile to the beach and launched it successfully, although when he clambered aboard, the 'boat' promptly sank.

After school at Berkhamsted, Robin Knox-Johnston failed the Civil Service Commission examination for entry to the Royal Navy and instead joined the British India Steam Navigation Company. Some years later, while stationed in India, he saw plans for a sailing boat in a yachting magazine (another parallel with Bardiaux) and sent off for them. The plans that arrived were of another boat entirely, a stubby canoe-stern craft based on a Norwegian lifeboat built to a 1924 design by American William Atkin.

Knox-Johnston had the boat built anyway, out of Indian teak, using traditional methods and tools. He named her *Suhaili* after the south-easterly winds that blow in the Gulf of Arabia and launched her using a coconut while the artisans who had built the boat sang ancient chants to bring her good fortune. With his brother and one other crew, *Suhaili* sailed from India to South Africa in stages. In November 1967, they took her on a 12,875-kilometre (8,000-mile) non-stop voyage from Cape Town to England, taking 74 days.

Knox-Johnston had one major problem if he were to take on the round-the-world challenge. Was *Suhaili* a suitable boat? Ideally, he wanted a steel boat, and a steel boat of sufficient size would cost in the region of £5,000 – then a considerable sum and one far beyond his reach. He thus tried other means, but despite writing 50 letters, Knox-Johnston could not attract a sponsor. He also tried convincing his employer to sponsor his entry in the Golden Globe Race. His employer declined.

Time was pressing and money was tight. If he was going to attempt the voyage, he had no choice but to do so in *Suhaili*. This had its advantages: he knew the boat inside out, she was tough and she was seaworthy.

Knox-Johnston, four chapters into writing a book, called his agent, George Greenfield, to tell him about the proposed voyage. He could not, he told the agent, commit to finishing the book. Greenfield immediately saw the potential of another book, about the Golden Globe voyage itself, and wasted no time selling the rights to British and American publishers. An apparent inconvenience now turned to Knox-Johnston's advantage – the advance for the new book would cover the cost of a major refit of *Suhaili*.

The *Sunday Mirror* was also interested in following Knox-Johnston's progress. George Greenfield thus arranged lunch on a Thames restaurant boat so Knox-Johnston could meet and persuade representatives of the *Sunday Mirror* to back him. At the meal, the wake of a passing tug set the restaurant boat rocking, whereupon Knox-Johnston lost his balance and fell off his chair. The silence that followed was thundering. Knox-Johnston, acutely embarrassed, thought he had blown it judging by the looks of disbelief on the faces of the newspaper executives, but his luck seemed to be holding when, despite the unfortunate mishap, the *Sunday Mirror* did eventually sign up.

Knox-Johnston departed on 14 June 1968. Two other competitors had already left: John Ridgeway on 1 June, and Chay Blyth one week later on 8 June. Six others followed, including Bernard Moitessier on 22 August. Moitessier worried Knox-Johnston the most for several reasons: for his ability as a sailor; for his experience, with a Cape Horn rounding already under his belt; and for his boat, *Joshua*, which was faster than *Suhaili*. Knox-Johnston therefore set his departure in advance of Moitessier's to compensate for *Joshua*'s speed and get him to Cape Horn in January, the tail end of the austral summer.

Knox-Johnston found trouble early. Close to the Canary Islands, *Suhaili*'s keel had worked loose. The remedy required Knox-Johnston to go over the side and caulk between the planks – difficult enough underwater without breathing equipment, but even more so with the boat bobbing about, and now, with a predatory shark circling in the depths, the job took on a huge element of danger.

Approaching Madeira, Knox-Johnston tried putting in a radio call, but without success to Alec Rose, who was heading in the opposite direction on his way home. Later, on 11 July, Rose sent Knox-Johnston a message of good luck and a warning: 'to watch out in the Southern Ocean'.

About 1,125 kilometres (700 miles) south-west of Cape Town, at 42° south, *Suhaili* was hit by a Southern Ocean storm and, as Knox-Johnston slept, the boat suffered a knockdown. In the pitch black, he struggled out of his bunk just as the boat righted herself, hurling him across the cabin. He lit a kerosene lantern to inspect for damage. Water was streaming in onto the chart table. When the next wave hit, the stream intensified as the cabin roof, loosened from its fixings, shifted. If he lost the cabin roof, *Suhaili* would effectively become an open boat. On deck, he found his self-steering gear, which he had designed himself (a contraption of steel tubing anchored to the side decks supporting a windvane on each end and passing in front of the mizzen mast – an idea he had borrowed from David Lewis's self-steering arrangement on his catamaran, *Rehu Moana*), had been bent out of shape. To top it all, 68 litres (15 gallons) of drinking water in the tanks had become fouled and unusable.

Five gales swept past during the next 10 days. Knox-Johnston came to appreciate what Alec Rose had meant. By way of immediate repair, Knox-Johnston secured the cabin roof with the aid of a hammer and nails.

On 13 October, halfway between Cape Town and Melbourne, *Suhaili* encountered the worst weather of the voyage so far – huge seas driven by force 10 (52-knot) winds. The boat rounded up, lying beam-on to the seas. Waves smashed into the hull with bone-jarring power. Knox-Johnston was convinced 'that the boat would not last long'.

He let out warps aft, both ends of one tied to the kingpost forward and looping behind the boat in a bight. These brakes slowed the boat and brought *Suhaili*'s stern round to the seas. She was pooped twice – breaking waves crashing in over the stern – but otherwise settled. After repeated failures of the self-steering system, it finally packed up for good on 3 November, leaving Knox-Johnston to hand steer or leave the boat to steer herself with appropriate sail configurations until they reached their end destination, the UK, half a world away.

Just off Port Phillip Heads, Knox-Johnston managed to attract the attention of a pilot launch and hand over mail and newspaper articles for the *Sunday Mirror* for onward posting to London. It was his first human contact for 147 days.

On 17 November, Knox-Johnston tuned in to New Zealand radio to get the weather report – which promised some severe weather to the south of *Suhaili*'s position – and just as he was about to switch off the radio, a message came over the ether for the 'Master, *Suhaili*'. The message, from Bruce Maxwell, an Australian journalist working for the *Sunday Mirror*, relayed that it was 'imperative' he stop outside Bluff Harbour in daylight – the same port Alec Rose had been forced to pull into to make emergency repairs to *Lively Lady*'s rigging.

As Knox-Johnston approached Bluff, New Zealand radio forecast winds of force 9 rising to force 10. Suddenly, Knox-Johnston wished he had not heard the message from Maxwell – the worst place to be in a big blow is close inshore. After an all-night vigil, Knox-Johnston was forced to make for Otago, where he ran aground – an embarrassing event perhaps, but not the end of the world since grounding did not contravene race rules; only if Knox-Johnston had gone ashore would he have earned disqualification.

The most important bit of news that Maxwell brought when he finally tracked Knox-Johnston down and came out from shore in a hired boat was that Moitessier's position put him 6,440 kilometres (4,000 miles) behind *Suhaili*. Knox-Johnston calculated distances and estimated speed. He had a fighting chance of getting to the finish line first, but it meant pushing *Suhaili* very hard to Cape Horn.

Knox-Johnston was aware that icebergs at the Horn and drifting far to the north posed a major risk. His information put the mean ice limit at the 45th parallel, and this danger informed his choice of route towards Cape Horn. Therefore, rather than sailing in a straight line towards the tip of the South American continent, he opted instead to sail along the 44th parallel and then turn south at 100° west longitude.

Knox-Johnston's strategy was compromised immediately – instead of the expected prevailing westerly winds, *Suhaili* was headed by easterlies for almost three weeks. Progress towards the Horn became agonisingly slow. On the 200th day of the voyage, 30 December 1968, Knox-Johnston had hoped to be at Cape Horn. Instead, he anticipated that he would get there, eventually, sometime in February. The frustration irked him, and he spiralled into depression. In his log, he described his mood as 'murderous'. *Suhaili* was 'tacking north and south and making no progress at all, while somewhere to the west and probably not far away now, I'll bet the Frenchman [Moitessier] is having beautiful westerlies'. Cape Horn was still 2,400 kilometres (1,500 miles) east, but Knox-Johnston began preparing himself. He had read much of the literature from the time when Cape Horn had been a major shipping route, but surmised that conditions at Cape Horn, just like the rest of the Southern Ocean, were variable, a pattern of gales and lulls, which should not pose any insurmountable difficulties for *Suhaili*. As a precaution, though, he hacksawed off his now defunct self-steering rig at the roots and tossed it into the sea. Two of its four legs had already broken, and if the rest came lose at Cape Horn, it could take down the mizzen mast and rip up the deck.

On 9 January, Knox-Johnston picked up Voice of America on the radio and learned that his nearest competitor was 4,800 kilometres (3,000 miles) behind him. He presumed this must be Moitessier. Only one other true competitor, Nigel Tetley, was still in the race. All the other entrants had either quit or been forced to retire – all, that is, except for Donald Crowhurst, but he was still in the Atlantic and busy sending in false position reports. He would later commit suicide, unable to face the shame of failure.

Knox-Johnston's position in the lead might have been good news but he did not credit the report – he figured Moitessier was more likely to be only about 3,200 kilometres (2,000 miles) behind – but he still had a fighting chance of finishing first. That chance became slimmer when, in worsening conditions, the mainsail split and the steel-wire jib stay started to unravel. The wind was at force 8 (37 knots). Then the main gooseneck broke. Almost as bad, Knox-Johnston was down to his last 110 cigarettes, with 14,500 kilometres (9,000 miles) left to sail. 'The sooner we get past the Horn the better,' he wrote in his diary on 13 January. Luckily for him, the weather moderated, making it easier to get around the deck making repairs. By the time he was done, the barometer had begun to fall and the wind to rise, coming from the north-west, a sure sign of an approaching depression. Cape Horn was close – less than 320 kilometres (200 miles). 'I am worried,' he wrote on 15 January. 'It's never dropped quite like this before and we are in an area famous for its rough seas … I don't mind admitting I feel a bit scared tonight.'

Next morning, on 16 January at 5am, the wind had reached force 10 (52 knots). Calmly, Knox-Johnston shortened sail, streamed warps from the stern and returned to his bunk. He set the alarm for 8am but slept through it, waking two hours later. The winds and seas had abated. The barometer was rising.

Throughout the night and the following day the barometer kept rising and the wind continued to moderate. *Suhaili* passed eastwards over the longitude of Cape Horn in blissfully mild conditions. Knox-Johnston recorded the moment in his logbook: '17th January 1969: 1900: course by compass 090°: Wind direction W, Force 1–2. 1915: Cape Horn bearing north. YIPPEE!!!'

To celebrate, Knox-Johnston had a stiff drink and opened his aunt Aileen's fruitcake, which had kept for seven months in its tin. As an added bonus, his aunt had wrapped the cake in sheets of newspaper from *The Times* newspaper – so he had something to read as well.

Some claim that Moitessier made the first singlehanded non-stop circumnavigation by crossing his outward track first, but it was Knox-Johnston who arrived home first, crossing the finish line at Falmouth at 3.25pm on 22 April 1969 after 313 days at sea, the only competitor of the nine starters to finish. Whether his father had been right – that the first non-stop and unassisted solo circumnavigation would be the *last* great sailing prize – is arguable. It may not have been the last, but history suggests it is the greatest.

In 1995, Sir Robin Knox-Johnston received a knighthood. He has won the UK Yachtsman of the Year award four times, was named World Sailor of the Year by the International Sailing Federation in 1994 and was awarded the Blue Water Medal. After extensive involvement in ocean racing as both participant and organiser, Sir Robin Knox-Johnston co-founded Clipper Ventures, an international marine events company. The company's flagship event is a biannual round-the-world race for amateur crews on matched boats.

NIGEL TETLEY

'As every sailor knows, the sea can never
be conquered, merely held at bay.'

Born . . . . 8 February 1924
Died . . . . 2 February 1972
Nationality . . . . British
Date of Cape Horn rounding . . . . . . March 1969
Boat name . . . . *Victress*
Boat type. . . . . Trimaran
Designer . . . . Arthur Piver
Year of build 1963
LOA. . . . . 40 feet
Material . . . . Composite (wood/fibreglass)
Rig . . . . Ketch

Nigel Tetley, a 44-year-old British naval officer, was asleep in the family trimaran, *Victress*, on a Sunday morning in March 1968 in Plymouth harbour when his wife Eve reappeared in the cabin clutching the Sunday newspapers. One of them was *The Sunday Times*. Tetley devoured the leader article announcing the Golden Globe Race, and before he had finished reading, he had made up his mind to enter. He discussed it with Eve. She agreed.

Tetley then sought and received permission from the Navy to take unpaid leave to compete. He immediately wrote to potential sponsors to fund the costs of a new boat – he had in mind a 50-foot trimaran. His first approach, to a tea company – he thought the link between the old clipper tea trade and the race route offered a sound marketing opportunity – met with rejection, as did all his other efforts. With a few days of his current leave remaining, Tetley, his two sons from a previous marriage and Eve decided to embark upon a sailing trip to Ireland. In Penzance, Tetley crashed the boat, staving in the port bow. With no boat builders available, he settled for a coffin-maker to repair the damage.

With time short, Tetley came to the obvious conclusion. Like Knox-Johnston, he would have to go in his existing boat if he wanted to take part. Tetley had experience of sailing European waters and he had already modified *Victress*, adding a centre keel to improve steering. She was a sound boat, but her wood and fibreglass construction had him wondering how she would hold up in the violent Southern Ocean.

In early June, *The Sunday Times* reporter Michael Moynihan visited Plymouth to interview Tetley. After a demonstration of the boat's stereo system, Moynihan suggested a music company as a sponsor – Around the World in 80 Symphonies summed up the pitch.

A few days later, a passenger jet returning from the South of France to England got into difficulties. The captain was having trouble getting the landing gear down. One of the passengers on board that flight was Richard Baldwyn, a director at the music company Music For Pleasure, who had just read Moynihan's piece in the paper. Faced with a potentially life-threatening situation, he vowed that if the plane got down safely, his company would sponsor Tetley.

Fortunately for all concerned, the aeroplane landed safely and Tetley received a call from Baldwyn the following day. The sponsorship money was not sufficient for a new boat, but it did mean that Tetley could provision and equip *Victress* as he wanted.

In July, Bernard Moitessier arrived in Plymouth for the start of the race and he and Tetley quickly became friends. He did not mention it to Tetley, but Moitessier was dubious about a trimaran in the Southern Ocean. What if it capsized? There would be no chance of righting the boat. Indeed, so concerned was Moitessier that he demonstrated his emergency leak-repair method to Tetley, which involved mixing equal parts of cement and plaster of Paris with clay and water until the right consistency was achieved; then he showed him how to apply it by patching up holes in a bucket filled with water to simulate an underwater repair. Moitessier put together a kit of materials and instructions and presented it to Tetley the next day.

Victress departed on her long voyage on Monday 16 September 1968, crossing the start line at 10am exactly – a good omen, Tetley thought to himself as the sounds of a brass band boomed from the cockpit speakers. Tetley's limited experience of both singlehanded and long-distance sailing diluted his perceptions of the very real dangers ahead, particularly given that Moitessier was right – a small trimaran was not a suitable boat to venture deep into the wilds of the Southern Ocean. That said, an article by Knox-Johnston in the previous day's *Sunday Mirror* did slightly temper Tetley's optimism. Knox-Johnston gave an account of the storm he had encountered entering the Southern Ocean near Cape Town, describing the seas as the worst he had ever seen.

Tetley's mindset, to an extent, was reflected in the food on board. On the first day, once clear of Eddystone Lighthouse (Smeaton's Tower), he sat down to tackle 'some excellent smoked trout for lunch'.

By afternoon, *Victress* was flying a full mainsail and poled-out twin headsails, the poles attached either side of the foredeck with goosenecks. The wind increased to force 7 (30 knots). The boat was over-canvassed, so Tetley began taking in the starboard headsail. Now, under an unbalanced rig, the boat slewed. The headsail backed with a mighty punch and snapped the boom like a match. The deflated sail wrapped itself around the bow and dropped onto the sea's surface. The broken pole unhooked itself and drifted away. It was a dreadful mistake and Tetley felt 'suitably chastened by [his] bungling'. Not bothering with oilskins, Tetley got soaked into the bargain. Early the next morning, woken by the sound of banging on the mast, Tetley found that an upper spreader had also snapped off. He made a makeshift fix to the spreader and consoled himself with a dinner of 'Chinese-style chicken and beef, with onions, beans, tomatoes, mushrooms and peppers helped down by a half-bottle of Beaujolais'.

The next day, the saga continued. As he pulled in the trailing log to clean off some seaweed, the instrument slipped from his fingers and sank to the depths. *Victress* did carry a spare, but Tetley thought it better to leave it for now. Instead, he sat down to a meal of curried prawns and rice.

Despite the 'good omen' at the start line, Tetley's race start had been anything but auspicious. Near Cape Finisterre, *Victress* took a pounding, close-hauled in heavy conditions, and sprang her first leak, into the clothes lockers on the starboard side. Tetley was simply not mentally prepared for the challenge of a circumnavigation, admitting later that the full voyage – some 45,000 kilometres (28,000 miles) – was too much for him to grasp 'as a single entity', so he broke it into stages, the first one being the 800-kilometre (500-mile) mark. He celebrated this with a meal of roast duck (tinned).

On 2 October, the first real doubts and thoughts of giving up the race flared in Tetley's mind. He had become increasingly listless, even though he was less than three weeks into the voyage, and this only increased as *Victress* progressed southwards over the Atlantic. The boat also began to reveal its structural inadequacies against the demanding challenges of a circumnavigation. On 21 October, Tetley inspected the engine compartment to find it flooded and, as a consequence, the starter motor out of commission. He traced the leak to a fractured cooling-water skin fitting, and plugged it with a cork. Three days later, he found that both the boat's floats were shipping water in the forepeaks – several gallons a day in each. By 27 October, these volumes had increased to 136 litres (30 gallons). Two days after that worrying discovery, pieces of the bow moulding began to break off. This did not pose any immediate threat, but indicated that the boat was beginning to protest. If the fact that the person who had made the repairs in Ireland was a coffin-maker had not struck him as ironic at the time, it must surely have done so by this stage of the voyage.

Sea conditions were variable and so far occasional force 7 conditions were the worst Tetley had to deal with. Yet by 16 November, more bits of the hull were breaking off. The following day, Sunday 17 November, Tetley inspected the bilges in the floats, something he had not done previously because it involved moving considerable quantities of stores and equipment. He found 45 litres (10 gallons) of bilge water on the starboard side, but 318 litres (70 gallons) on the port side – usually the drier of the two. *Victress* had been lugging 360kg (800lb) of water. Tetley spent most of the following day rigging a pumping system to drain the starboard float into the main hull bilges and from there pump it overboard. Earlier doubts about continuing the race resurfaced. His mood plummeted, plagued by an almost overwhelming urge to retire from the race. 'The cold finger of reason points constantly in that direction,' he wrote in his log.

By now, Tetley was dreading the Southern Ocean, but the weather stayed moderate as *Victress* rounded the Cape of Good Hope in early December. The worst weather of the voyage so far came on 11 December, when winds escalated to force 9 (44 knots). The boat was not fully under control. Tetley decided heaving-to and relying on the boat's lateral stability offered the best option in the circumstances, rather than following Moitessier's suggestion – which the two men had discussed prior to departure – that in big seas with a following wind he should maintain boat speed. Tetley felt that tactics suitable for one boat did not necessarily apply equally to another.

Tetley maintained a course towards Australia north of the 40th parallel, sparing *Victress* from more severe weather further south. It was a good decision. *Victress* was never in much danger. Only when *Victress* dropped below the 40th parallel approaching Cape Leeuwin did Tetley encounter heavier weather with occasional short-lived episodes to force 10. He celebrated Christmas Day with a meal of pheasant bathed in a mushroom and red wine sauce, washed down with champagne.

By 13 January 1969, sailing in the higher latitudes of the Roaring Forties 650 kilometres (400 miles) south of Australia, *Victress* had had a taste of the new 'normal' – force 11 (60 knots). 'Rank after rank of spine-chilling waves marched towards *Victress*. Her and my destruction seemed a foregone conclusion.'

Doubts about whether he should continue with the race again bubbled to the surface. What seems to have chilled Tetley even more than the harrowing experience of a force 11 storm was the prospect of facing a further 11,250 kilometres (7,000 miles) of this to Cape Horn. On the following day, acknowledging that he 'had not expected to survive the tempest', he decided to make for Albany in Western Australia and call it quits. As he began to make his way northwards, feeling the chill hand of failure, he argued with himself. Hurricane-strength winds were usual at this latitude. The vicious storm of the previous day had not been some kind of divine conspiracy. Now, emboldened by his survival, he changed his mind again, altered course once more and determined to see if he could at least make New Zealand.

Despite his frightening experience of a near hurricane, Tetley was incredibly lucky with the weather – sailing for the most part with fair winds and seas. When conditions did creep over force 7, Tetley felt inclined to heave-to and wait out the worst. *Victress* paid a heavy price for these conservative tactics with repeated batterings.

Just as Knox-Johnston had done two and a half months before, Tetley called in at Otago to hand over mail, staying one night in harbour in the hope of avoiding Hurricane Corrie, which was forecast to sweep past Auckland. He felt reasonably positive, since the boat seemed to be holding up and he had made it to New Zealand. The decision became clear: *Victress* would continue on eastwards, to Cape Horn.

Tetley's good fortune with the weather persisted after leaving New Zealand. Hurricane Corrie spun off northwards, while to the south a deep depression flicked *Victress* with some short-lived gale-force tail winds. While he was sandwiched between these two systems, hove-to, Tetley celebrated his 45th birthday and retirement from the Royal Navy.

At times making fast passages, Tetley's hopes rose. He thought he might have an edge on Moitessier, perhaps even be gaining on the Frenchman. Tetley had received news by radio much earlier of a previous sighting of Moitessier off Tasmania. Computing average speeds and deducing his better rate of progress did much to hearten Tetley. He changed charts from one showing the western half of the Pacific to one of the eastern half and Cape Horn.

Two days later, his hopes were dashed when he received news of another sighting of Moitessier off the Falkland Islands. 'Either his boat had wings or the date given me for his sighting off Tasmania had been wrong. Instead of level pegging, he was a fortnight ahead. There was only the remotest chance of catching him now.'

A force 9 blew up on 24 February. Three times, following waves gripped *Victress* and slung her round 180 degrees, one almost capsizing the trimaran – tipping the boat to a 50-degree heel. Just in case the boat did capsize, Tetley had a procedure planned. A grab bag secured in the wheelhouse contained a wetsuit and mask, and if the boat flipped, he would don the wetsuit. Once he had gained the upturned hull he would flood one of the floats so the boat turned through 90 degrees, bringing the mast parallel to the surface. He would then launch the liferaft and use the halyards to try to lever the yacht upright.

Unnerved by the near-capsize, Tetley nevertheless turned south-east for Cape Horn on 27 February. With 1,600 kilometres (1,000 miles) still to go to the Horn, *Victress* was hit by a storm. Tetley recalled: 'I particularly noticed one large over-hanging crest as it broke near *Victress*: if she had been underneath, it would have smashed her open like an egg box.' In such dangerous conditions, Tetley deployed his usual tactic and heaved-to.

The storm raged for two days and, alarmingly, as waves roared beneath and against the trimaran, Tetley heard 'the sound of wood cracking below. A long piece of joinery had sprung away from the cabin side.' The next morning at 6am, another wave smashed into *Victress* square-on, punching through the 1.8-metre-wide (6-foot-wide) starboard cabin window, flooding the cabin, and dislodging stores and equipment. Spilled rice clogged the electric bilge pump so, in desperation, Tetley had to bail by hand. Finally, when he had time to inspect the boat for further damage, he found the starboard deck edge had sprung, two frames had split and the cabin housing had separated at deck level.

The extent of the damage, from one wave, brought home the realisation that *Victress* was 'insufficiently robust for the Southern Ocean', and Tetley decided that he would 'retire from the race, make for Valparaíso, put the trimaran up for sale and fly home'.

Sailing north towards Valparaíso the next day, a new mood of obstinacy took root and Tetley swung the boat back round to head south-east once more. He patched up the shattered window and tidied the boat, yet every time a wave hit, water spurted into the cabin from the sprung joins, wood splintered from the stringers, and the boat groaned in protest. Later, Tetley wrote: 'Only the proximity of Cape Horn and the prospect of kinder weather beyond kept me going.' But Cape Horn was still several hundred miles south, deep, deep into the savagery of the Southern Ocean, and unless Tetley was extremely fortunate, *Victress* would break up in the murderous seas.

The weather moderated and amazingly stayed that way, winds at force 3 to 6, all the way to the Horn. Tetley's mood lifted. He occupied himself sewing sails, making bread and listening to Chilean rhumba on the radio. *Victress* approached Cape Horn on a moonless night, 17 March, sailing quietly past the Ildefonso Islands in calm conditions. At 1pm the following day, Tetley 'could just make out land ahead'. One hour later, the sky cleared, and 'there was the Cape sticking up among the islands of the Hermite group like a sore thumb'.

Even more astoundingly, positioned at the heart of the world's most dangerous stretch of water, Tetley felt nothing in particular. For him, '… the Horn was just another headland to round, more of a navigational problem than anything else…' He had steered *Victress* along a route allowing a 24-kilometre (15-mile) clearance of Cape Horn, a safe distance off just in case the boat was becalmed. Whatever gods of fortune were grasping Tetley's hand, they kept their grip. The wind died to a zephyr and *Victress*, all sail lowered, and borne on the Cape Horn current alone, drifted past the mighty pyramid of rock as if she were on a Sunday-afternoon potter. In his typical gourmet style, Tetley rustled up a feast complemented by a bottle of wine, and with Cape Horn lost in the veils of night, ate his fill and retired to bed.

Victress made it as far as the Azores without encountering severe conditions. Then, on the night of 20 May 1969, a storm blew in, winds screaming at force 9 (44 knots). A peculiar scraping sound roused Tetley from sleep close to midnight. The port bow had come adrift, leaving a gaping hole in the hull. *Victress* had given up the fight. The hull was flooding. Tetley knew instantly any attempt to keep the boat afloat was futile. He had to abandon ship and immediately put out a Mayday distress call. He was exactly 1,770 kilometres (1,100 miles) from Plymouth. Water was slopping around his ankles. The boat was dead in the water. Tetley launched the liferaft, grabbed essential survival gear and abandoned his long-suffering yacht.

An Italian freighter, the MT *Pampero*, picked Tetley up that evening at 6pm.

When he returned to England, Tetley immediately set about building another trimaran, obsessed with the idea of completing a circumnavigation, but the project faltered for lack of money.

Nigel Tetley died on or shortly before 2 February 1972, when his body was found hanging from a tree in a wood near Dover, Kent. The circumstances surrounding his death were mysterious. The coroner recorded an open verdict.

THE LEGACY OF THE GOLDEN GLOBE RACE

In the wake of the Golden Globe Race, a better-organised singlehanded around-the-world race was inaugurated in 1982. Sponsored by the British Oxygen Company, the BOC Challenge Race – unlike the Golden Globe Race – was completed in stages and run every four years. With changes in sponsorship, the race was rebranded to Around Alone in 1998. Robin Knox-Johnston's Clipper Ventures acquired the race rights in 2001. Velux stepped in as sponsor for the 2006 event and the race changed its name to the Velux 5 Oceans Race.

The winner of the inaugural BOC Challenge Race, Frenchman Philippe Jeantot, also won the 1986–1987 event and was third four years later. He saw the potential for a non-stop round-the-world contest in matched boats and founded the Vendée Globe Race. The true successor to the Golden Globe Race, the Vendée Globe follows a similar eastward route south of the great capes but starts and finishes in Les Sables d'Olonne, France. The first edition of the race was held in 1989, the second edition three years later in 1992 to synchronise timings midway between each running of the BOC Challenge Race, and since then the race has been run every four years.

Racing along routes taking in Cape Horn, whether singlehanded or crewed, generates another layer of risk. Boats built for speed, with inevitable compromise to strength and thus security, are sailed at the extremes of their capabilities, although this is not uniquely the case. For instance, Sir Chay Blyth's Challenge yachts, constructed of steel and robustly engineered to meet the rigours of the Southern Ocean, prioritised safety. However, the Challenge race route was 'uphill' around Cape Horn, westward. Dangers on the eastward routes are, to a degree, mitigated by sailing downwind, deploying boat speed as a principal defence. The advantages of sophisticated weather routing from shore-side support teams directing boats into the Cape Horn area under more favourable weather conditions cannot be overstated, though accidents do still occur, tragedies even – Harry Mitchell lost his life during the 1994–1995 BOC race.

SIR CHAY BLYTH

'When that moment arrives and I'm lying in bed looking at my toes, I'll be asking those toes some hard questions. Have I enjoyed life? Have I taken all my opportunities? Have I done all that I wanted to do? Unless all the answers are yes, I'm going to be really, really pissed off.'

Born	14 May 1940
Nationality	British
Date of Cape Horn rounding	December 1970
Boat name	*British Steel*
Designer	Robert Clark
Year of build	1970
LOA	59 feet
Material	Steel
Rig	Ketch

Chay Blyth entered the Golden Globe Race on a whim. Although he had never sailed a boat in his life, he was no stranger to adventure. Born in Hawick, Scotland on 14 May 1940, Blyth left school at 15 to work as an apprentice in a knitwear factory. However, he saw no future there and left to join the 3rd Battalion, the Parachute Regiment three years later. In 1966, by now a sergeant, Blyth volunteered to join one of the regiment's officers, Captain John Ridgeway, in rowing a 20-foot open dory, *English Rose III*, across the Atlantic. They departed from Cape Cod on 4 June and arrived at Kilronan on Inishmore off the coast of Galway, Ireland 92 days later.

Ridgeway had originally asked David Johnston, a journalist also planning a transatlantic row, to join him. Unable to get on with Ridgeway, though, Johnston opted to team up with fellow journalist John Hoare. They left from Chesapeake Bay on 21 June and were never seen again.

When John Ridgeway signed up for the Golden Globe Race two years later, Blyth, now out of the army and with a failed business venture behind him, decided he would give it a go too. He wanted to enter the 1968 OSTAR but changed his mind when the opportunity of sailing around the world presented itself. His decision to sign up for the Golden Globe Race was never about the sailing. It was about the thrill, the adventure, the desire to test himself and, somewhere in the recesses of his mind, the idea that this might just be a way of making a name for himself and creating a platform for a brighter future.

Westfield Engineering had lent him a boat, *Dytiscus III* – a fibreglass, bilge-keeled, 30-foot production boat – for the Atlantic race but agreed to let him have it for the altogether bigger challenge of a circumnavigation. No one thought to tell the novice sailor that such a boat was about as unsuited to the rigours of the Southern Ocean as it was possible to get without straying blindly into suicide territory. When asked about his reasons for going, Blyth, perhaps unwisely, commented that he was not particularly fond of the sea, '… it's just a question of survival'.

It seems odd that a man who was not particularly fond of the sea should want to sail around the world. In a much later interview for a business magazine, Blyth said: 'I was never much interested in sailing, it was just a way of making money.' Whatever Blyth's ultimate motive, though, his focus and determination remained undimmed.

On the day Blyth left, 8 June 1968, friends came aboard to help him raise the sails and set the self-steering gear. He followed other friends on another boat as he left the Hamble River, adhering to their earlier instruction: 'Whatever you see us doing, do the same.'

Blyth got lost during the very early stages of the voyage but managed to find his way out of the English Channel and down towards Madeira where, in moderate conditions, the boat displayed its vulnerability by broaching. Blyth, unnerved, went below to consult sailing manuals on what to do. 'It was like being in hell with instructions,' he recalled later.

Dytiscus III was leaking badly, things were breaking and finally, on his 92nd day at sea, on 6 September, the self-steering system packed up. Blyth had just entered the Roaring Forties, near Cape Town, and it became clear that to continue would be nothing short of madness.

Earlier, on 15 August, Blyth had stopped at Tristan da Cunha to take on fuel, assistance expressly forbidden in the race rules. Technically disqualified and unable to win, Blyth nevertheless chose to continue because he had already taken a pummelling and was curious to test himself. And test himself he did, to the point of near extinction. Sailing over the shallow waters of the Agulhas Bank, *Dytiscus III* was knocked down 11 times. Eventually, common sense prevailed and he put into East London on Friday 13 September, accepting a tow from the harbour pilot launch.

During his brief sojourn in East London while waiting for his wife Maureen to fly out from England and sail *Dytiscus III* back to England with him, Blyth hooked up with an ex-army friend who had emigrated to South Africa. The two discussed another idea Blyth had, another adventure – to cross the Andes and canoe the length of the Amazon. While this notion was brewing in the back of his mind on the sail back to England, Maureen suggested he might try sailing a solo circumnavigation against the prevailing winds and currents, having listened to her husband complaining about the difficult handling characteristics he had experienced while sailing *Dytiscus III* downwind.

Back in England, the two schemes vied for prominence in Blyth's mind. Then he met a PR man, Terry Bond, at the Birmingham Boat Show and in the ensuing weeks the sailing project emerged as the preferable option. With a considerable dollop of chutzpah, the two approached the then state-owned British Steel Corporation to sponsor the build of a new boat, of steel, for Blyth's attempt to sail a westward solo circumnavigation. Blyth had none of the communion with the sea of Bernard Moitessier, none of the experience of Chichester and none of the seamanship skills of Knox-Johnston. What he did have, though, was nerve, a good line in persuasion, uncommon self-belief and a record of adventuring – even if rowing a boat had about as much to do with sailing as kite-flying. What he wanted more than anything else was to make a name for himself. For the British Steel Corporation, the promise of a glowing aftermath in the vein of Chichester's, Knox-Johnston's and Rose's voyages, together with the fact that this would be a marvellous advertisement for their product, as well as providing wonderful marketing opportunities, with a man at the helm with some decent sailing experience and the guts to give it a go, together constituted an enticing inducement. They agreed.

Frenetic activity ensued. Blyth was eager to have the boat built and sea trials completed ready for a departure in the autumn of 1970. His reason was clear. 'I wanted to be the first to sail alone non-stop round the world from east to west, and if I were delayed – if my start had to be postponed for a year – someone else might get in ahead of me.'

Robert Clark designed the boat, a ketch-rigged 59-footer, weighing 14.5 tons. George Philip & Son at Dartmouth built her and launched her on 19 August 1970. Her name, predictably enough, was *British Steel*. Weeks of hectic activity followed – victualling, sea-trialling and final preparations – before *British Steel* was introduced to a man who had done it all before. On 30 September, Blyth took Sir Alec Rose out for a sail on *British Steel* and benefited from some wise counsel. Rose was encouraging but remained deeply sceptical. Others were not so sanguine. To sail round Cape Horn eastward, from the Pacific to the Atlantic, with the wind behind and the currents favourable, is challenge enough. To go westward, against winds and currents, is arguably crazy. Earlier, Blyth had received a letter from Bernard Moitessier imploring him not to attempt the venture – to try and go westward round Cape Horn would be madness and Moitessier proffered his opinion that an east-to-west circumnavigation 'could not be done'. Chichester described Blyth's proposed route westward and south of the great capes as 'impossible'. Despite these opinions, however, Blyth and *British Steel* set out from the Hamble on Sunday 18 October 1970.

Within 48 hours, after spending the first day tacking head-to-wind, Blyth had compiled a list of things that had already gone wrong, including a broken log and failure of the mainsail shackle. On the fourth day, a running pole broke. This meant Blyth would have to change the pole over each time he gybed when running downwind.

During times of extreme frustration, Blyth reminded himself how fortunate he was in a wider context. A man of deeply held religious beliefs and grateful for the food on board, he decided to say grace before each meal, noting in his log: '… this is something I think all families should do – we are jolly lucky to be able to have meals, and we really ought to be grateful.'

In early November, the second running pole broke. Downwind progress would slow without the running foresails boomed out. Blyth felt it a suitable moment for prayer. He then repaired the poles.

The critical timing factor behind Blyth's departure date was Cape Horn – *British Steel* needed to make her rounding in the austral summer. South of Madeira the winds died, leaving the boat becalmed for long periods. On 5 November, his repaired running pole broke again and Blyth, already disconcerted, began to worry about the integrity of the main mast. He also began thinking about Cape Horn and the best route to approach the Drake Passage – east of Staten Island or through Le Maire Strait? Whatever eventually happened, he decided that his best strategy was not to drive the boat too hard.

Blyth's black mood surfaced in his log. '5th November 23.30hrs … I'll have to play it safe to get round [Cape Horn]. At the end somebody will say, "Why didn't you drive the boat harder?" I'll clout the bastard.'

After a difficult, squall-filled passage through the Doldrums – including electrical storms that Blyth admitted frightened him and that he dealt with by 'drawing strength from prayer' – *British Steel* crossed south over the equator on 14 November. Next day, Blyth changed his charts over to the new set – equator to Cape Horn. The same vexed question raised itself again: which route to choose to approach Cape Horn? To go east round Staten Island would mean an additional 100 kilometres (60 miles) of beating into the wind once he made the turn. A short cut through Le Maire Strait might prove unproductive if he found himself pitted against strong currents, just as Marcel Bardiaux had experienced. Even worse, if the wind was against tide, the seas could kick up into vicious, steep waves. The other concern that played on Blyth's mind was the target size – Le Maire Strait being only 32 kilometres (20 miles) wide. To navigate his way precisely to the target after 11,250 kilometres (7,000 miles) using a sextant would be a challenge.

Blyth encountered his first storm on 21 November, near the coast of Brazil – not a particularly severe storm, with the wind building to force 7, but several things went wrong at once. The self-steering broke and the mainsail, which Blyth had left up because he did not think the falling barometer would amount to anything given the relative infrequency of storms in the area, jammed halfway down as he tried to reef the sail. Blyth was becoming increasingly concerned about the rig, particularly when the mainsail track started pulling away from the mast. He again sought solace in prayer.

The catalogue of mishaps to which he always seemed to find some kind of answer or, in Blyth's mind, solutions provided by God to get him out of a tight spot, moved him to write in his log: 'No one will ever say to me that there is no God without my remembering all these situations.'

Off the coast of Argentina, Blyth, who had been advised about the 'pamperos' (the sudden katabatic squalls spilling off the mainland), ignored the warning signs and was hit with 55-knot winds. Again, the mainsail jammed as he tried to wrestle it down. He was in a dilemma – to keep the main permanently reefed or hand it altogether? Alternatively, if a sudden violent blow caught the boat over-canvassed, the consequences might be catastrophic. Blyth went up the mast to see if he could identify the problem, but he could not discern any obvious cause. He sandpapered every rough area he could find and liberally applied lubricant to the track.

Soon after this, a rising wind from the south brought with it thousands of moths and cobwebs, which caught up in the rigging. Blyth recalled that this was a sign of a severe pampero, but before he could prepare the boat for the onslaught, the wind struck at 60 knots. Unlike his previous encounters with the pampero phenomenon, this one 'really scared' Blyth. *British Steel* was dumped over onto her beam ends. The mainsail, fully raised, thumped frantically in the screaming wind and from below came the sounds of equipment and stores crashing around in the cabin. He could only wonder that the rig survived.

As *British Steel* drew ever nearer to Cape Horn, Blyth busied himself preparing his emergency equipment and consolidating it in one place.

On 19 December, unsure of his exact position, Blyth again argued with himself about whether to go into Le Maire Strait or round Staten Island. In the end, nature made the decision for him. The wind persisted from the south, meaning *British Steel* would be head-to-wind transiting Le Maire Strait. So, reluctantly, Blyth bore away eastward to go round Staten Island on 21 December. With the north coast of Staten Island 32 kilometres (20 miles) off, a force 6 blowing and confused crossed seas, Blyth became anxious. At the eastern end of the island, dangerous overfalls extend many miles seaward. For this reason, Blyth decided to give the area a wide berth.

He stayed up through the night, and at 1.10pm the following day, 22 December, turned right, dropping south past Staten Island, ready to face the long upwind haul towards Cape Horn. As she cleared the lee of the island and faced her bows towards the Horn, a force 7 westerly wind greeted *British Steel*. Girding himself for tough sailing ahead, Blyth was even more disconcerted to see whales diving beneath the boat. As a precaution (and a nod to his military training), Blyth had depth charges on board to frighten off the whales if they ventured too close. He wondered, though, whether the explosives might just aggravate the whales and provoke an attack.

Fortunately, the whales, losing interest, left the area and took the wind with them, leaving Blyth to edge his way westward and find time to open a 'Cape Horn parcel' from Maureen. Inside he found a tin of pâté, a tin of potatoes, another of mandarins, some puzzles and a cake.

HMS *Endurance*, a small Royal Navy icebreaker stationed at the Falkland Islands, had left port to look out for *British Steel*. It found her on 23 December. Cape Horn lay 135 kilometres (85 miles) to the west. The ship circled the yacht twice, a helicopter went up to get an aerial view and a ship's boat came alongside, took Blyth's mail and film and gave him a bag of fresh fruit, bread and two bottles of whisky. Later, Blyth cited this episode as one of the highlights of his life. To have human company, even briefly, so close to the prospect of facing down the legend of the Horn had filled Blyth with a sense of normalcy that lifted his spirits for the trials ahead. The visit from HMS *Endurance* was not down to luck, as far as Blyth was concerned. There was only one explanation: 'God willed it.'

With little sleep, only two hours in the last two days, Blyth continued in light conditions to edge westwards. On Christmas Eve, having crept northwards, *British Steel* passed the longitude of Cape Horn at 14.50 local time, only 8 kilometres (5 miles) off and in danger of being caught in the adverse currents and, worse, had the winds backed to the south, tight on a lee shore. Staring at the Horn in benign conditions, Blyth felt the acute loneliness of the place. Nevertheless, he toasted his passage with a glass of wine and proclaimed, 'Excellent – Atlantic – Pacific.'

Once he was past Cape Horn, the winds did back to the south-west, worrying Blyth because he lacked sea room to the north, and especially because none of the islands carried navigation lights. The wind was strengthening, but not enough to cause him alarm, and instead, in the evening, he sat down to his Cape Horn meal: crab, a tin of ham, potatoes and a glass of wine. Lack of sleep had left Blyth feeling decidedly lethargic, and even though the cabin was a mess, he could not summon the energy to do anything about it, despite his natural inclination towards tidiness.

If Blyth had any thoughts of a peaceful Christmas, they were quickly dispelled as the weather deteriorated on 25 December with winds at force 8 gusting to force 9 (37–44 knots), heaping the seas into monstrous waves. The enormous scale of the seas was a new and disturbing sight to Blyth and the ocean's power became apparent all too quickly when a huge wave hit *British Steel*. Blyth was topside when it struck with sufficient power to damage the self-steering gear beyond repair and shock the boat into a sudden stop, hurling Blyth across the cockpit. He bashed his forehead on the companionway, opening a deep laceration.

The wound would mend – the self-steering gear would not – and in that instant of realisation, Blyth plunged into a trough of despair. Unless he hand steered, *British Steel* could not get close to the wind under sails alone. The consequences meant short tacking, with the result that the voyage would take inestimably longer to complete and the amount of time spent in the treacherous Southern Ocean would greatly increase, putting man and boat in jeopardy. There was, of course, no prospect of Blyth hand steering for anything like extended periods, because – even if he had the stamina – the bitter cold was too much for long periods to be spent on deck.

As Blyth sank into a bitter funk, knowing that he faced the probability of having to abandon his attempt, he heard his name mentioned on the Merchant Navy radio programme – it was a request by Maureen and his tiny daughter Samantha to play 'Moon River'. Reinvigorated, an obstinate determination took hold.

The wind on Christmas night howled unrelentingly, forcing Blyth to heave-to, sparing the sails from further thrashing. He also needed to spare himself and, in desperate need of sleep, he curled up in two sleeping bags, one placed inside the other.

On Boxing Day, the wind veered to the north-west, slightly lighter at force 7, but forcing *British Steel* to head southwards, away from the jagged rocks of the islands but into dangerous iceberg territory. Huge waves slamming into the boat stopped her in her tracks, stressing the rigging and plunging Blyth into another state of misery. Gradually, though, over the ensuing days, the winds moderated and when the sun finally showed itself, Blyth was able to take a sight and calculate his position. He was surprised by how far west *British Steel* had travelled, to 78°10'W, clear of Tierra del Fuego. The wind toyed with *British Steel*, playing games with Blyth – if he made westing he also had to go further south. To go north, away from iceberg country, he would have to accept some easting. To Blyth's way of thinking, the only thing to do was pray. So he did.

The wind, as if by command, shifted into the south-west, freeing *British Steel* to make a course of 283° – west with a touch of north. 'What is needed,' Blyth wrote, 'is faith and belief in God.'

Blyth and *British Steel* endured many more storms on their westward passage across the Southern Ocean but completed the route around the world, arriving back at the Royal Southern Yacht Club on the Hamble River on Friday 6 August 1971 after 292 days at sea.

Chay Blyth went on to found the Challenge Business in 1989, an organised race for paying crew on board identical yachts and following his westward track around Cape Horn but with stops en route. The first race began from Southampton in September 1992 and opened the door for dreamers to turn into reality what might otherwise have remained tantalisingly beyond their reach. It was every four years, and the fourth and final race took place in 2004–2005, before the Challenge Business went into administration.

THE SQUARE-RIGGERS

Making a Cape Horn passage on the square-rigged ships of the 19th and early 20th centuries was clearly a risky business. Seamen, driven by poverty, on the run from the law or simply because they knew no other life, could mitigate the risk to an extent by knowing which captains had a better safety record – those who nurtured their crews, ensuring they were well fed, well rested and competently supervised. But most had to succumb to chance – either they got lucky or they found themselves employed on the watch of a brutal 'Bucko mate' – the name for ships' mates who drove their crews with the power of their fists. The term applied particularly to the mates on American ships plying the New York or Boston to California runs after the discovery of the California goldfields in 1848. Life on board could be hell.

Prospectors could reach California overland, but the journey was long, arduous and fraught with danger from Native American Indians. Better to go by sea, and the prospectors paid handsomely for their berths, with demand increasing further following the discovery of the Australian goldfields in 1851. This heightened demand created fierce competition between ships to make fast passages around Cape Horn. The more trips a ship completed, the higher the profits rolling into the coffers of their owners. Many owners appointed masters and mates on whom they could rely to drive crews to the limit, and sometimes beyond, in their search for speed. These men did not spare their voices, fists or rope-ends to keep their crews at work whatever the weather. Many seamen in these ships went to their deaths in the seas around Cape Horn, mainly because exhaustion caused them to miss their footing on the yards when working the sails in a gale.

Alongside the ships ferrying prospectors were the coal ships from Wales sailing to coal-bunkering stations at Valparaíso, San Francisco and a network of other bunkering depots and ports along the western coasts of the Americas. There were closer sources of coal, but the coal hewn from the Welsh valleys was the best steaming coal in the world; it burned hotter and longer than other coals, making it the most economical fuel for shipping and industry.

The County of Peebles, a four-masted square-rigger, built as a fast deep-sea trading vessel and launched in 1875, made regular runs between Cardiff and Chile carrying coal on the outward leg and retuning laden with copper ore. On an eastward, downwind rounding of Cape Horn, one crewman wrote:

> On this voyage she seemed to be alive ... tearing through the
> mountainous greybeards at 15 or even 16 knots, the irresistible force
> driving her cutter through the boiling seas, the wake of white foam,
> the board-like stiffness of her sails, the roaring hissing rollers, lifting the
> stern, passing the ship, and surging ahead with sea and air filled with
> ozone laden flying spume, every sail, spar and rope humming, roaring or
> whistling the song of the gale.

The ship survived her Cape Horn ordeals. Sold to Chile and renamed *Munoz Gameno*, she is today preserved in Punta Arenas by the Chilean Navy.

Many of the coal ships did not escape either the Cape Horn torment or the natural tendency of coal to self-combust. Self-heating of coal caused by oxidation can trigger ignition. This can happen wherever coal is stored, but on board ship the danger is amplified. The resulting temperature rise leads to emissions of methane which, being lighter than air, rises. Elsewhere, this flammable gas might disperse. Within the sealed hold of a ship, however, methane gathers as an explosive layer above the cargo. Once alight, these methane fires are notoriously difficult to extinguish. A case in point in the USA is the Centralia mine fire, probably caused by spontaneous combustion in 1962, which still burns today.

By the time the crew detected a fire it was often too late, particularly on a ship constructed from wood. On later steel-hulled vessels, short of running for port, the only way to deal with the problem was to open the cargo bays and shovel the coal on deck until the fire was found, isolated and extinguished. With the cargo bays open, the ship was at the mercy of the weather, vulnerable to boarding seas. At Cape Horn, the weather can turn very quickly, far too quickly to allow a straining, exhausted crew to manhandle tons of coal back into the hold. A fire in the Cape Horn area spelled total disaster.

One of those to succumb to this fate was the *Patmos*, an American barque, which now languishes somewhere on the seabed of the Drake Passage, an unseen testament to the double danger of hauling a combustible cargo into the teeth of a Cape Horn storm.

Captain Charles Nichols was 25 when he took charge of the *Patmos* in 1876. It was his first command and on board was his new wife, Millicent. They sailed east across the Atlantic to England carrying export goods and, after discharging the cargo, the ship sailed on to Cardiff, loaded up with coal and departed for Valparaíso. After eight weeks of uneventful passage-making, the ship sailed past the Falkland Islands on approach to Cape Horn. As is typical of the area, the *Patmos* made good westing, powered by the favourable winds of a trailing Cape Horn storm that was vanishing rapidly eastwards. Captain Nichols was pleased until, abruptly, the wind changed direction, coming straight in over the bow. Before long, the crew was fighting a full gale and the ship was forced south while the temperature plummeted.

Tendrils of smoke began to permeate the fo'c'sle housing the galley and crew quarters. The coal was alight, the fire spreading. Captain Nichols ordered the crew to batten down, and the helmsman to tack north. The west wind hurled sleet into the faces of the desperate men scampering over decks made slick with boarding seas. Soon, the rising heat of the fire beneath burned out the oakum caulking between the deck timbers and began to melt the sealing pitch. Water quickly found its way below decks, adding weight to the hold. The ship became sluggish and less responsive to the helm. The charred hatch covers collapsed under the assault of pounding seas. The deck was in danger of collapsing altogether. The captain ordered the heave-to on port tack. Fire broke out on the quarterdeck. This was the death knell. The men lowered the longboat, provisioning with beef and hardtack from the galley now choked with smoke. With daylight fading, the storm's ferocity intensified.

The crew assembled on deck while flames streamed to leeward, ripped from the carcass of the ship by the frightening wind. Captain Nichols carried his young wife to the deck rail. How long would it be before the masts were aflame? Already the staysails were burning. Through the dense pall of smoke only the topsails remained flying. Captain Nichols decided to wait until first light before taking to the longboat in the forlorn hope that somehow the ship might yet come through this ordeal. His hope was in vain. The grey light of dawn illuminated the hopelessness of their situation – swirling clouds of black and yellow smoke staining the frigid air like a giant bruise. The *Patmos* was going down, her stern settling ever lower in the broiling seas. There was no choice but to abandon ship and get clear.

Captain Nichols, his wife and the crew held off in the longboat. Might the sea yet extinguish the fire? Even if it did, no one in that longboat could know what fire damage there might be to the hull timbers below the waterline. The storm continued to rage, the crests of breaking waves streaming away on the wind and dousing the longboat in icy spray. For the duration of that day and throughout the night, the crew spelled one another at the oars, and bailed and tried to bat away the waves with an assortment of makeshift washboards. By the following morning, the ship had gone, lost beneath the waves.

With the dawn light came another forbidding sight – the jagged coast of Tierra del Fuego, visible when the relentless rolling march of the combers lifted the longboat high.

Their boat lashed by the spindrift, whipped by the raging wind and battered by the heaving seas, the sight of land was no guarantee of safety to the crew. If any of them went into the water that would be the end. Making landfall on treacherous rocks carried just as much risk. And then what?

'Sail ho!' a crewman cried. All heads turned to spy the distant canvas of lower topsails, close-hauled. The ship was downwind and to leeward. Captain Nichols and his crew redoubled their efforts, clawing their way towards a doubtful salvation. Would the ship even spot them in the maelstrom?

Then, despite the scream of the raging storm, the distinct sound of a gun. A signal! The ship had seen the longboat. Men lined the rail of the *Pretricia*, an iron ship under a British flag, hurling rope ladders over the side. They hauled Millicent aboard, and the exhausted crew of the *Patmos* clambered gratefully onto the deck of the *Pretricia*, forced over to her scuppers by the wind. As soon as Captain Nichols was safe, the half-swamped longboat fell away and capsized.

Safe was a relative term, though, because the *Pretricia* was in desperate trouble herself. She was so close to a lee shore west of Cape Horn that the low booming of crashing surf thundered above the cacophony of the wind. The *Pretricia* had been losing ground for hours, driven ever closer to the rocks that would rip open her iron belly. The men aboard were as exhausted as the crew of the *Patmos* they had just plucked from the sea, but now there were more of them – all seamen, except for Millicent.

Like her hull, the *Pretricia*'s masts were of iron tethered with steel rigging. The men piled on the canvas. When the staysails blew out, more were brought up and bent on. The mizzen topsail exploded into shreds and fluttered silently away. With four men at the helm, they brought her head as close to wind as they could get. Her lee scuppers found the water from the press of the wind while her weather bilge shuddered from the booming impact of the pounding seas, but the ship was making headway at last, inching forwards.

Through the night, the men drove the ship into deeper water, while Cape Horn battered them with equal ferocity. With the dawn came a shift in the wind, into the south. With the wind abeam and streaming in over her port quarter, the *Pretricia* now had a fair slant and she was round. Like the *Patmos*, she was laden with Welsh coal, and like the *Patmos*, she was bound for Valparaíso. Unlike the *Patmos*, the *Pretricia* eventually made port with all hands safe.

Captain Nichols went on to other commands and made numerous Cape Horn roundings, but never was he engulfed in so much danger as he had been that first time.

The stories of the *Patmos*, the *Pretricia* and many others led to the renaming of a pub in Swansea as The Cape Horner, a meeting place for the seamen who had ventured to the end of the earth. It is still there, just beyond the dock gates.

Captain Nichols was a decent man, not given to hounding his crews until exhaustion led them to make fatal errors. Plenty of others did, however. The sailing ships plying the Cape Horn route created an unenviable record – an estimated five per cent fatality rate, a figure extrapolated from the records of individual shipping companies. Moreover, it is likely that some captains and shipowners did not report or record all losses at sea, keen to downplay the risks for fear of discouraging crews from signing on, particularly given that many crewmen were itinerants. No one would ask questions. Had a central record office existed, the probable fatality rate among the Cape Horners would likely have been some way north of five per cent.

With the increasing dependence of international trade on the Cape Horn route tempered by concern at the dreadful toll in lost crew, wooden ships gave way to the windjammers. Built initially of iron and then of steel, these were the grandest of all merchant sailing ships and featured new technologies in shipbuilding that allowed them to carry huge cargoes and to withstand the battering they could expect heading into wind on a westward rounding of Cape Horn.

The *British Isles* was one such ship, a three-masted brute at 309 feet in length, with a 44-foot beam and weighing in at 2,530 tons, and launched in 1884. Many experienced hands were, however, wary: the colossal main deck would catch an unimaginable weight of water in the Cape Horn seas.

All years are bad weatherwise down at the Horn, especially in winter. Bad is the norm. In winter, gales occur 30 per cent of the time. The Beaufort wind scale puts a gale at force 8, with mean wind speeds of 37 knots, a probable wave height of 5.5 metres (18 feet) – maximum wave height 7.5 metres (25 feet) – and a sea-state described as very rough/high.

The *British Isles* sailed from Port Talbot on 10 June 1905, bound for the Chilean port of Pisagua and laden with 3,600 tons of coal, under the command of Captain James Barker, with a company of two mates and 20 crew.

None of them could know that 1905 was destined to be one of the worst years at Cape Horn. To make things worse, added to the inherent dangers of a Cape Horn passage were the dire living conditions. The pay for a deckhand was £3 a month, but a raft of petty offences spelled out in their contract meant the crew were liable to fines. The men ate and slept in a steel deckhouse, vulnerable to boarding seas, and which contained two rough tables but no benches – the men's sea chests doubling as seating. Rations were meagre, and the berths were little more than shelves with a low wooden side to keep a sleeping man from falling to the floor with the roll of the ship.

Traditionally, a Cape Horn rounding begins from the latitude of 50° south on one side (that is, the Atlantic for a westward rounding, or the Pacific if coming downwind eastwards) to 50° south on the other – a distance, at its shortest, of approximately 1,500 kilometres (930 miles). For the square-riggers, the distance was considerably greater – 2,400 kilometres (1,500 miles) at least – for they had to get well west of Cape Horn before turning north with sufficient sea room. Cutting the corner meant courting the danger of a lee shore with few if any navigation marks and no lights.

According to Captain Barker (who recounted his experiences during the 1905 voyage of the *British Isles* to his son Ronald in 1933), the *British Isles* had passed the latitude of 50° south in the Atlantic after 45 days' sailing. This conflicts with an account by an apprentice on board, William Jones, who was 15 at the time and later to become a master himself, and who recorded that 57 days had passed since leaving Port Talbot. Indeed, in Jones's book, *The Cape Horn Breed*, published much later, in 1956, there are many points that differ with Captain Barker's account. One discrepancy is the number of lives lost during that winter rounding of Cape Horn. Jones claims six: four at sea and two others dying later from their injuries. Barker (in agreement with the official log) cites four: three at sea – a 25-year-old Chilean named Juan D'Alencon and John McCarthy, an American from Boston aged 39, both lost over the side. The third, a 42-year-old Englishman named GJ Harrhy, died from his injuries. The fourth, a Swedish seaman, L Lindquest, aged 52, died later in hospital in Pisagua. Either way, the loss of four men out of a company of 20 not including the officers is an alarming rate – 20 per cent. Moreover, the inconsistency suggests how captains may have underplayed the dangers.

In Barker's recounting, *The Log of a Limejuicer*, he describes how one man went to his death:

At that moment the moon, which had been hidden behind a thick blanket of scurrying clouds, broke through a rift to reveal a scene which caused me to gasp with astonishment and awe ... there, stretching endlessly north and south, a mighty wall of water, towering high above its fellows and making them appear insignificant by comparison, was rolling towards the *British Isles*.

So far as the ship was concerned nothing could be done, for she was hove to under fore and main lower tops'ls, and a storm fore topmast stays'l. The helm was hard down, with relieving tackles hooked on to the tiller; under which conditions the duty of the man-at-the-wheel was simply to stand on the grating, gripping a spoke tightly in each mitten-covered hand. Making a lee drift of seven points, she was creating that swirl and smooth to windward which has often proved the salvation of sailing ships.

The greybeard was racing towards us at a speed of not less than forty miles an hour, and only a few minutes would elapse ere it reached us. The members of the second mate's watch, down on the main deck clearing up running gear, were in imminent danger of being swept away to death.

'On the main deck there! Let everything stand! Jump into the rigging – quick! Climb high, and hang on for your lives!'

In response to my orders, I had the satisfaction of seeing dim forms mounting the ratlines to the maintop. When I felt sure that everybody had left the main deck I again turned and looked to windward, where I saw that the space between us and the onrushing wall of water had greatly decreased. I then ran to the wheel, urged the helmsman to hang on, and myself grasped the spokes to await the inevitable impact.

The suspense was an agony to me, as I thought of my family lying helpless in the cabin below. The colossal greybeard seemed to approach with tantalizing slowness during these last few moments; but finally the ship slid down into an enormous hollow, and the water to windward, rising like a frowning cliff and blotting out the moon, cast us for perhaps a split second into deep shadow…

Thoughts flashed through my mind: 'The end of the voyage for us all – the old ship's gone!'

The foaming crest rose and curled over with a vast sigh, and in the curling seemed to touch the tips of the lower yardarms. My God, what a sea! The ship fell over so far and so deep down to leeward that I expected her to turn turtle.

There was a terrific roar. Then – chaos! The ship was completely engulfed in the swirling maelstrom fore and aft. Overwhelmed by that depth of water, not a single elevated structure along the whole length of the decks could be seen. That the helmsman and myself were not swept overboard like match sticks seemed miraculous to me, for the sea had rushed over the poop more than a fathom deep. I raised my bruised body from beneath the smashed wheelbox. The helmsman was jammed hard under the tiller and relieving tackle; but apart from being half drowned he appeared to have suffered no serious injury, for he pulled himself from his uncomfortable position and with nothing more than a throaty curse resumed his station at the undamaged wheel.

As the ship and her crew recovered from the great shock, I heard the faint cries of a man in dire distress. Not from anyone caught and bodily injured on the main deck did those pitiful wails come but, even above the droning of the wind, from out of the darkness far down to leeward… Whoever he might be he was doomed, for we aboard the *British Isles* were helpless to render any assistance.

The man who vanished over the side was either the Chilean, Juan D'Alencon, or the American, John McCarthy.

In all, the *British Isles* battled Cape Horn for 71 days before finally getting clear.

Many ships turned and ran for the Falklands, Montevideo or Rio and others gave up altogether and turned eastwards, going instead by way of the Cape of Good Hope.

Although much earlier, HMS *Bounty* had to resort to similar tactics after she approached Cape Horn on 2 April 1788 en route to Tahiti. Her mission: to stock up with breadfruit plants for cultivation in the Caribbean to provide a cheap food source for plantation slaves. Despite repeated attempts to make a westward rounding, severe storms defeated the ship. On 22 April at five o'clock in the evening, *Bounty*'s commander, Lieutenant William Bligh, ordered that '... the helm be put a weather, to the great joy of every person on board.' The ship eventually made Tahiti by the eastward route round the Cape of Good Hope.

Bligh recorded in his later account of the infamous mutiny, *A Voyage to the South Sea*, published in London in 1792, that the weather at Cape Horn 'exceeded what I had ever met with before'.

The four-masted vessel *Edward Sewell*, launched in 1899, was the last American square-rigged ship to make a westward passage around Cape Horn, in 1914.

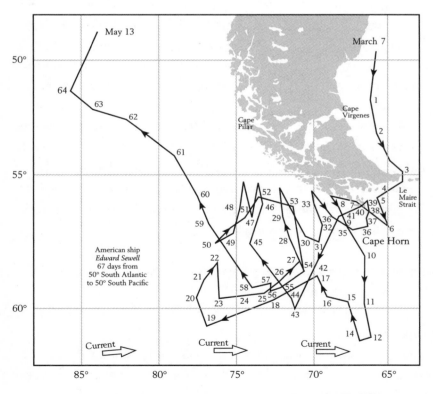

The track of *Edward Sewell* battling west around Cape Horn in 1914

The voyage from Philadelphia to Seattle took 293 days, from 18 October 1913 to 5 August 1914. Sixty-seven days were needed to get round Cape Horn. Six years before, her sister ship, the *Arthur Sewell*, had been lost at Cape Horn with all hands.

DR DAVID LEWIS

'The call comes to the adventurer and he must by his nature answer it. But he reduces any element of risk to an absolute minimum, acting out his destiny in spite of anxiety and fear.'

Born . . . . 16 September 1917
Died . . . . 23 October 2002
Nationality . . . . New Zealand
Date of Cape Horn rounding . . . . January 1973
Boat name . . . . *Ice Bird*
Designer . . . . Dick Taylor
Year of build 1962
LOA . . . . 32 feet
Material . . . . Steel
Rig . . . . Sloop

Dav256id Lewis was 54 when he decided to circumnavigate Antarctica, alone. Born in Plymouth in 1917 but raised in Rarotonga (the largest of the Cook Islands) and New Zealand, Lewis was possessed by a need for adventure from an early age. For instance, to celebrate the end of his time at boarding school, he built a canoe and planned a 725-kilometre (450-mile) expedition back to his parents' house in Auckland by way of river, portage (using a cradle constructed from bicycle wheels) and sea coast. When Lewis informed the headmaster of his plan, it was vetoed, but his parents wrote to the school giving their consent, and their son duly canoed his way home. Lewis went on to study medicine at Otago University and while there scaled 19 unclimbed peaks in the South Island. He completed his medical training in England, at Leeds Medical School, and saw out the end of World War II as a parachute medical officer.

Despite a continued longing for adventure, Lewis now braced himself for a life of predictability and settled into medical practice in London, becoming involved in setting up the National Health Service. But try as he might, the hankering for wild places and open sky remained, hidden perhaps, but never dimmed.

Restlessness is a corrosive state. Lewis's marriage disintegrated and with that came the realisation that his true self, the 'very essence', as he later wrote, of his character, lay not in medicine but in adventure. The opportunity to express that aspect of himself came in 1960 when Francis Chichester and Blondie Hasler conjured up the idea of a singlehanded transatlantic race. Fascinated and appalled by the perceived difficulty, not least because of his inexperience, Lewis bought a 25-foot boat, *Cardinal Vertue*, signed up for the race and, despite a series of early mishaps, including a dismasting, placed third, completing the course from Plymouth to New York in 55 days and 50 minutes.

After this triumph, there was no going back for Lewis. He sold *Cardinal Vertue* and his house and put all his savings into building an ocean-going catamaran he named *Rehu Moana*, Maori for 'Sea Spray'. He tested the boat during a trip to Greenland before entering her for the 1964 transatlantic race. This time, he placed seventh out of fifteen starters but made the crossing in the much faster time of 38 days, 12 hours and 4 minutes. His second wife and their two young daughters (aged one and two) met him in New York and, *en famille*, they set off on a circumnavigation aboard *Rehu Moana* by way of the Strait of Magellan and the Cape of Good Hope, a voyage lasting three years and the first circumnavigation in a multi-hull.

Lewis, an elfin figure with a piercing intelligence and an enquiring mind, had long been fascinated by the traditional navigation methods of the Polynesians – no instruments, no sextant, no charts or pilot books; just star paths, the patterns of ocean swells, the migration routes of whales and the flight of birds. In response to this, the Australian National University in Canberra awarded Lewis a four-year research fellowship to investigate and record these methods. For the 'field work', he traded *Rehu Moana* for *Isbjorn*, a 39-foot, gaff rigged ketch.

With the collapse of his second marriage, Lewis's mind strayed back to adventuring on the high seas, specifically to Antarctica. Lewis perceived this land of ice as a wilderness whose siren call was too enticing to resist and the Southern Ocean surrounding it as the last great bastion against which he might pit himself. He planned to sail alone and yet discover '… what manner of man remained after the familiar supports of society had been stripped away. Would there be a worthwhile man there at all?'

The challenge he set himself was immense – the first solo circumnavigation of Antarctica – and with it as the means to expunge his failed relationships and his inability to simply accept the well-trodden path of family and career, and the chance to satiate a terrible thirst for experience that would keep him anchored in the moment, living life on the edge, extreme and exhilarating. 'I had long been obsessed with the fascination of the frozen Southern continent; to reach it, relying entirely upon my own resources, was to accept the ultimate challenge of the sea.'

By 1971 Lewis was ready to plan his quest. His boat, however, was not. *Isbjorn*, under the command of his son Barry (from his first marriage), had been plying the Gilbert Islands as a trading vessel for three years and was en route to Sydney when she broke up in heavy seas and was lost. A freighter picked up Barry and his crewmate. Lewis, unconcerned about the loss of the boat and immensely relieved that his son and his mate were safe, set about finding an alternative boat. He preferred steel, to better deal with ice and provide a measure of psychological reassurance, given the recent exposure of the comparative frailty of wood.

Lewis's departure point, Sydney, lay 9,650 kilometres (6,000 miles) from the Antarctic Peninsula, with Cape Horn in between. To reach the Drake Passage at the optimal time of year would necessitate leaving Sydney in mid-October. He would be sailing, for the most part, in the extreme high southerly latitudes, south of 60°. Route-planning required a juggle between encountering ice and weathering fearsome storms. Lewis made a study of as much meteorological data as he could lay his hands on, deciding his best course would be to make easting, towards the Antarctic Peninsula, through the Drake Passage and into Cape Horn territory, by following the 60th parallel, where the westerlies were consistent and *relatively* less intense than those found further north in the Furious Fifties. In the Soviet *Atlas of Antarctica 1966*, Lewis read that very large waves in the area could be expected. Lewis thought 9 metres (30 feet) was big but not impossible, until he re-read the annotation more carefully and found the '30' referred to metres, not feet. A chill slithered down his spine. Waves that size were monstrous. He did not sleep well for the next two nights, '... so vivid and horrifying were the pictures that persistently haunted my mind.'

Around the same time, Sir Vivian Fuchs, head of the British Antarctic Survey, whom Lewis had met years previously, was in Australia for a conference. When Lewis told Fuchs of his intended voyage, Fuchs retorted: 'If I spot you waving your shirt from an ice floe, I'll assume your trip isn't going so well!'

Lewis had two major problems: since the loss of *Isbjorn* he had no boat, and he had very little money – just the remnants of his fellowship grant. The possibility of a book advance offered some hope, though, in reality, Lewis doubted any publisher would agree to a book ahead of him actually achieving the voyage on the reasonable presumption that he would probably be dead. Loading his meagre possessions into the back of his old Morris van, Lewis drove to Sydney, to Rushcutters Bay, where his friend Jos Doel ran the chandlery. He then began to search for a suitable boat in earnest, scouring the Sydney boatyards and inland marinas with no way of knowing how he was going to pay for one.

Eventually, the search led back to Rushcutters Bay; his perfect boat was there all along, moored close to his parked van: a 32-foot, Dick Taylor-designed steel sloop built in 1962 and constructed from ⅛-inch steel plate throughout. Lewis put down a deposit against the A$7,500 asking price, paying with the last of his funds. He rechristened her *Ice Bird*.

Media interest in Lewis's forthcoming voyage was immediate and, to his great surprise and relief, helped secure a book advance, which went towards paying for the boat. His one-time lawyer and friend in London offered to make up the balance (in much the same way Vito Dumas had funded his voyage in *LEHG II* 30 years earlier). At the very last moment, he sold the Australian newspaper rights. He also sold his van for the princely sum of A$250.

Lewis set about strengthening *Ice Bird* and incorporated a Perspex dome over the main hatch. He would have all-round visibility and be able to steer by lines running from the tiller through blocks and holes drilled in the washboard without having to leave the cabin. A small army of helpers materialised to prepare the boat. Many volunteers offered to pay for bits of equipment, including a Hasler-Gibbs self-steering rig, as well as food and a liferaft. After a flurry of last-minute I-dotting and T-crossing, including a one-day trial sail with his two young daughters, Lewis set off on Thursday 19 October 1971.

At the end of the first week, *Ice Bird* crossed south over the 40th parallel and into a force 8 (37 knots) head-on. Lewis had an uneasy feeling that '… this was only an introduction, an overture to what waited below New Zealand.'

Lewis made an overnight stop at Stewart Island to call Australia – his radio being too underpowered for the job – then set sail again only to discover that the bilge pump had given up the ghost, as had both manual back-ups. The bilges, stuffed with tins, left little space for bilge water to collect. Soon the cabin sole was awash. Lewis shifted and re-stowed the tins and for the rest of his time at sea had to bail the bilges by hand.

After this unwelcome addition to the daily routine, Lewis read Moitessier's *The Logical Route*, absorbing his tactics for running before the wind in big seas. Lewis knew Moitessier – the two had met in Tahiti.

As *Ice Bird* plunged over the 56th parallel (Lewis was now just further south than the latitude of Cape Horn) and eastwards across the International Date Line, the first severe storm of the voyage burst over the boat. Lewis was fearful, but in the measured way of a man who questions whether he has taken every conceivable action to mitigate risk. *Ice Bird* reached 60° south exactly four weeks out from Sydney. Lewis needed to be careful with his course from here on, keeping, as far as possible, to the 60th parallel so as not to wander into the easterlies to the south and in order to avoid the worst of the prevailing westerlies to the north. The ambient temperature now dropped below zero, freezing the drips of condensation inside the cabin.

Ice Bird continued through a succession of gales and snow, working her way eastwards, flying only a storm jib and occasionally the storm trysail. On 26 November, Lewis encountered the worst weather to date – a force 10 north-wester, blasting the small boat with 50-knot winds that, with the much higher air density at these high latitudes, punched into the boat with alarming force. Waves broke against *Ice Bird*. Anything loose in the cabin went flying, making Lewis thankful for one precaution he had taken – fitting steel plates over the cabin windows.

He set the self-steering so the waves advancing from astern met the boat at an angle of 20 degrees, watching almost disbelievingly how *Ice Bird* was able to rise, just in time, in front of a marauding wave that then swept beneath and past the boat. Lewis was following the tactics Dumas and Moitessier had used – run before the wind with headsail only – but he was also widely read on the subject of sea adventure and recalled the dismasting of *Pandora* near the Falklands, *Tzu Hang*'s pitchpole and later capsize, and the mishap that befell the French boat *Damien*, which capsized off South Georgia. He had also read WHS Jones's book, *The Cape Horn Breed*, which recalled that in 1905, of 130 commercial sailing vessels to leave Europe for the US Pacific coast, four were lost and 54 were still missing in Cape Horn waters four to six months later. Yet, here he was, 'traversing even stormier waters than they. No wonder I was scared.'

Permafrost (as Lewis described it) coated the interior of the cabin. A wave hit the boat, laying her over. She righted quickly enough, but to his consternation, Lewis watched the barometer begin to fall. He was exhausted, cold, wet and battered. Worse still, he was also carrying an old skiing injury that made his left hip 'ache intolerably'. As the bottom fell out of the barometer, Lewis knew that 'something altogether new had burst upon us'. Lewis remembered his research. The Russian atlas proclaimed this exact area home to 30-metre (100-foot) waves. The seas built with unbelievable rapidity and Lewis knew that nothing he had ever experienced had prepared him for this. *Ice Bird* was 2,400 kilometres (1,500 miles) west of Cape Horn.

When it came, as Lewis knew it inevitably must, the wave was a seething bomb of broken water crashing over the stern. Lewis, below decks maintaining his vigil, hauled on the control cords he had rigged to the tiller. The boat did not respond. *Ice Bird* slewed down the wave face, veering dramatically to starboard. Overtaken and submerged by the violent water, she went over on to her port side. In the cabin, the galley shelves tore from their mountings, and tins, jars and implements hurtled through the cabin space like missiles. Lewis was flung about, disoriented and shocked. When he recovered and peered through the Perspex dome, he saw with dismay that the self-steering gear had gone. All that remained was a tangled mass of bent, misshapen tubing.

The wind continued to rage, rising to 70 knots – force 13, hurricane strength. As he fought to regain some control over the boat using the tiller lines, Lewis's world exploded into mayhem. A moment later, a cascade of water streamed through the forehatch, which had been ripped open by the force of the sea; the stove sat inverted on twisted gimbals; water sloshed about on the cabin sole – *Ice Bird* had rolled over, 360 degrees. Desperately clambering among an assortment of flotsam, Lewis poked his head through the hatch. The devastating sight confirmed his worst fears. The mast, snapped 2 metres (7 feet) above deck, lay among mangled rigging over the starboard guardrails, its tip in the seas. The impact had staved in the starboard side of the cabin, opening a vertical slit between the windows. Seawater spurted in like an arterial bleed.

In a daze, Lewis bunged the split with a rag, retrieved his soaked charts and began to bail, for hour after hour. After six hours of relentless effort and near to collapse through exhaustion – mental and physical – Lewis found himself flying through the cabin, and then crumpled to the sole. The cabin was once again awash.

Ice Bird had been knocked down again, this time to starboard. Lewis, operating like an automaton, began the laborious task of bailing once more – 10 hours in all before the boat was more or less dry. A quick glance into the cockpit and Lewis saw the liferaft had gone, ripped from its lashings. Crawling to the deck, lying flat against the violent motion of the boat that was made worse without the balancing effect of the mast, Lewis set about freeing the broken rig. In the numbing cold, he fought to separate the shrouds from the rigging screws until finally the mast and jumble of steel wire fled over the side and into the deep. Working without gloves, his fingertips succumbed to frostbite.

The next day, 1 December, Lewis sorted through the deck wreckage for pieces with which to construct a jury rig – the 3-metre-long (10-foot-long) spinnaker pole would serve as a mast, stayed with rope and halyards. Cold and hunger forced a retreat to the cabin, where he miraculously got the stove to work and heated a stew and some coffee. Sleep had to come before anything else, and the wind was still too strong to get the jury rig up.

Lewis erected the makeshift mast the following morning, raising the No. 2 storm jib. Finally, *Ice Bird* was underway again. His main concern became the danger of infection from his frostbitten fingers, compounded by the loss of the self-steering gear, which meant standing long watches to hand steer, 12–14 hours at a stretch. The only thing he could do was swallow huge doses of tetracycline, a powerful antibiotic, and hope.

Four days later, the jury rig came down and now, with hands and fingers permanently numb with cold, Lewis took a day and a half to untangle the mess of rigging to get the thing to stand back up. For all his efforts there was reward: a torturous pace of 1 knot. Lewis pragmatically assessed his chance of survival as 'negligible'. The next day, he wrote: 'Surprising no fear at almost certainly having to die, a lot of disappointment though.'

Lewis maintained a gallant but, to his mind, pointless fight, constantly bailing or scrambling onto the freezing deck to sort out some nonsense with the pitiful rig or tending his exquisitely painful hands, all the while clawing eastwards towards hoped-for but never seriously contemplated salvation.

On 13 December, two weeks after the first capsize, the wind again began screaming at force 11 (60 knots). On deck, the puny scraps of sail flogged themselves to death. Lewis went topside into the maelstrom and lashed the sails more tightly, hoping *Ice Bird* could steer herself under her bare pole. She turned broadside to the weather, starboard side-to. Down below, everything that could be lashed, stowed, wedged and shut was secured. Lewis collapsed onto the port bunk, bracing himself against the bulkhead, waiting, while outside the sea had built into mammoth, heaving waves, so steep as to be almost flat-fronted.

The detonation came at 3pm, a hissing prelude, the roaring approach followed by the shattering explosion. *Ice Bird* tumbled over. Lewis found himself hurled onto the cabin roof, encased in blackness, before *Ice Bird* regained her feet and rolled back upright, dumping him on the floor.

Miraculously, the tiny 3-metre (10-foot) spinnaker pole-cum-mast was still standing proudly, but the main hatch had jammed partially open, so Lewis, dressed in bulky, insulated clothing, had to squeeze in and out, making the task of bailing even more difficult and time consuming.

The storm abated during the night, though the sea was still running high and dangerous. Lewis clambered topside to inspect the rig. The base of the spinnaker pole was crumpled and split. He sat on the coach house (not wearing a lifeline – what was the point?) to consider the problem, when suddenly he was lifted bodily by a boarding wave and smashed against the starboard stanchions, immediately feeling burning, breath-halting pain in his ribs. Slithering though the narrow opening of the jammed hatch, Lewis could not afford to rest – the bilges had filled and needed bailing, again.

Beset with the agony of his frostbitten hands and bruised ribs, Lewis became so demoralised that for three days he did not venture out of the cabin, despite the wild thrashing of the sail threatening to tear down the makeshift rig and surely consign him to death.

Lewis had saved the strong wooden boom after the dismasting. It was too heavy for him to manhandle into position as a temporary mast, and opting instead for the lightweight aluminium spinnaker pole, he had lashed the boom on deck. Now, as he lay on his wet bunk, resigned to death, his salvation came to him in a moment of clarity. As soon as the weather calmed, he clambered topside. The base of the spinnaker pole was clearly disintegrating. It could not last much longer. Lewis disassembled the jury rig and transferred the halyards, ropes and wires to one end of the boom. This would be the new mast top. He lifted this end and set it in the boom cradle over the cockpit. Then he set the other end of the boom, the foot of the new mast, into the mast shoe, the boom/mast now canted at an angle of 15 degrees. Next, he led a line from the raised end of the boom, the mast top, to the bow, through a block shackled to the forestay deck fitting and back aft to a winch. Now for the moment of truth: Lewis began to wind on the winch. Would the angle of 15 degrees be sufficient to give lift or would the boom simply be pulled forwards? As he wound in the line, the boom began to lift. The boat heeled, the mast base slipped and the contraption collapsed. Tears of exasperation hazed his vision – getting to this stage had taken eight and a half hours of work, non-stop, in the bitter cold.

The problem with his frostbite seemed to have worsened. His right thumb was disgorging large volumes of pus – Lewis diagnosed necrosis in the terminal bone of his thumb, posing a real danger of gangrene – so he continued the only treatment option available, swallowing huge doses of antibiotics.

He reset the boom/mast in the cradle and tried winching it up again. It rose, slowly, to the vertical. Joyous, Lewis tightened the stays and shrouds, raised the sail and set the boat on a heading for the American Antarctic Palmer Station on Anvers Island.

The weather, as expected, was variable, but *Ice Bird* did not experience the kind of extremes that had twice capsized her. On 18 January 1973, Lewis recorded in the log: 'Cape Horn rounded 360 miles to the north.' His latitude was 62° south and, as if with a twist of brutal humour, *Ice Bird* found herself becalmed in the Drake Passage.

On 29 January, after approaching Anvers Island through a minefield of jagged rocks and barely submerged reefs, *Ice Bird* finally entered the sheltered water of Arthur Harbour at 2.30am. Since the dismasting, the boat had struggled for 4,000 kilometres (2,500 miles), averaging 66 kilometres (41 miles) per day. The Palmer Station buildings were just up the beach. A pier jutted into the harbour, a minesweeper, *Calypso* – owned by Jacques Cousteau – tied alongside. Lewis was about to drop anchor but, worried it might drag, decided to go alongside the pier. He called out towards the buildings. The door opened and a startled figure emerged and ran to the pier.

Calypso's crew appeared. Quickly, they made *Ice Bird* fast and plied Lewis with hot coffee and rolls.

He had achieved the first singlehanded voyage to Antarctica.

Unable to continue, David Lewis flew to Australia, where he spent the next 10 months, returning to Palmer Station in November 1973. With the assistance of the station's personnel, *Ice Bird* was refitted and re-rigged in quick time and departed Palmer Station on 12 December. His plan: to continue eastwards to Australia and thereby complete an Antarctic circumnavigation.

Ice Bird passed northwards over the 50th parallel in early February, thus completing an official rounding of Cape Horn. Lewis did not pay much heed to this – he had another, more pressing concern. Sitting in the cockpit to steer for long hours – or sitting anywhere for that matter – had become a painful experience. Clad in clothing unchanged for weeks and impregnated with salt, Lewis's backside had become inflamed and sore. Unwilling to use precious fresh-water reserves for washing, Lewis found inspiration once again, this time by recalling the Marlon Brando film *Last Tango in Paris*. With fresh Australian butter on board, he 'anointed himself liberally and found immediate relief'.

Despite the lower latitudes, *Ice Bird*'s travails were far from over. On 23 February, the barometer plummeted. By early morning the following day, Lewis found himself once more in the teeth of a ferocious storm – winds screaming at 80 knots, the seas a heaving cauldron. The eye of the storm passed directly over *Ice Bird*. 'I was terror struck,' Lewis recorded in his log. When the eye passed, *Ice Bird* re-joined the storm. Twice in quick succession, waves knocked the boat flat. Then the inevitable – at 4.15pm, *Ice Bird* capsized for the third time and dismasted once again. Lewis rigged a jury mast with what he could salvage and headed north. 'There was now time soberly to consider longer-term plans, and the inescapable conclusion was depressing. The voyage would have to end in Cape Town.'

Ice Bird, battered and dented, and her skipper bruised and depleted, limped into Cape Town on 20 March 1974. Lewis's son, Barry, later sailed *Ice Bird* back to Australia.

Dr David Lewis defined the personal dreaming of an Australian Aboriginal as: 'doing that which is nearest to his heart – as fulfilling his own destiny'. After his return to Australia, Lewis continued writing and researching. Sitting in the cab of his Land Rover at a desert rock hole, appropriately called Old Man's Dreaming, Lewis concluded that 'the destiny of my personal dreaming has been pretty well fulfilled'.

He died in Australia in 2002, aged 85.

ALAIN COLAS

'Cape Horn, as every seaman knows, allows passage
only to those who are worthy.'

Born . . . . 16 September 1943

Died . . . . 16 November 1978

Nationality . . . . French

Date of Cape Horn rounding . . . . February 1974

Boat name . . . . *Manureva*

Boat type. . . . . Trimaran

Designer . . . . André Allègre

Year of build 1968

LOA. . . . . 67 feet

Material . . . . Aluminium

Rig . . . . Ketch

From his earliest memories, Alain Colas felt an inescapable urge to venture on the sea. As his experience and skill as a yachtsman developed, the pull increased and the ultimate goal crystallised:

> Anyone who gives himself wholeheartedly to sailing knows there is one place he will have to go if he has any sense at all of the tradition he has inherited. To anyone who knows the sea, it is not necessary even to name that place. It is a Mecca, an almost mythic place that every seaman carries in his heart.

The challenge of Cape Horn represented to Colas the 'supreme test of seamanship'. It drew him through his life like a dim flash of a distant lighthouse far beyond the horizon, coaxing him ever onwards until, at last, he might be bathed in its brightness, safe and secure in a fulfilment that only few could know: 'to become one of that heroic – and sometimes anonymous – group that is the subject of ancient legends'.

Like Marcel Bardiaux, Colas was born in central France, in Clamecy, on 16 September 1943. His father always encouraged the young Alain to pursue his dreams, told him that dreams are meant to be chased and caught. Not given to itinerant dreaming, Colas was methodical and understood the need to build towards a goal, to win experience and knowledge that would minimise risk and establish a platform for success. The history of sailing, particularly the era of the square-riggers and its importance in the development of world trade, held a fascination for Colas that coalesced into his desire to somehow become a part of it.

Like Bardiaux, Colas became a keen kayaker, founding the Clamecy Canoe Club. After studying English at the Sorbonne, Colas emigrated to Australia aged 22, to teach French at St John's College, University of Sydney, where he first took to sailing and discovered a passion for racing. A year later, in 1966, he met legendary French yachtsman Éric Tabarly, winner of the 1964 singlehanded transatlantic race, who was in Australia to compete in the annual Sydney–Hobart race aboard his new boat, *Pen Duick III*, a 57-foot aluminium schooner. After victory in the race, Tabarly invited Colas to join the crew as cook for a voyage to New Caledonia.

Colas did not hesitate; he quit his teaching job and had his first experience of long-distance offshore sailing. In France in 1968, he joined Tabarly again to prepare his new boat – *Pen Duick IV*, a 67-foot aluminium trimaran with a ketch rig – for the upcoming OSTAR. This was the boat Knox-Johnston and others suspected Tabarly might use to have a crack at a singlehanded non-stop circumnavigation. The race was a disaster, a collision with a cargo ship in the English Channel forcing *Pen Duick IV* to withdraw. After the boat was repaired, Colas crewed for Tabarly, sailing across the Atlantic to Martinique and then across the Pacific, from Los Angeles to Honolulu. In Honolulu, Tabarly put the boat up for sale. Colas loved *Pen Duick IV*, saying, 'The boat was fantastic.' It was in Honolulu that the idea of taking part in the next OSTAR occurred to him, with *Pen Duick IV*. He had learned a lot from Tabarly and felt certain he could handle the boat on his own. The problem was the price tag. Undeterred, Colas entered as many races as possible, including the 1969 Fastnet, offering himself as crew. No matter how many other boats he sailed, though, there was only one boat for him. 'Between *Pen Duick IV* and myself I had immediately sensed the existence of a relationship that left absolutely nothing to be desired.' Colas used all his savings and took out a bank loan to buy the boat, making the monthly payments by writing magazine and newspaper articles. To provide fodder for his stories, he embarked on a round-the-world voyage, meeting his future wife Teura in Tahiti.

Colas entered the 1972 OSTAR and won the race in a new record time. With victory came accolades in France. Feted as a hero, Colas found himself in demand and soon in a position to pay off the debt on the boat. Now the next challenge beckoned. 'For my boat and myself, the time had come to measure ourselves against Cape Horn.'

Modifications were needed. And what better place to 'Cape Hornise' the boat, as he put it, than at the original builder's, the Perrière shipyard in Lorient. While he had no debt on the boat, though, Colas was still short of money to fund the extensive and costly requirements – a new suit of sails, hull strengthening, reinforcing the rig, and 'humanising' the cabin. In time-honoured fashion, he relied on the goodwill of technicians, craftsmen and patrons to help him in return for nothing beyond an act of faith and the promise of involvement in something greater than themselves. Colas's main concern about sailing eastwards around Cape Horn was the danger of pitchpoling. To mitigate this, he came up with a novel idea – welding hollow deflectors to the bows designed to increase buoyancy and improve wave-piercing action. This would prevent the bows digging in and establishing a fulcrum for the stern to flip over. He also added watertight bulkheads in the central hull and an inside steering position with all-round visibility through a Plexiglas dome. To improve the chances of at least one of the two masts surviving a capsize, he rigged them independently. The other critical modifications involved strengthening the bracings between the central hull and the port and starboard pontoons.

Key to Colas's preparations to ensure the boat survived whatever Cape Horn might throw at it was the answer that came when he asked himself the question: what if the boat capsizes? Because the boat was a trimaran, he knew that if she flipped over she would not be able to right herself, like a beetle on its back. The watertight bulkhead in the main hull served to isolate the central living area containing the communications equipment, food and water. With Colas in this section, he would be able to survive for an extended period until help arrived. That was still not enough. *Pen Duick IV*'s aluminium construction meant she had no natural buoyancy. If the pontoons either side of the hull flooded, the boat would sink with him entombed in the central watertight section of the main hull. To get round this, Coals partitioned the pontoons into sections with watertight bulkheads. If one flooded, the others would act as buoyancy devices and keep the whole structure afloat.

To determine whether the newly installed pontoon partitions were in fact watertight, the French Atomic Energy Commission agreed to test the boat by pumping air out of each partitioned section and replacing it with nitrogen. Nitrogen monitors positioned outside the section could then detect any nitrogen leaks through microscopic cracks or pit corrosion. X-ray and ultrasound tests added to the overall hull analysis. The results showed up one very thin (and therefore weak) weld and 20 leakage sites around the boat. These structural faults were marked and sealed with new welds.

In the spring of 1973, another well-known French sailor arrived in Lorient – 47-year-old Loïck Fougeron, one of the nine original starters in the Golden Globe Race of 1968. Fougeron was manager of a motorcycle company in Casablanca and a close friend of Bernard Moitessier, and he and Moitessier had started the Golden Globe Race together from Plymouth on 22 August 1968. By 31 October, Fougeron was in deep trouble. Lying a'hull in a merciless storm, his 30-foot steel cutter called *Captain Browne* – named after James Browne, an American square-rigger captain on the Cape Horn route whom Fougeron had met in Casablanca – capsized. Petrified that he was going to die, then finding he hadn't, Fougeron abandoned the race on 27 November and dropped anchor at Saint Helena. Obsessed with a desire to round Cape Horn after his failure in the Golden Globe, Fougeron had set sail from Lorient on 27 August 1972 on a new, larger boat, *Captain Browne II*, a 40-foot steel ketch. This time he was not alone. Betty Blancquaert, an air hostess with Sabena Airways, accompanied Fougeron as crew even though she had never before set foot on a boat. The plan was a non-stop eastward circumnavigation, but a severe storm six days west of Cape Horn forced Fougeron to turn away north. He made the return to France via the Panama Canal, his dream of becoming a Cape Horner like his mentor and spiritual father, Captain James Browne, still unfulfilled.

Colas wrote later: 'There was immediate affinity between the sailor who had just rounded Cape Horn, and the one who was about to round it.' There seems to have been some confusion on Colas's part – perhaps he meant to say, referring to Fougeron, 'the sailor who had just *attempted* to round Cape Horn…' Either way, the two men got on famously and Fougeron was instrumental in advising Colas on modifications to *Pen Duick IV*.

Discussing the matter of capsizing in the trimaran, Fougeron made a suggestion. If the trimaran turned turtle and Colas was in the watertight living area of the main hull, he would need an air supply. He would also need to be able to get a radio aerial out of the boat to send distress messages, so why didn't he cut a hatch into the bottom of the main hull that could be opened if the boat went over? Colas agreed this was an excellent idea and had a hatch-opening cut in.

To 'humanise' the boat, Colas imagined living aboard for months on end and what he would need to make his life comfortable. The first aspect was food, and he compiled lists and menus to provide interest and variety in his diet. He also considered comprehensive medical supplies essential. In addition, a robust heating system and good all-weather clothing to combat the cold of the high latitudes and, finally, he gave a lot of thought to how he could 'distract and entertain' himself.

By the end of August 1973, the boat emerged from her refit re-christened *Manureva* (pronounced man-ou-ray-va), which in Tahitian means 'bird of passage'.

For the start of his voyage, Colas moved the boat to Saint-Malo, home of the *Amicale Internationale des Capitaines au Long Cours Cap Horniers* (International Association of Cape Horners – IACH). *Manureva* set sail on Saturday 8 September 1973, but just before she slipped her lines, Colas heard his name called from the crowd. A giant of a man with a voice like thunder emerged – Captain 'Mainmast' Gauthier, a veteran Cape Horner and presiding president of the IACH. He handed Colas a stiff, yellowed marine chart. 'This chart has been used in twenty-two passages around Cape Horn, all of which ended in a safe arrival in port,' Gauthier said, handing the chart to Colas. 'I turn it over to you, with a prayer that you will bring it home safely again!'

That first evening, *Manureva* was hit by a violent gale. Four battens in the mainsail snapped. 'A great beginning!' Colas wrote later.

No one before or since has made ready a boat so exactingly and specifically to meet the rigours of the Southern Ocean, and Cape Horn in particular. As part of his preparations, Colas had travelled to Greenwich to see *Cutty Sark*, the doyenne of the clipper ships and the record-holder for the fastest passage from Plymouth to Sydney – 72 days. As well as nursing a dream to round Cape Horn, being an instinctive racer, Colas set himself a target: '... to beat the record [106 days] set by Francis Chichester.'

To mimic the clipper route, Colas too planned to stop in Sydney, lay over for one month, then begin the second leg of the voyage in late December or early January for his date with destiny at Cape Horn '... when *Manureva* enters the narrow strait that separates the South American continent from

Antarctica – where the sea seems to shrink only to gather force to punish trespassers for their insolence.'

Colas's concerns about safety also influenced the timing of his voyage. Just as he set off, so the inaugural Whitbread round-the-world race fleet left on the same date from Portsmouth, with stopovers planned in Cape Town, Sydney and Rio de Janeiro. Colas calculated that the Whitbread boats, faster than *Manureva* but slowed up by the stop in Cape Town compared with his anticipated steadier progress, meant that he might have company going round Cape Horn and, if the worst happened, an increased chance of another boat close by that could rescue him. Among the Whitbread race fleet was *Pen Duick VI*, skippered by his old mentor, Éric Tabarly.

Manureva covered 1,365 kilometres (848 miles) in the first week, very slow and nowhere near fast enough if Colas was to have a serious crack at Chichester's record, but he remained completely calm, rationalising that after eight months of hard work, stress and exhaustion readying the boat, a leisurely start while he recuperated was perfectly reasonable. One aspect of *Manureva*'s performance did please Colas. Sailing close-hauled, the least efficient point of sail for a trimaran, he overhauled *Guia*, one of the Italian Whitbread boats. Out of 19 starters, *Guia* would finish fifth overall.

On 16 September, his 30th birthday, Colas was happy to learn via Radio Luxembourg that *Pen Duick VI* was leading the Whitbread, some 320 kilometres (200 miles) ahead of Chay Blyth, who was sailing on *Great Britain II* with an amateur crew drawn from his former unit, the Parachute Regiment.

Another of the Whitbread boats, *33 Export*, was co-skippered by Dominique Guillet, a friend of Colas. With the state-of-the-art radio on board *Manureva*, Colas was able to maintain regular contact with Guillet, and at the end of a good second week's run of 2,150 kilometres (1,335 miles), he was thrilled to learn that *33 Export* was only 12.8 kilometres (8 miles) ahead.

The radio contacts were very important to Colas, to keep up his morale. 'I may be a hermit by inclination, but I do like to know that there is something around me other than the sea.' The contacts also served as something of a warning when he learned that one of the crew on another French Whitbread boat, *Kriter*, had been knocked over the side by a flaying spinnaker sheet, at night, and only saved himself by grasping the sheet and being dragged through the water until finally someone saw him and hauled him back aboard. 'Everyone needs such warnings from time to time; and I more than most people.' The crewman did not have his lifeline attached.

On Saturday 29 September, Colas learned the *Pen Duick VI* had been dismasted and was diverting to Rio de Janeiro. *Manureva* crossed the equator on 1 October – Colas was pleased. The clipper ships usually took between 21 and 26 days. Chichester had taken 26, but *Manureva* had been at sea for only 22 days.

Colas used his solitary time at sea to explore a deeper understanding of himself – a philosopher as well as an adventurer, Colas came to know that while he sought to beat Chichester's record, he also recognised that his boat was faster and stronger and his equipment more technologically advanced so that even if he broke the record, 'I will never equal his performance.' He also acknowledged the transient nature of success – the glow of the 1972 transatlantic race victory soon faded – and that to keep stimulated and learning, and thereby growing, challenges would have to become ever greater. This was his appreciation of why he was now battling to get to Cape Horn. As to solitude, Colas appreciated that 'one is never so close to humanity as when one is alone'.

His bent towards a philosophical outlook allowed Colas to be content with himself whatever setbacks he faced – calms, equipment failure, cold, extreme weather. On 16 October, after a broach that afternoon nearing Cape Town, he wrote: 'I'm in a kind of ecstasy and nothing seems to bother me.' *Manureva* had been travelling at 12 knots. The broach could have caused very serious damage but, as Colas remarked, 'I took it all in my stride.' His morale was boosted by *Manureva*'s performance, which almost matched that of *Cutty Sark* and placed him among the leaders of the Whitbread fleet.

Despite his stoicism, a sequence of nasty squalls as *Manureva* passed round South Africa's Cape of Good Hope – with winds regularly over 50 knots generating big seas – forced Colas to admit: 'These waves, with all the luffing and sudden heeling, make me break out in a cold sweat ... like something out of a nightmare.'

To maintain some semblance of normality, Colas cooked extravagant meals, including *pigeon aux champignons, riz d'oignon* and a selection of *cuisines chinoises* in addition to a variety of pre-prepared meals made by a restaurateur friend, his mother and Teura. These were stored in sealed glass jars. He also slept, whenever he could, in pyjamas, with a sheet and blankets under his sleeping bag.

The violent motion of the boat woke Colas on Friday 2 November. The wind was screaming. He sprang from his bed and dashed on deck, still in pyjamas and barefoot despite the freezing air. He needed to reef the sails and fast, becoming frozen to the bone, breaking several sail battens and shredding his pyjamas in the process. Even with minimal sail, *Manureva* was surfing at 30 knots down the waves. The vicious conditions of the Roaring Forties had taken Colas by surprise. 'I didn't expect things to be quite so difficult or to last so long. This is really a sea of troubles, where the waves toss boats around and the winds blow without relief and without mercy.'

As *Manureva* slid eastwards towards Sydney, the Southern Ocean was relentless in its attacks. 'The sea is becoming really dangerous ... *Manureva* occasionally heels so that my hair stands on end ... some of the gusts of wind are incredible ... it is now a matter of survival.'

Colas arrived in Sydney on Tuesday 27 November, having travelled 23,560 kilometres (14,640 miles) in 79 days – a new solo record and faster than some of the clipper ships; not quite as fast as *Cutty Sark*'s fastest time, but quicker than some of her other runs.

The 14 remaining yachts in the Whitbread race left Sydney at 6pm on Saturday 27 December. Colas departed one hour later on the second leg of his voyage, '... this leg that will be the solemn moment which will make of us, simple seamen that we are, knights of the sea with the title, "Cape Horners".'

His stay in Sydney, which had been joyous (he had been reunited with Teura and his family, who had flown out from France, and had been able to sort out numerous problems on the boat), was marred by one terrible event: his friend Dominique Guillet, co-skipper of *33 Export*, had been lost overboard, swept from the deck on 24 November.

Soon after departure, Colas received another piece of bad news. *Pen Duick VI*, with a new mast fitted in Rio de Janeiro, was dismasted again only five days out of Sydney, having won the second leg from Cape Town. This marked the end of the road for Éric Tabarly.

Colas was obsessive about maintaining his radio in good order, keeping channels open with the Whitbread race fleet and ensuring that his family were kept up to speed with his progress and condition. These were all positives in Colas's mind, morale-boosters that allowed him to express his natural friendliness and hold on to human contact in the inhospitable and remote areas of the oceans. On the negative side, the radio was a constant reminder of imminent danger. On Wednesday 9 January, Colas contacted Chay Blyth on *Great Britain II* to offer his sympathies after learning during a radio chat with the French boat *Grand Louis* that one of Blyth's crew, Bernie Hosking, had been lost.

Two days later, a violent gust tore the mainsail cars from the track. Colas reduced sail to a minimum to keep the boat heading downwind and retreated to the cabin, observing the storm through the Plexiglas dome.

> I saw a gigantic wall of green water rise from nowhere. When it struck, we were tossed about like a piece of straw. My heart jumped into my throat, my knees felt weak, and a shout escaped my lips, 'My God!' It was half-exclamation, half-prayer … I feel a certain tension in my guts; and I have a feeling that it won't go away until I've rounded Cape Horn.

A huge concern for Colas was icebergs. The further south he went, the shorter the route to the Horn but the greater the threat of ice. On Sunday 13 January, *Grand Louis*, sailing along the 57th parallel and south of *Manureva*, reported seeing the first iceberg. Hearing this, Colas opted to stay further north while the Whitbread fleet, all of which were able to maintain a 24-hour watch, went south.

Not only was Colas sailing towards Cape Horn in the expectation of fulfilling his dream, his perception of near-death experiences in the Indian Ocean had fundamentally altered his perspective. The pursuit of records, and his recklessness in doing so, seemed diminished, a trivial legacy. He and Teura had decided, in Sydney, to have a baby together. Now, his altered responsibilities demanded a more prudent approach to his task of getting home safely.

Colas began his official Cape Horn rounding at noon on Thursday 17 January, crossing south over the 50th parallel to be met with 50-knot winds and the constant anxiety of icebergs. *Manureva* was equipped with sophisticated weatherfax, which race rules prohibited on the Whitbread boats, and Colas found himself acting the role of general weather adviser to the Whitbread fleet. They in turn reported back that icebergs were dotting their paths with increasing frequency. The winds accelerated to 60 knots. Running before with just a storm jib and his autopilot malfunctioning forced Colas to hand steer from the inside helm with his head encased by the Plexiglas dome, adjusting the boat's attitude to keep her stern to the waves. 'We are heeling at a frightening angle and I feel absolutely helpless under my bubble ... gigantic waves occasionally manage to hit us broadside with a deafening roar.'

Indeed, such was the ferocity of the waves that when one hit the boat the chain plate securing the mainmast forestay 'shattered like a piece of glass'. Colas was amazed, and hugely relieved, that the mast did not come down. He cobbled together a fix, working on it for two hours in buffeting wind, drenched by boarding seas and frozen stiff.

HMS *Endurance* patrolled the Cape Horn area on standby, awaiting the Whitbread fleet in case a rescue became necessary. She was also radioing weather reports that Colas picked up and he was relieved, after the brutal approach, that 'the weather at the Horn is all that could be hoped for'. He was pleased for the Whitbread crews who, on the shorter routes further south, were now, on 23 January, passing through the Drake Passage. He still had another 2,900 kilometres (1,800 miles) to go.

Of central importance to Colas's frame of mind was the ongoing relationship he had with the boat. 'There existed between my boat and myself a perfect accord ... This may sound ridiculous, but I really believe that captain and boat must be tuned to each other if they are going to make a go of it together, and that this mutual understanding is based both on habit and on an intuition that is impossible to explain.'

Through the enduring cold and exhaustion of weeks on end in the cauldron of the Southern Ocean, Colas tried desperately to maintain his morale mainly by cooking, particularly the food prepared for him by his mother and Teura, because 'the heart is warmed by the heat of recollected love'. Colas nonetheless felt lethargic as *Manureva* closed with Cape Horn. The repeated problems on board, constant worry about icebergs and the sense that things were not completely under his control gnawed at his enthusiasm.

HMS Endurance was reporting good conditions on Thursday 31 January. *Manureva* was 725 kilometres (450 miles) from the Horn, experiencing a strong swell but with no waves breaking. Forty-eight hours later, on Saturday 2 February, *Manureva* passed the Diego Ramírez Islands.

After a seemingly endless succession of difficulties with the rig, the generator and the autopilot – despite the exacting preparations of a large and dedicated team, each setback faced with good humour, patience, fine cuisine, the love of family and an instinctive understanding of the undefeatable nature of the sea – Colas met Cape Horn in near-perfect conditions. It was as though the stupendously powerful forces at work in this forlorn place contrived to rest a while and reward a man, in tune with his boat and the wider world around him, with a glimpse of his prize. Cape Horn was 'majestic in its forbidding solitude ... a watchdog, bestriding the howling fifties, a tragic precipice beaten by the fury of the winds, its very appearance making it a mystic place, a Holy Grail'.

Colas retrieved Captain Gautier's chart with its faint pencil tracings of 22 roundings and with a trembling hand wrote '*Manureva*' and added his course to the course of history.

Manureva sailed through the night, making a rendezvous with HMS *Endurance* just west of the Horn. The British ship dispatched a technical team in one of the ship's boats. Invigorated by the company of the British sailors, Colas drank a toast to Cape Horn with champagne. They then got to work on the generator and quickly had it working again before taking their

leave so that Colas would be alone passing the longitude of Cape Horn, '…
which, as seamen, was the best gift they could have given me.'

The clouds parted to reveal the azure sky, the wind died and there, only
a few miles off the port beam, stood Cape Horn. 'Everything is going well.
Our approach is slow, as is fitting for the great moments in life. I am at peace
with myself. I feel somewhat lightheaded, and my respiration is perhaps a bit
more rapid than usual. I can barely take my eyes from that great rock that I
have so often seen in my imagination.'

Then the cloud came down. 'My eyes strain, but there is nothing but the
mist and spray.'

Alain Colas arrived back at Saint-Malo on Thursday 28 March 1974,
greeted by a huge crowd, his family, and his wife, Teura, radiantly pregnant
with the first of their three daughters, Vaimiti.

As soon as he had reacclimatised to life ashore, Colas began his next big
project, the construction of a giant 246-foot, four-masted yacht for the 1976
OSTAR. He found himself again in the company of Éric Tabarly, this time as
an adversary. Before the start of the race from Plymouth on 5 June, Colas had
been delighted to learn that his friend Loïck Fougeron had finally achieved
his dream of becoming a Cape Horner.

Fougeron had left France on *Captain Browne II* on 11 October 1975
for his third attempt at an eastward circumnavigation and had passed the
longitude of Cape Horn on 13 February 1976. After the initial euphoria had
died away, Fougeron said: 'I had a feeling of emptiness. I had accomplished
what I wanted to do and there was nothing. That was the purpose of
my life.'

Colas, ever the sympathetic philosopher, understood exactly what this
meant for Fougeron – a deep contentment would emerge in time, after the
sense of deflation that often follows the attainment of a long-held goal.

Colas sailed brilliantly on the 1976 OSTAR, but with a lead of 480
kilometres (300 miles), a rigging problem forced him into Halifax, Nova
Scotia. Colas was given a 58-hour penalty for accepting help by being
given a tow, and the race was given to Tabarly. Colas was relegated to fifth
place overall, a devastating blow, but one which Colas bore with grace and
equanimity.

Two years later, Colas entered the inaugural Route du Rhum, a singlehanded transatlantic race starting from Saint-Malo and finishing at Pointe-à-Pitre, Guadeloupe, this time reunited with his beloved *Manureva*. On 16 November 1978, in the lead south of the Azores, he radioed: 'I'm in the eye of the cyclone, everything is an amalgam of elements, there are mountains of water around me...'

It was to be his last radio transmission. No trace was ever found of Alain Colas or *Manureva*.

PROFIT AND LOSS

During the 19th century and the early part of the 20th century, the congestion in the sea lanes around Cape Horn was driven by the avarice of European traders. The Chinese, Arabs and Polynesians, all capable explorers and mariners, had been content to colonise and trade closer to home along sea routes established centuries earlier. Before the advent of the Suez Canal in 1869 and the Panama Canal in 1914, the shortest route to the Indies was via Cape Horn, the alternative being a long haul around Southern Africa's Cape of Good Hope. For this reason, and in keeping with the business mantra that time is money, the Cape Horn route established itself as the most profitable, on paper at least.

By the 1850s, the Cape Horn route had become a thoroughfare, spurred by the lucrative trade in wool, grain and timber from Australia, coal from Wales, nitrates from Chile, and the China tea trade that gave rise to those sleek speed merchants, the clipper ships, the most famous of which, *Cutty Sark*, now rests gracefully in dry dock at Greenwich in South London.

Carrying English silver, the clippers sailed from London to India, traded silver for opium, then raced on to China, where they exchanged their cargoes of euphoria-inducing opiates for tea and silk. The final leg of this money-making cycle was a charge across the Pacific Ocean, an eastward rounding of the Horn and back to London, where the tea and silk were sold on for eye-watering profit.

The cost was high, paid for in lost ships, lost cargo and lost crew. There are no official records detailing the losses, but from the fragmentary evidence it is clear that the numbers were great. The discovery of Cape Horn in 1616 by Dutchmen Schouten and Le Maire opened the new trade route, but no records exist of the first ships to venture so far south in search of profit, nor is it known how many ships and lives were lost during that early period. The Hydrographic Service of the Argentine Navy lists the earliest ship lost at Cape Horn as the Chilean-registered *Constitucion*, an 86-foot, three-masted schooner bought in the USA. This was equipped and armed as a privateer, and commanded by one Oliviero Russel who, together with his 45 crew, planned to harass Spanish merchant shipping in the Pacific, inspired most likely by the earlier exploits of Francis Drake. They never got the chance; *Constitucion* went down in October 1815 with the loss of all hands.

The record lists 59 ships lost up to 1929, the last being a German vessel, *Pinass*. Collectively, these lost ships fell under nine national flags, though the majority were British. However, there are large time gaps in the record. For example, there is no recorded loss of any ship between 1826 and 1852. Taking the wider Cape Horn area to contain the labyrinthine channels of Tierra del Fuego – including the Strait of Magellan and the treacherous Staten Island at the eastern entrance to the Cape Horn area – the International Association of Cape Horners puts the losses at more than 800 ships and more than 10,000 lives.

In 1869, two significant events spelled the beginning of the end of the Cape Horn route: the opening of the Suez Canal and the completion of the US transcontinental railroad. These meant that European ships could find

Pamir

quicker, safer passage by way of Suez, while prospectors on the hunt for gold no longer needed to risk their lives getting to California.

The completion of the Panama Canal in 1914 finally did for Cape Horn, to the probable relief of mariners everywhere. The SS *Ancon*, carrying a mix of cargo and passengers, became the first ship to officially transit the 77-kilometre-long (48-mile-long) canal on 15 August 1915.

Pamir, a German steel-hulled, four-masted barque, became the last commercial sailing ship to round Cape Horn, sailing from Port Victoria, Australia to Falmouth, England in 1949.

WEBB CHILES

'A sailor is an artist whose medium is the wind.'

Born .... 11 November 1941
Nationality .... American
Date of Cape Horn rounding .... December 1975
Boat name .... *Egregious*
Designer .... Bruce King
Year of build 1974
LOA .... 37 feet
Material .... Fibreglass
Rig .... Cutter

Webb Chiles was born in Saint Louis, Missouri on 11 November 1941. His start in life was not an auspicious one – when he was aged only eight, his father took his own life. He lived with his mother, joined later by a step-father. An only child, cocooned in a shroud of loss and sadness, he was plagued with myriad silent unanswered questions. He later commented: 'The worst part of my life was my childhood. I don't dwell on it.'

Chiles graduated from university with a degree in philosophy. 'I then worked for eleven years at unimportant jobs that gave me time to write. I was frugal, saved money and made long term plans.' He bought his first boat, an Excalibur 26, with a small down payment and a five-year loan.

Two years later, he traded up to a 35-foot, sloop-rigged Ericson and in 1973 – while Dr David Lewis was recovering from the first stage of his Antarctic ordeal – purchased an Ericson 37, a cutter rigged with a fin keel and spade rudder, which he named *Egregious*. Chiles lived aboard his various boats, teaching himself to sail and navigate in San Francisco Bay while harbouring a burgeoning ambition to become the first American to sail a solo circumnavigation by way of Cape Horn. As to the 'Why?', Chiles remarked:

I have learned that 'Why?' is not a good question. People either understand instinctively or they don't understand at all. Our species has evolved to figure out 'how?' rather than answer 'why?' I believe that societies need most people to maintain stability, and a few to explore physically and mentally. I consider myself an artist – a sailor is an artist whose medium is the wind – and the essential function of the artist is to go to the edge of human experience and send back reports.

Like David Lewis, he found the unsettled life of an adventurer did not accommodate happy, stable relationships. With two failed marriages behind him, Chiles set sail on his quest from San Diego, California on 2 November 1974, without sponsors, with no shore team, with no PR agent and with no way to call for help. Neither did he want any fanfare from friends or family, nothing that might require him to put on any kind of act or pretence that might detract from the quiet contemplation of his goal.

Chiles's goal was simple – to sail the fastest solo circumnavigation, setting himself a target of 200 days. He felt this was possible because, in his words, 'I have a fast boat, I sail her aggressively and I keep her in racing trim.' He did not know then how hopelessly inadequate the boat would prove to be. It was a dream that had begun much earlier, when he was 11 or 12 – though 'there was no specific influence that led to that act of will, no relative who sailed, no motion picture or book I sought to emulate'.

His voyage quickly came to mirror his life – an unfortunate start followed by a catalogue of unhappy incidents. Unused to being alone offshore, Chiles began almost immediately to worry about unseen, unheard dangers. 'Imaginary ships loom out of the night. The compasses – all three of them – enter into a conspiracy: and instead of heading offshore, we are actually about to drive headlong on to a rocky Baja beach ... I know that such notions are ridiculous, but still I go on deck to look around more often than is actually necessary.' The next day, he was violently seasick.

Chiles's choice of name for his boat was a curious one. In a literal translation from Latin, *egregious* means 'illustrious' or 'remarkable', standing out from the crowd, perhaps reflecting his desire for aloneness despite the worry generated by being alone at sea. It also reflects a desire for acclaim.

He kept things simple on board – his boat was not equipped with an engine, and it had no through-hull fittings below the waterline, no electrical system (and therefore no radio), no lifelines on deck, no pushpit or pulpit and no toilet – he preferred the 'bucket-and-chuck-it method'.

Ominous sounds began emitting from the rudder, and the gland sealing the rudder post was leaking. Repeated efforts at isolating the source of the problem revealed nothing. On day nine, 10 November, Chiles went to inspect the bilge, expecting to see a gallon or two of bilge water. The shock came quickly when he saw the water almost at the level of the cabin sole. The leaky rudder gland had sprung. Chiles tightened all the screws around the collar, reducing the water flow to a trickle.

Egregious sailed on, crossing the equator and keeping to the ambitious schedule Chiles had set for the voyage. His confidence was dented once more when, on 19 November, he found the bilge again brimming full, and this time the rudder was not to blame. The only explanation, Chiles reasoned, could be a crack in the hull. Worse was to come. Late that evening, the two bolts securing the mast to the deck sheared. Chiles tried to steady the mast, which was gyrating in its footing, by cutting and hammering wooden wedges around the base, but they were quickly pulverised. The worry here was that the boat had yet to be tested in really severe weather.

Chiles eventually found the source of the leak now filling the bilges twice daily – a hull crack where a steel fibreglassed to the inside of the hull reinforced the bulkhead separating the galley from the main saloon. Chiles deliberated on his options, eventually deciding to press on southwards. Then the tang – a tongue of metal securing the portside shroud – failed.

To continue south, to Cape Horn, to the savagery of the high southern latitudes, would be crazy. Chiles, despairing, turned the boat west for Tahiti, 2,900 kilometres (1,800 miles) distant, the nearest place with facilities to fix the boat. Before then, ill fortune had one more surprise in store: the self-steering system failed on 26 November. The coupling linking the vane and the servo-rudder had broken and, worse, Chiles could not remove the offending part to replace it with the spare he carried on board.

With the various equipment and structural failures on board, *Egregious* was taking an early opportunity to express her unsuitability for the task set by her skipper and, as if in parallel, Chiles's frame of mind collapsed:

I would become the greatest solo sailor the world has known.
Foolishness. I came to find solitude and grandeur and victory. Instead
I have myriad petty breakage and despair and defeat.

My vision of myself has formed my life. I have benefited by it, and
now I suffer from it. Through a process of self-deception for twenty
years, I am become a victim of my grandiloquent dreams.

I have no intention of quitting. But that is as much because I can
think of nothing else to do with my life as because my 'indomitable will'
is unshaken.

Chiles made it to Tahiti, mooring up in the harbour at Papeete on 5 December. It would be almost three weeks before the boat was ready to sail again. *Egregious* edged her way out of the harbour and south for Cape

Horn on 24 December; Chiles's ambitions to continue the voyage were rekindled.

The two bolts securing the mast, replaced in Papeete with spares flown out from the USA, quickly started working loose. On 6 January, a failure in the rigging, this time the tang for the starboard lower shrouds, spelled the end of progress. The bolt holes at the base of the mast were by now so enlarged as to render the bolts themselves useless. The mast was visibly moving. Chiles replaced the tang. The new one broke three days later, the excessive movement of the mast creating too much stress in the steel wire and too much torque for the tang. Chiles, faced with an almost certain dismasting if he persisted, turned again, this time north and back towards San Diego. 'There is no chance – none at all – that the rig will survive 16,000 more miles in the Forties and Fifties.'

Chiles plunged once more into maudlin introspection, angry at his boat: 'She has cost too much of my life to have failed so badly.'

Egregious limped back into San Diego on 6 March 1975, mission aborted, her skipper full of disillusionment and bitter regret.

Chiles spent the next few months re-preparing for his voyage, fixing what he could, ensuring the boat was as seaworthy as possible, getting himself into the right frame of mind. Short of money, Chiles could not afford a bilge pump. It was to prove an almost fatal omission. He set off again on 18 October with a silent vow: 'I will not see San Diego again until the Horn and the world are behind me even if that means I will never see San Diego again at all.'

Despite remedial work on the boat, the leak through the rudder-post gland still persisted, shipping 136 litres (30 gallons) daily into the bilge. By 1 November, 650 kilometres (400 miles) north of the equator and pounding to windward, the leakage into the boat had worsened, upwards of 364 litres (80 gallons) a day. Again, Chiles revisited the collar around the rudder post, tightening the screws. It made no difference. Water was now coming in at an even more alarming rate – 4.5 litres (5 gallons) an hour, close to 450kg (1,000lb) in weight during each 24-hour period. With no bilge pump, he had to bail by hand. Numerous searches on board to isolate the source of the leak proved fruitless. Some interior parts of the hull were inaccessible.

The only way to inspect the hull would be to go over the side. Chiles did exactly this on 17 November while *Egregious* sat becalmed. 'To be almost certain in mid-ocean that your hull is cracked is one thing, but it is another and quite shocking thing actually to see it ... For about three inches, the trailing edge of the keel, where it joins the main body of the hull, looks as though someone has carefully sliced it open with a knife.'

Applying putty, both internally and externally, did not help much, the stuff working loose before it could set. Chiles had little choice but to continue south, now plagued by a constant worry – would the hull hold together? Prudence suggested he should make for port and get the problem sorted out, but Chiles was too committed to his pursuit of a personal ideal that, in his mind, could only manifest if he continued on, for he was determined '... to get past the Horn or sink.' He never abandoned his ambition to complete a circumnavigation, but a successful rounding of Cape Horn assumed ever-greater importance. If he could achieve that at least, and become the first American singlehanded sailor to do so, then that would provide a measure of satisfaction.

Chiles claimed not to be depressed or even subdued, but he thought often of death. On 18 November he recorded in his diary, 'By December 18th we will either be past Cape Horn or broken. Or both. Sail on, *Egregious*. Sail on, you beautiful bitch.'

Crucially, Chiles also came to recognise how utterly mismatched his boat was for the task he demanded of her. 'Living with *Egregious* is like living with a very beautiful, very sensual, very insane woman. Life is exciting because of the great pleasure and because you know that at any moment without warning she may try to kill you. There is no longer any question in my mind that I chose the wrong boat for this voyage. Wrong, perhaps, in design, but certainly in execution.' This acknowledgment was vital because, if only subliminally, Chiles treated the boat differently, sailing her more conservatively now that his confidence in her was spent.

Three days later, the mainsail tore along almost the entire length of the lowest and longest seam.

On 4 December, with her mainsail stitched up, *Egregious* sailed south over the 50th parallel and so, at last, began her official quest to round

Cape Horn. The next day greeted *Egregious* with a 'symphony of violence', the wind at gale force, ripping away the wave tops. Chiles had never seen seas like this. From among the crowd of 4.5-metre (15-foot) waves, three 9-metre (30-foot) ones, their crests breaking, swept past. A day later, another seam in the mainsail split, this time near the top. Chiles handed the sail to make a repair and, with the boat making 7 knots under bare poles, kept the mended sail lashed down. To make matters worse, Chiles ricked his back, his hands and feet swelled with the cold and sleep became difficult. By 8 December, *Egregious* had reached latitude 55° south, almost level with Cape Horn. Having steered a course to stay well off the west coast of Chile, a dangerous lee shore, Chiles now turned east.

So far, the leak from the hull had not appreciably worsened, but bailing out the bilges three times a day had become routine drudgery, the near-freezing water numbing his fingers so they tingled persistently. The mainsail continued to split along its seams, twice on 9 December, necessitating quick mends while the wind held off. By 10 December, Cape Horn lay 320 kilometres (200 miles) to the east. *Egregious* was holding a course of 100° to take her south of Horn Island with enough sea room to be safe. The boat was taking some terrific hits from breaking waves, and the unwelcome thought of the crack in the hull played on Chiles's mind. The winds became variable, the course swinging wildly in the wind shifts, making dead reckoning nigh on impossible.

The following day, Chiles thought to cheer himself up by baking biscuits. As he shoved the dollops of mixture into the stove, the sun peeked out. Without bothering getting into oilies, he grabbed the sextant to take a sight, but the rolling motion of the boat and the uncooperative clouds had other ideas. The smell of burning wafted up from the cabin. Just about to go below, Chiles was doused by a freezing wave. He retrieved the biscuits and dried himself, then another roll of the boat sent all the biscuits bar one flying into the bilge.

By noon, between sleet showers, Chiles got a sextant sight and plotted his position. The Diego Ramírez Islands were four hours distant. He spotted them at 4.45pm, 24 kilometres (15 miles) ahead. By 7pm *Egregious* was south of the islands with the wind blowing at a reasonable 25 knots, and Cape Horn a mere 100 kilometres (60 miles) to the north-east.

The long-awaited moment he had dreamed of since childhood and that had been thwarted twice before came on 12 December when Webb Chiles finally passed eastwards over the longitude of Cape Horn. 'At 5.00am we were due south of Cape Horn. Those are the finest words I have ever written.'

Aside from the acknowledgement to himself, his grim satisfaction did not lend itself to celebration. He felt that it was not even appropriate to contemplate his achievement. Instead, he saw it as a day 'for survival', and with good reason. Despite the relatively mild conditions of the night before, and given the sometimes too-personal way in which Chiles accepted the whims of the weather, he could be forgiven for believing that bisecting the Horn's longitude had triggered the fury of Cape Horn. 'Ashore, I had imagined I would have a glass of my best brandy and pour one for the sea; but I felt no desire to honour in victory the gods I steadfastly denied in defeat.'

By dawn, the wind was tearing at 50 knots. Almost predictably, the mainsail ripped. A vicious cross-chop rendered the 6-metre (20-foot) breaking seas even more dangerous as the wind-driven wave sets from the south-west collided and merged with a distinct set from the north-west, knocking down the boat repeatedly. Boarding seas swamped the cockpit. For the first time, Chiles tied himself in as he steered, arcs of water sprouting from the self-steering rudder as *Egregious* surfed perilously down steep wave faces.

The wind eventually died 12 hours later, decreasing to 30 knots. Only then did Chiles, frightened and exhausted by his rotation at the tiller, hand over to the self-steering gear and enjoy a brief celebration – hot stew. His mood did not stay triumphant for long. Soon he felt deeply depressed, bereft of the goal 'on which my life had been focussed for almost as long as I can remember'.

The Cape Horn pounding had exacted a price – the hull crack had widened. Chiles was soon bailing six times daily. On 21 December, *Egregious* again crossed the 50th parallel, this time northwards in the Atlantic, her rounding of Cape Horn now truly complete. In this crippled state, *Egregious* had yet to face thousands upon thousands of miles of storm-whipped Southern Ocean wilderness if Chiles was to gain the totality of his ambition and complete a circumnavigation.

Aside from the hull crack, *Egregious* sustained other damage, most notably on the forward bulkhead, which had sprung. Thoughts of the boat sinking were never far from Chiles's mind, suggesting that a stopover in Cape Town might be prudent, if he got that far. Chiles eventually resisted temptation, passing well to the south of the African continent and maintaining a course close to the 40th parallel.

On 21 January 1976, *Egregious* became engulfed in a brutal storm and capsized. The storm jib shredded. Fourteen hours later, the boat suffered a second capsize. Chiles, hit by some object in the cabin, was bruised, black-eyed and dazed. Unable to make way without a headsail, *Egregious* lay a'hull. The storm continued its pounding, fuelled by 60-knot winds. On the only occasion Chiles went on deck, to take in the shredded remains of the storm jib, the huge seas knocked down the boat twice in rapid succession. Chiles clung to the mast as it met the water. The storm lasted four days. By the end of it, Chiles could barely believe his boat was still in one piece, wondering how '… one of these killer waves has not already found her wound and split us wide open.'

As to that wound, Chiles gave up even inspecting the crack: 'If it is too gaping, I would only become frightened; and if it is not, what is the point of looking?' Thoughts of death returned: '… sometimes I think I will not survive.' The split in the hull, a breach in the very carapace that was protecting him, and the weakness and exposure it reflected, ensured that a deep sense of vulnerability was Chiles's unwavering shadow.

On 12 February, the strongest winds yet encountered on the voyage slammed into *Egregious*. 'This is too much, simply too much. It is too bad no one will know that I got this far, that I rounded the Horn before I was killed.' The fierce wind lasted only an hour but the mast bolts had again worked themselves loose and the self-steering gear was shattered beyond repair.

By now, the crack in the hull was letting in water at the rate of 136 litres (30 gallons) an hour. This meant only a 30-minute respite between long bouts of bailing. *Egregious* was crippled. Chiles had to think seriously about the consequences if he pushed the boat much further. Partially inflating the liferaft and readying supplies and what equipment he could take with him seemed a prudent measure if, as seemed likely, abandoning the yacht became his only option. New Zealand was 480 kilometres (300 miles) distant. Bailing had become an almost constant necessity – 3,000 litres (660 gallons) a day (almost 3,175kg (7,000lb) in weight). Chiles's body, weakened by the physical effort of transferring such weights from bilge to cockpit using a bucket, was deteriorating like his boat: his skin had become pocked with salt-water boils.

On 16 March, *Egregious*, near derelict, limped into Auckland's Waitemata Harbour, all her sails split, the cabin sole awash, the mast skidding at its base, and Chiles mentally and physically spent. At 2pm, he steered the boat alongside King's Wharf. He commented afterwards that the greatest moments of his voyage were: 'Rounding the Horn and reaching Auckland alive.'

Chiles tied the knot on his circumnavigation on 26 May 1976, when he sailed into the harbour at Papeete in Tahiti.

Now in his 70s, Webb Chiles has circumnavigated five times on different boats. He has been married six times, but the sea remains his most alluring mistress. He spends a good deal of time on his own, living on a small boat in New Zealand's Bay of Islands between periodic trips home to the USA.

DAME NAOMI JAMES

'I rarely listen to the news and when I do listen it doesn't concern me deeply. I live my own life, and I'd prefer the rest of the world to live theirs.'

Born . . . . 2 March 1949
Nationality . . . . New Zealand
Date of Cape Horn rounding . . . . March 1978
Boat name . . . . *Express Crusader*
Designer . . . . EG Van de Stadt
Year of build 1968
LOA . . . . 53 feet
Material . . . . Fibreglass
Rig . . . . Cutter

Naomi James (née Power) grew up along with her two sisters and one brother on a remote dairy farm in Hawkes Bay, New Zealand. A shy, timid girl – by her own admission – Naomi liked to wander endlessly through miles of near-virgin countryside criss-crossed by rivers and streams. The family's annual pilgrimage to town was the only occasion when she experienced crowds and, more often than not, she had to be prised from the car.

Bored and disinterested at school, Naomi left early to work an apprenticeship at a local hairdresser. Being among gossiping women most of the day went some way towards being a cure for shyness, but the narrowness of the conversations and the limited lives they reflected stirred a desire in her for something different: what exactly, Naomi was not sure, but something, anything. Obstinacy is one of her character traits, as was demonstrated by her tenacity when she 'inherited' a nasty-tempered pony from her sister, who was fed up with being constantly thrown. Naomi was thrown too, repeatedly, and repeatedly she climbed back into the saddle until the pony gave in and let her ride.

In 1970, aged 21, she had saved enough money to get to Europe. 'I think I inherited wanderlust from my father who was from one of the Irish Power families and who had left County Waterford at the age of sixteen to find work in New Zealand.' She and her sister Juliet left together on New Year's Eve that year. Naomi knew one thing for certain: she wanted to have control of her own future – 'to choose, not to accept'.

After a five-week passage to England aboard ship, the sisters made their way to Richmond in Surrey, found work and, on visits into London, experienced a big city for the first time. Naomi did not like it much. She yearned for open space and after ten months headed for Tyrol in Austria, landed a job waitressing for the season, but became frustrated by the lack of any opportunity to ski, which had been the whole point of going. A move to Vienna and work hairdressing again led to stultifying boredom. The women's conversations were identical to those of her previous customers in Hawkes Bay. Still uncertain of her future and how to fulfil herself, Naomi did know one thing for sure – she preferred to be alone, she wanted adventure and escapism, and she found deep satisfaction in self-reliance.

Quitting her dull job and now armed with a motorised bicycle, Naomi set off across Germany, then through Switzerland and eventually ending up in Greece – the first time she had ventured anywhere completely alone. Juliet was still in Vienna working as a language teacher. By now short of funds but reasonably proficient in German, Naomi returned to Vienna and took up a job alongside Juliet as a language teacher, bluffing her way a lot of the time.

Two years later, in the summer of 1975, Naomi had come to some sort of concrete decision: she liked animals and she preferred to be outdoors, so working in a zoo or a wildlife park seemed like an answer, and rather than Austria, the best place to go would be England. Back on the trusty motorised bicycle, she travelled through France as far as Saint-Malo, arranged for the bike to be sent to Juliet in Vienna, and went in search of the ferry-booking office. A young Frenchman, seeing her clearly lost, offered to show her the way. As they walked along the quay, a girl poked her head from the companionway of one of the yachts, calling out to ask whether anyone wanted coffee. The girl, who, as it transpired, was a fellow New Zealander, had meant her call for the rest of the crew on deck, but with typical French chutzpah, Naomi's guide immediately accepted the 'offer'.

Chatting on the quayside, Naomi forgot about the ferry office. The Frenchman, figuring his luck had expired, took his leave. With the habitual hospitality found among those who sail, the crew invited Naomi on board.

Knowing nothing of sailing, having never ventured on a boat (with the exception of the passage from New Zealand to England five years before), Naomi knew little of the exploits of the adventuring mariners who, during the previous decade, had set world firsts and records in solo expeditions. She had vaguely heard of Chay Blyth – newspapers, magazines, TV, radio … she could not remember where – and was astonished to find herself drinking coffee in the cabin of the now eminent yacht *British Steel*, on charter in Saint-Malo.

The crew roused the skipper from his bunk and Rob James came through to the saloon to meet his impromptu guest. Their rapport was instant and they talked late into the night. *British Steel* was due to leave port next morning. Naomi stayed on board, sleeping in the forecabin with one of the female crew and next day caught the ferry to England, with plans to meet up with Rob in Weymouth.

Rob signed Naomi on as crew aboard *British Steel* for the remainder of the charter season before the boat set off on the Atlantic Triangle Race. She proved adept at handling the boat: a quick learner, competent and enthusiastic, but as she'd found on board ship, Naomi was 'paralytically' seasick. While Rob was away sailing, Naomi returned to New Zealand, shearing sheep with her brother, Brendon. As a child at school, Naomi had spent most of her time daydreaming. Now, it provided an escape from the monotony of shearing. After crewing on *British Steel*, she had read about Chay Blyth's round-the-world voyage and her daydreaming slowly morphed into something else – fantasy. How would it be, she wondered, if she could one day claim to have sailed alone around the world?

Books were the best way to learn, so she read those by Robin Knox-Johnston, Sir Francis Chichester, Dr David Lewis and any others she could get hold of.

She returned to England six months later, just in time to see *British Steel*'s arrival in the Solent, and stayed with Rob's parents. Rob and Naomi then made a momentous decision, and six weeks later they married. Naomi worked as crew on another boat Chay Blyth had bought – *Spirit of Cutty Sark*, a boat that Naomi would quickly grow to love; on it, in partnership, she would be propelled to the front pages.

It was shortly after the wedding that Naomi broached the idea with Rob of her sailing a circumnavigation – the plan being to attempt a non-stop run and become the first woman to do so. After some thought, he agreed. He knew instinctively that she had already made the decision. The two approached Chay Blyth. He thought the idea had merit. The drive to find a sponsor to fund a new boat began, all this despite Naomi being a complete neophyte, but if anyone knew how to pull it off, it was Blyth. With Rob as her mentor and trainer, Naomi learned the basics of seamanship and navigation on yacht deliveries and charters, experiencing severe weather for the first time on a delivery run from Dartmouth to the Canaries, including a knockdown in force 9 winds in the notorious Bay of Biscay.

Bad news awaited Naomi on her return to England. The sponsorship drive had proved fruitless. The sum sought was considerable – £60,000 – and no one was willing to put money behind a novice. The Whitbread round-the-world race was due to start on 27 August, a few weeks hence. One of the entrants was *Great Britain II*, a 77-footer owned by Chay Blyth and skippered by Rob – the same yacht that had raced the Whitbread in 1974 and that had kept in contact with Alain Colas. At a barbeque at Blyth's house in Dartmouth one evening, talk – liberally fuelled by Yellow Bird cocktails – turned to Naomi's adventure. The suggestion came that she join the crew of *Great Britain II*, gain real blue-water experience and position herself more favourably to attract sponsorship after the race. Another suggestion was tabled. Why not go for a lesser amount, £10,000, to cover costs and charter a boat for her proposed circumnavigation? That way, together with the experience she would gain on the Whitbread, Naomi would have a much better chance of success. At that point, with everyone tight on Yellow Birds, one of the dinner guests, Quentin Wallop, announced that he would sponsor Naomi for the £10,000 if she could find a boat. Chay Blyth, perhaps recalling the almost insurmountable difficulties he had faced getting his project off the ground with *British Steel*, then added the rejoinder that he would let her sail *Spirit of Cutty Sark*. Naomi James could not believe her luck. It was 2 August 1977.

Any thoughts of gaining experience in the Whitbread race were kicked into the long grass. While her husband continued with last-minute preparations on *Great Britain II*, Naomi began to prepare for her own voyage. The idea she had nurtured all along – which was similar to Alain Colas's way of thinking – was to leave at or about the same time as the Whitbread race fleet, but in her smaller, slower boat, and gain ground while the bigger boats were in the various ports en route for one-month layovers. She set a departure date of 2 September, which, being just a few weeks away, was ridiculously ambitious.

During this time a late sponsor did emerge: the *Express* newspaper. Incredibly, with the help and support of many people, Naomi James was ready and crossed the start line on the River Dart on 9 September, only one week behind schedule, to a gun fired by the Royal Dart Yacht Club, her boat rechristened *Express Crusader*.

As part of the *Express* sponsorship deal, Naomi had to make several rendezvous (RV) along her route, the first one being off the harbour entrance at Gran Canaria. The voyage until that first RV was uneventful – niggling problems with the self-steering gear (a Swedish Sailomat), some untraceable but minor leakage into the bilges, and her unsettling seasickness during the first few days. Her skills as a navigator still needed refining, so she was in turns thrilled to get to the rendezvous and then livid – 'I was so angry I could have murdered someone' – when the *Express* photographer missed it and Naomi had to drift around, hove-to close offshore, overnight. When she handed over her film and articles for the newspaper and ITN news broadcasts, there was no mail for her in return. Her disappointment was immense. She discovered later it had been left behind in England by mistake.

Long voyages alone, which Robin Knox-Johnston described as 'solitary confinement with hard labour', did not worry Naomi in the least. On the contrary, she revelled in being alone and came to understand her true nature fully, recording in her log: 'I can very well do without people ... I find that I don't even have the patience to talk over the trivialities of life with people I find as uninteresting as their topics of conversation ... this doesn't mean I dislike all people; on the contrary, there are people who interest me enormously and in whose company I find great pleasure, albeit in small doses.' The one exception was her husband Rob, with whom Naomi was deeply in love, and 'with whom I could spend every minute of my life in perfect ease'.

With a library of hundreds of books on board, one in particular resonated with her: Chris Bonington's *Annapurna South Face*. Naomi identified closely with his motives for mountaineering: '... the soothing balm of solitude ... the undercurrent of danger ... staking one's life on one's judgement ... going into a potentially dangerous situation but then, through his own skill and experience, rendering it safe.'

Naomi was not strictly alone – she had a companion on board, a kitten called Boris. On 8 October, while trying to call Rob, who was newly arrived in Cape Town, her radio died. She still had the VHF, but that line-of-sight radio had limited range. The only option would be to call into port and have the radio fixed, the nearest being Liberia 580 kilometres (360 miles) away. That would mean delay and an end to any hope of achieving a non-stop circumnavigation, and it would upset the pivotal timing, on which her voyage depended, for getting to Cape Horn. She had to be there no later than March – otherwise it might prove impassable in the austral winter. She pressed on.

Juliet had stashed a number of parcels on the boat, each for a specific occasion, and there was one for 'Happy First Equator Crossing', which Naomi achieved at 5pm on 16 October. The package contained a book of short stories by DH Lawrence and a lollipop. She ate it immediately, celebrating later with a three-course meal washed down with a half-bottle of champagne.

Naomi was still very conscious of her relative inexperience: '… I feel far more confident about handling sails generally and hope that when bad weather comes I shall be able to avoid the catastrophes that arise from inexperience…' Along with Naomi's growing confidence, her fondness for *Express Crusader* was also deepening: '… she is a marvellous boat and I feel an overwhelming affection for her.' Boris, too, had become a focus for affection, jealously guarding his territory whenever flying fish slapped on to the deck or birds alighted for a rest; even whales and dolphins close by raised his hackles. As for her own well-being, Naomi found an antidote to worries about bad weather in the high latitudes. She read David Lewis's *Ice Bird* and, comparing her own journey with his, her voyage seemed like a 'summer cruise'.

Boris had taken to dancing along the toe rail. On 29 October, from the corner of her eye, Naomi saw him go over the side while she was making a sail change. Boris was visible 50 metres (165 feet) away. In the few seconds it took to start the engine, she lost sight of him. She searched for two and a half hours, motoring in ever-increasing circles. Nothing. She had no radio and no companion. Naomi was now, for the first time, utterly alone. As a precaution, she trailed a floating line from the stern. If the same thing were to happen to her, at least she would have a fighting chance if she could grab the line as the boat went past. She elaborated this further by also hanging a rope ladder from the stern.

Naomi was becoming increasingly concerned that her fixed positions were at variance with dead reckoning. She went through her astro calculations and found that all the while she had been making a fundamental error – adding magnetic variation to compass error, when compass error is a combination of magnetic variation and compass deviation – in other words, she had been adding magnetic variation twice, throwing her plotted position wildly out. Despite this elementary error in her workings, identifying and correcting the mistake went a long way to boosting her confidence. 'I feel in an exceptionally good temper at present having now solved the problem of the compass error and its influence on my weird positions.'

On 3 November, *Express Crusader* got her first taste of what to expect in the Southern Ocean – 60-knot winds. The Sailomat worked well, getting the boat back on course after repeated impacts from breaking waves and two accidental gybes. Naomi had left the reefed mainsail up to act as a storm trysail, which she acknowledged had been a mistake. Worse, she had '… been waiting for the boat to capsize…' She later wrote: 'But to overcome the cold lethargy that crept over me while I waited for something to happen demanded a willpower which I wasn't certain that I had.'

After the storm, Naomi re-read passages from Chay Blyth's book, noting in her log:

> … Chay and I differ, especially in our concern for the welfare of loved
> ones … he had a wife and baby to consider. Perhaps I'm a natural loner
> because as long as I know that Rob is alive and well I don't really worry
> about him.

Religion was another subject on which Naomi had definite views, which differed markedly from Blyth's:

> Chay is moderately religious whereas I am not. He said I would change
> my mind about religion before the end of the voyage, but I can't
> imagine it.

On 18 November, Naomi's ambition to sail her circumnavigation without stopping ended. The Sailomat was broken beyond repair, and she had to put into Cape Town. The stopover was a concern. Naomi decided on a maximum of three days to get the repairs done. 'I just couldn't afford any more time and feel confident about getting round the Horn in decent weather.'

A minesweeper and a warship led *Express Crusader* to the harbour entrance. Two tugs took over to guide her in along with the rendezvous boat carrying reporters. A woman journalist asked her if she was glad to see people again. Naomi did not answer directly but later wrote: 'I'm afraid I pulled a face.'

Express Crusader sailed from Cape Town on Tuesday 27 November with repaired self-steering and a working radio. Two days later, in light winds, she finally spoke to Rob, who had just arrived in Auckland, anxious about meeting his in-laws.

As *Express Crusader* made her way steadily eastwards, following the 44th parallel, she was treated to a succession of gales and lulls. Naomi could not reconcile her fixed positions against the log. The fixed positions suggested she had travelled much further each day than the mileage ticked off on the log. Rob came up with the reason during a radio call to Auckland – she had been measuring distance on the chart's longitude scale at the bottom instead of on the latitude scale on the side. This Naomi greeted with the one characteristic invaluable to any singlehanded sailor – self-deprecation: 'I had to laugh at myself, me the big-shot navigator! It's a wonder I have managed to come this far ... Still, if I've succeeded in getting here as an idiot, perhaps I'll survive the whole journey as one.'

On 21 December *Express Crusader* suffered her first knockdown, just as Naomi came up from below, water crashing into the cockpit and slamming the companionway doors in her face. The Sailomat was damaged, but not beyond repair – she had picked up plenty of spares in Cape Town – but it was a nagging concern.

A lucky escape followed the next morning. Facing sternwards while tightening the windvane, Naomi was leaning against the railing when the guard wire gave way and she fell forwards over the stern, grabbing the windvane just in time. She was not especially worried because she was wearing her harness. Only when she recovered did Naomi see that she had forgotten to attach the strop to the boat. Had she not grabbed the windvane, she would have been in the water, just like Boris. The realisation of how close she had come to going overboard shocked her deeply.

Just after Christmas, the Sailomat shed a rudder. Naomi had only one spare left and half the world to get round. At the second rendezvous, scheduled for

15 January 1978 at the Maatsuyker Islands, South Tasmania, she gratefully took on board a bunch of spares for the Sailomat, including rudders flown from Sweden.

Shortly after she left the rendezvous, extreme winds battered *Express Crusader* – the worst she had yet experienced. This provided Naomi with an opportunity to stream warps behind the boat as a storm-handling technique. Vito Dumas and Bernard Moitessier may have frowned, but the tactic worked for her. This increasing confidence in her own abilities led to more reflection, and she noted in her log:

> My limits are the extent of my physical and psychological make-up.
> I succeed or fail by my own endeavours without any influence from
> the outside world. I like being a free agent and an individual which is
> perhaps why I am against all religion and political doctrines which try to
> impose their will on mankind.

The physical toll was beginning to tell – that and the prospect of Cape Horn. Naomi's thoughts often turned to Rob who, now that her radio was working, had been such a constant source of praise and encouragement. Her introspection led her to note in her log:

> Rob taught me to sail and navigate just over two years ago and by
> now must have faith in my ability. And so must Chay. But do they
> really know? I wonder how they can possibly know what I am really
> capable of. This business doesn't only depend on skill, and besides,
> they know that I am not that skilful. So what makes them think I
> can sail a boat around the world alone? Is it because I say I can do it?
> Yes, I think that is the answer. They believe I can do it because I say
> I can. And such a belief in a person's determination is an incredible
> expression of faith. But if I fail, then, in the eyes of the world, they
> will be the ones to blame. And they won't be able to exonerate
> themselves by saying she died because she made a mistake, even if
> it were the truth. Poor Rob. I'll have to make it. It would be just too
> terrible if I didn't.

Delays and forced stops had thrown out timings. The Whitbread fleet was past Cape Horn. On 20 February, Naomi was able to speak to Rob in Rio. He was just about to leave for Portsmouth on the final leg of the race. The call bolstered her morale as the weather around her deteriorated. She did not think it could get any worse and she was confident that 'Express Crusader could handle any sort of weather conditions'.

Four days later, Naomi rushed on deck in response to an alarming, unfamiliar banging noise. The mast was swaying dangerously. Bundled in a confused heap on the side deck were the starboard lower shrouds. She quickly set up a jury rig using the spinnaker guys, led back through blocks on the side deck to the winches. She winched the guys tight. The mast stopped swaying. While she contemplated how to make a more permanent fix to the shroud tang (which had snapped), the barometer began to slide. The problem compounded itself when Naomi finally managed to get out the mast through-bolt (which held the tangs), only to discover a crack in the portside tang in the same place where the starboard one had failed. With the weather threatening, all she could do was rig jury lines on the port side and hope.

The next day, Naomi managed a temporary fix, but the starboard shrouds soon failed again. The Horn was looming. Would the mast hold up? A Chilean port was a possibility, but that meant windward sailing and more stress on the rig. A return to New Zealand offered another option, but the consequence would be a year's delay before trying for the Horn and, more immediately, 4,830 kilometres (3,000 miles) of windward sailing. To add to her problems, the main rudder had developed excessive play – was it loose, about to fall off? A final idea struck. How about forgetting the Horn and going via the Panama Canal instead? The downside – there were no South American coastal charts on board – the Panama option would necessitate a return to New Zealand, getting the rigging fixed and sourcing the appropriate charts, but at least that way she would not lose a whole year and at least, she figured, that option would turn 'defeat into something less than defeat'.

It was 26 February. Winds screamed at 50 knots. Waves were breaking over the boat. Naomi set Express Crusader to lie a'hull to spare the rig. Her new dilemma – continue to lie a'hull, or rig a storm jib, flattened fore and aft, and steer downwind? It was now 8pm. She did not know what to do: go for the Horn, turn back to New Zealand, lie a'hull, run before… she decided to do nothing and sleep on it.

At 5am the following morning, with winds raging at force 10 (52 knots), a wave approached with a 'deafening roar', smashed into *Express Crusader*, and Naomi's worst nightmare manifested: the boat capsized. She was hurled out of her bunk. Water cascaded into the bilges as *Express Crusader* righted herself. The sails, lashed to the guardrails, were dragging in the water; one spinnaker pole had gone, the other broken; but, miraculously, the mast was still standing. Taking the helm but facing sternwards to better judge the approaching 9-metre (30-foot) monsters, Naomi stood watch for six hours. Dodging boiling, spuming water that might easily roll the boat again, she periodically darted below to pump the bilges among the chaotic mess in the cabin until finally the heart went out of the storm and the winds moderated to force 8.

The capsize crystallised thoughts in Naomi's mind. Her rationale for turning back and her doubts about the boat had been born of fear, fear that had subliminally dogged her all along. Her survival, the boat's survival, and the calmness with which she had handled the situation all combined to drive out the fear. She set *Express Crusader* on a course for the Horn.

Despite her renewed commitment, though, fear did take root once more. On 8 March, Naomi wrote: 'If I live past the Horn I still have to clear the Southern Ocean. How I dread this ocean … My life has narrowed to a single theme – getting through each day till I round the Horn.' Having read of Chichester's experiences at Cape Horn, sailing quite close in and experiencing some of the worst conditions of his voyage, aggravated by the shallow water over the continental shelf, Naomi decided to head much further south and give the 'brooding, malignant rock' a wide berth. She preferred the risk of tangling with icebergs instead.

Naomi got a fix on 17 March and then put the boat on a heading to pass 24 kilometres (15 miles) south of the Diego Ramírez Islands, relying on dead reckoning to keep her course because she could not be certain of when she might be able to take another sun sight. With the bitter cold limiting periods on deck to 10 minutes, Naomi was grateful for a half-moon the next evening so she could 'see where I'm going'.

The weather turned squally, driving *Express Crusader* at 7 knots with the storm jib and deep-reefed main flying. In the early morning of 19 March, the wind died. Naomi took the opportunity to grab a nap, getting up at 2am as the wind rose from the west. She handed the main and steered all day in driving rain, too 'keyed up for the final battle' to worry about the weather. As they were hidden by poor visibility anyway, she reckoned she must be past the Diego Ramírez Islands, and at 4pm decided to hold course until she judged the boat past Cape Horn itself, 100 kilometres (60 miles) north-east. By evening, now over the continental shelf, the seas became steeper and shorter. Assessing her position by dead reckoning, she gybed *Express Crusader* onto a north-easterly heading, believing she must now be past Cape Horn, 'the focal point of all my fears and apprehensions of the last four months'. Despite the danger of icebergs, the relative proximity of Cape Horn and the unpredictable weather, Naomi turned in at 11.30pm and slept for four hours – her longest uninterrupted sleep during her six months afloat and a reflection of the magnitude of the obstacle that Cape Horn represented to Naomi. Now that she had successfully navigated her way past it, sheer relief allowed some respite from the tension.

Navigating by dead reckoning, Naomi could not be sure of her exact position or know with certainty whether or not she had actually passed Cape Horn. A sun sight on 21 March gave her a fix – 16 kilometres (10 miles) south of Staten Island. To make certain, she climbed the mast and 'saw its dim mountains twenty to thirty miles away'.

To celebrate, Naomi broke open a bottle of Riesling, poured a glass and hurled the wine into the sea.

Express Crusader put in at Port Stanley in the Falkland Islands for rigging repairs. Naomi spoke at length with Rob, now home in England, the Whitbread completed – *Great Britain II* having won on elapsed time.

Naomi's absence from Rob was now a major factor – she yearned to be back with him. 'I don't need religion, but I certainly need Rob,' she wrote in her log shortly after leaving the Falklands. Rob flew to the Azores for an early reunion with Naomi before her final dash for home, 1,930 kilometres (1,200 miles) away.

Naomi James guided *Express Crusader* past the finish line, Rob close by on an escort vessel, at 9.15am on 8 June 1978.

After her triumph and a damehood from the Queen the following year, tragedy hit when Rob died at sea, drowned after falling from a trimaran off the Devon coast on 22 March 1983. He was 36. Ten days later Naomi gave birth to their daughter.

Naomi gave up sailing after her husband's death and went to live in Ireland in a cottage on the south coast they had bought together. She received a PhD in philosophy from University College, Cork in 2006 and is developing a philosophical therapy, 'a model for a common sense approach to find a way through the clutter in everyone's life'.

FIRST SMALL-BOAT ROUNDINGS
OF CAPE HORN

As Cape Horn gave way to the Panama Canal as a commercial trade route, its notorious reputation began to attract small-boat sailors, provoking a challenge that some ardent adventurers, seeking to test themselves in the most extreme marine environment, could not fail to accept.

For yachts powered by sail, the danger of sailing upwind in breaking seas comes from broaching. Downwind, pitchpoling is a constant threat, a sweeping sea gathering and lifting the stern, forcing the bow to dig in and slowing the boat while the following wave continues on somersaulting the boat stern over stem. In the relentless, brutal conditions of Cape Horn, equipment failure and crew exhaustion increase the likelihood of a catastrophic error.

The era of small-boat passages around Cape Horn began with the voyage of *Pandora* in 1910. Built along similar lines as Joshua Slocum's *Spray* and yawl-rigged, *Pandora* sailed on 3 May from Bunbury in Western Australia. At the helm was her English owner and skipper, George Blythe, accompanied by his crew, Peter Arapakis, a Greek-Australian. Blythe's intention was an eastward circumnavigation by way of Cape Horn and the Cape of Good Hope. They stopped first in Sydney to make final provision, before setting out again on 10 July.

In the tempestuous Tasman Sea, the boat suffered a knockdown and limped to New Zealand, where the pair spent a month repairing the damage. Eventually, on 2 October, they set off once more, making the transit of the southern Pacific Ocean via Pitcairn and Easter Islands. Cape Horn beckoned with a succession of gales, and *Pandora*, running before the wind and mountainous seas, passed Cape Horn, 6.5 kilometres (4 miles) off their port beam, on 16 January 1911. Six days later, with the weather worsening and the crew exhausted, *Pandora* was running under bare poles, having climbed north towards the Falkland Islands, when a giant wave rolled up from astern and capsized the boat. Blythe and Arapakis were below at the time, which happy coincidence arguably saved them both. While *Pandora* lay stricken and inverted, both masts broke off before another wave rolled her upright. Desperately, Blythe and Arapakis cut away the mangled rig and decided to trail much of the clutter of wreckage as an impromptu sea anchor. Drifting hopelessly before the west wind with a real prospect of being swept into the vast emptiness of the South Atlantic, they were sighted by a Norwegian whaler, which towed *Pandora* to West Falkland. For the second time on her voyage, *Pandora* underwent extensive repairs.

She set sail once again on 4 March 1911 bound for New York, stopping en route at Saint Helena and Ascension Island. Blythe planned to make an eastward trans-Atlantic passage to London before heading south again to round the Cape of Good Hope. *Pandora* left New York on 30 July. She was never seen again.

Although Cape Horn had almost destroyed the boat, *Pandora*'s successful rounding did much to encourage others. Despite this, perhaps because she did not complete her proposed circumnavigation, *Pandora* quickly disappeared from consciousness and most credit Conor O'Brien – a maverick Irish aristocrat, sometime adventurer and gunrunner during the Irish rebellion – with the first small-boat rounding of Cape Horn. His, in fact, was the second.

Saoirse, which in Gaelic means 'freedom', was designed by O'Brien himself along the lines of an Arklow fishing smack. He had made some of his gunrunning expeditions in these boats and he modelled *Saoirse* on them as much for reasons of familiarity and sentimental attachment as for their open-water sea-keeping qualities, despite his intention of sailing a circumnavigation. The boat measured 42 feet overall (37 feet on the waterline), had a 12-foot beam and drew almost 2 metres (7 feet) of water when loaded. She was planked with pitch pine over oak frames with iron fastenings.

O'Brien, along with a crew of three, sailed from Dublin on 20 June 1923. By all accounts an acerbic character, O'Brien mistrusted his crews and sought to change them repeatedly as he made his way around the world.

In Melbourne, one of 12 stops he made en route, two new recruits joined the boat: a Swedish-American and a former British naval officer, both of whom O'Brien grew quickly to dislike. His plan was to stop over in New Zealand for some mountaineering, but when he arrived there it was too late in the season for climbing. Instead, O'Brien made ready for the South Pacific passage and Cape Horn. About 240 kilometres (150 miles) out, he discovered that a line dragging astern had fouled an albatross. This was a portent of ill fortune, a long-held superstition among mariners since Samuel Taylor Coleridge penned *The Rime of the Ancient Mariner* in 1797. As if to lend flesh to the bones of the superstition, one of the crew badly injured his elbow and it was clear to O'Brien the man needed urgent medical attention. Other calamities ensued. The weather deteriorated. Another crew member injured a leg, which turned septic. Water found its way into the cabin, wetting all the matches, so O'Brien could not light the stove. Shortly afterwards, a bag of coal was washed overboard. This was the last straw. O'Brien gave the order to turn about and head back to New Zealand. In Napier, he discharged one of the injured crew and sailed to Auckland. There, he got rid of the rest of them.

Now it was too late to go for Cape Horn, so O'Brien decided instead on a more leisurely passage, taking on a crew of Tongans who wanted to get home, and a couple of Irishmen. In Tonga, O'Brien became concerned about wood rot and corroding iron fastenings in the hull. Without crew, he came to a hard decision – to abandon the voyage. With that, he put *Saoirse* up for sale. No one was interested. Taking on a new crew of Tongans, including one man called Kioa who turned out to be a first-rate sailor, a competent cook and a hard worker in contrast to practically every other crewman O'Brien had employed up to that time, *Saoirse* headed back to New Zealand. Here, with the exception of Kioa, O'Brien replaced the crew again, taking on 'W', who was running away from his wife.

Saoirse left Auckland on 22 October 1924, homeward bound via Cape Horn. Despite all the earlier misfortune, the Cape Horn passage was notable only for one breakage – when the rudder chain parted – and *Saoirse* rounded the rock itself on a fine, clear day. She arrived in Stanley Harbour on 6 December, having sailed 9,330 kilometres (5,800 miles) non-stop.

Despite the varying experiences of these two earliest pioneering voyages, the unrelenting succession of storm systems meant that to venture into the Cape Horn region before the advent of sophisticated weather forecasting and without the means to communicate that information to mariners by satellite phone and email was to take a chance, a risk, to play Russian roulette with nature.

Conor O'Brien knew he had been lucky. He later recalled the words of Herman Melville: 'Ye lucky livers, to whom, by some rare fatality, your Cape Horns are as placid as Lake Lemans, flatter not yourselves that good luck is judgement and discretion: for all the yolk in your eggs, you might have foundered and gone down, had the Spirit of the Cape said the word.'

Alain Colas, the renowned French sailor, put it another way:

The Horn is not an enemy. It is not even an adversary in the sporting sense of the term. Rather, it is a symbol – a symbol of that which is difficult, of a certain anguish and fear to be overcome, of a great reward to be won, step by step. It represents more than an individual victory. It is part of a heritage which must be accepted and preserved. Generations of men have fought and sometimes died here. And, though we as amateurs cannot pretend to compare ourselves to them, we are privileged to continue their line. The legend of Cape Horn must be kept alive and, if no one dares any longer to confront the Cape, then it will become nothing more than a black dot in geography books. Things must be experienced, if they are to have reality.

LES POWLES

'Some people thought I was an idiot but I couldn't
care less. It's what I wanted to do.'

Born . . . . 24 October 1925

Nationality . . . . British

Date of Cape Horn rounding . . . . February 1981

Boat name . . . . *Solitaire*

Designer . . . . Bruce Roberts

Year of build 1975

LOA . . . . 34 feet

Material . . . . Fibreglass

Rig . . . . Cutter

Les Powles has always felt himself a loner, '… never feeling I belonged.' Perhaps, then, it is not too surprising that he was drawn to the oceans where, as a singlehanded sailor, self-reliance becomes not a sporadic manifestation but an everyday way of living. Powles, now in his 90s, completed three circumnavigations between 1975 and 1996, the latter two eastwards by way of Cape Horn, and all on his self-built 34-foot fibreglass boat, *Solitaire*.

Born on 24 October 1925 and brought up in Birmingham, 'about as far from the sea as you can get', Powles went to work in an aircraft factory aged 14 with dreams of becoming a pilot. Three years later he joined the Royal Air Force, though qualifying as a radio operator and gunner rather than as a pilot, and too late to see active service in World War II. After serving in the military, he started and ran a number of businesses, including a garage, a haulage firm and various shops. Nothing held his attention for long. An opportunity to work abroad took him to South Yemen, where he worked as a radio engineer for two years from 1966 until 1968 when, with a newly discovered penchant for golf but dissatisfied with playing the game on sand, he flew to South Africa to try the game on grass.

One Sunday morning in Durban, now working for an electronics company, Powles wandered along the yacht-club jetty, stopping often to gaze at the moored boats under flags from many parts of the world. As he watched the boats, Powles experienced a new liberation, the crystallisation of myriad latent frustrations keeping him pinned down to a conventional if widely travelled existence. The boats represented freedom. 'They were not shackled to land by chains whose links were forged by careers, mortgages and fashion.' He felt a sudden compunction to throw his arms wide and shout out at the sudden realisation that he had found the key to unlock … freedom! The boats promised a new and different way of life, home and transport combined, and achievable at considerably less cost.

Powles had never sailed but decided he would buy a boat. He returned to England in early 1969 only to find that his £2,000 savings would not stretch to the sort of boat he wanted. So, with his fall-back as a radio engineer, he took a job in Saudi Arabia and increased his savings to £4,500, but within just two years, inflation had done its work and kept a suitable boat beyond his means. Back in England once more, he met a couple about to embark on a round-the-world voyage on their 45-foot sloop. They invited Powles to join the boat as crew. Excited, he agreed, only to experience an unremarkable passage as far as Gibraltar made largely under power, and 'a strong desire to sail alone'.

No concrete plan had yet emerged to circumnavigate; Powles was more inclined towards pottering around the world, sailing wherever and whenever the fancy took him, more governed by the simple desire to be free than by anything else. Whatever loose ideas of romanticised abandon were floating around in his mind, he still had one major problem: Powles needed more money. So for the next two years he worked, again in Saudi Arabia, until he had increased his bank balance to £8,500 by the beginning of 1973. More frustration awaited. The price of the type of boat he wanted had now increased to around £12,000. It seemed to be a never-ending game of returning to the table only to find his arms too short to reach the food. Then fate, with its peculiar tendency to offer succour if sufficient frustration is first experienced as a kind of qualification, stepped in. Powles saw an advertisement in a boating magazine: 'Come to Liverpool and build your own Nor-West 34, hull and deck, £1,300.'

Powles drove to Liverpool. The shed, when he eventually found it at Liverpool docks, was near derelict, but the promise of escape and freedom, as Powles perceived it, was overpowering. Here, he would be able to build a boat within his budget. He paid a £400 deposit, bought a caravan to live in for the duration of the build and cobbled together help from friends to lay the fibreglass. The job took nine days, leaving the remainder of the month, the period for which Powles had rented space in the shed, for applying and sanding the outer coatings made up of resin and talcum powder. Some time during the build another DIY-er pitched up. His name was Rome Ryott, an RAF pilot. The two liked each other immediately and agreed to exchange labour on their respective boats. Of the many people who drifted in and out of Powles's life during that time in Liverpool, Rome was to become a constant.

Taking a job as a quality-assurance engineer with British Leyland, Powles moved closer to Birmingham to look after his ailing mother and completed the fit-out of the boat there. Rome Ryott meantime had taken his boat to Lymington. Powles visited him on the south coast and, seeing it was as fine a place as any, launched his newly named *Solitaire* in the Lymington River. Now aged 49, Powles had no qualms giving up his well-paid job despite knowing he would have difficulty finding another. The dream hatched in South Africa six years before was as strong as ever. He had little tolerance for the talkers – 'tomorrow's people' he called them: 'We're off tomorrow … when we've bought a new mainsail. We're off tomorrow … when we've painted the topsides. We're off tomorrow … when we've bought a bigger boat.'

Powles took *Solitaire* out with Rome for the first time in the spring of 1975 and was eager to get underway round the world when Rome, observing his (lack of) sailing skills, suggested he wait a year, but then revised that to two years. Powles ignored him, too eager to be off and gone.

In the late summer of 1975, with funds running low, Powles took lessons from Rome on celestial navigation, and finished kitting out the boat with a Hydrovane (self-steering gear), radio, gas bottles and provisions. With a vague idea of how to get to Barbados, he set sail on Monday 18 August. 'The wind blew free with no bills to pay at the end of the month for that! Oceans lay ahead like orchards of succulent fruit: we could gorge ourselves and feast.'

It was a beautiful day, the sky blue, the wind calm. By evening the wind picked up and the seas became choppy. After dark, fog descended. The lights of ships moved swiftly up and down the Channel. By the following morning, Powles was completely lost. He eventually made his way to Brixham, then Falmouth, then across the Atlantic – aiming for Barbados but ending up in Brazil through a minor mistake in reducing a sun sight, which led him to believe he was on latitude 14° north when in fact his latitude was closer to 2° south, almost 1,600 kilometres (1,000 miles) off track. With no charts of the area and believing himself to be among the Windward Islands, Powles approached the coast, piled into a reef, suffered dreadful sunburn trying to get the boat off and ended up moored in a river and spending two weeks in hospital. When he discovered his mistake, Powles was mortified, but proceeded to sail around the rest of the world via the

Panama Canal, Tahiti, Gladstone and Darwin in Australia, Durban and Cape Town, finally arriving back in Lymington on 30 April 1978 after 54,700 kilometres (34,000 miles).

It was while he was in Tahiti that Powles began to shape an idea that would form the basis for his future sailing. Entering the harbour at Papeete on 19 June 1976, Powles circled round several times looking for a space. The harbour was packed. The Bastille Day celebrations were not far off and many boats had arrived in anticipation of the festivities. He spotted a space next to a bright yellow Ericson 37. A tall, lanky man appeared on deck. 'Can I moor next to you?' Powles shouted across the water. 'Are you singlehanded?' came the American-accented response. When Powles said he was alone, the man waved him in.

The next day, Webb Chiles, who had sailed from Auckland and arrived in Tahiti on 26 May, introduced himself. Learning of Chiles's circumnavigation on his near-sinking boat – the first true circumnavigator Powles had met – the idea of a second voyage, a circumnavigation non-stop via Cape Horn, took root, primarily because such a voyage would atone for the near-disaster of hitting the reef off the coast of Brazil. 'These chats with Webb dictated the route for my next attempt – around Cape Horn … I was finding it increasingly difficult to live with my errors. I wanted to square the account which made me believe a second voyage around Cape Horn might help.'

Powles, by trial and error, tenacity and endeavour, had developed into a competent sailor. It is not so surprising, therefore, that he sought a greater challenge. The very idea of becoming a Cape Horner was irresistible. In the spirit of true exploration and adventure, Powles did not seek fame or records, but instead felt a deeper yearning for freedom and the inevitable desire to test himself and his vessel.

Once he arrived back in Lymington, his intention to sail a non-stop circumnavigation via Cape Horn was still firm. With money tight, Powles took a job to fund preparations. He wanted to change the rigging on *Solitaire* from that of a sloop to that of a cutter to provide a more diverse selection of sail plans. He also needed a new suit of sails, 'strong enough to take me round Cape Horn'.

When the sails were ready for collection, Powles was so appalled by the poor quality that he had no choice but to sue and, worse, the delay meant he could not sail in time to be at Cape Horn for the austral summer. The court case dragged on for two years. Powles could no longer afford to convert his rig in the way he wanted and did not receive any compensation for the botched sails.

He ordered another suit of sails, this time expertly made by Peter Lucas of Lucas Sails, and after two years of almost perpetual struggle, *Solitaire* was finally ready to depart in July 1980. If Powles needed any further inducement to justify getting on his boat and sailing away, his last two years in England – ripped off, denied justice, tangled in bureaucracy – more than provided a reason.

Rome had taken time away from his RAF duties to crew on the British yacht *Adventure* in the 1977–1978 Whitbread round-the-world race (the same race in which Rob James skippered Chay Blyth's *Great Britain II* to victory). Now returned, Rome and his new beau, Annegret, came to see Powles off with armfuls of gifts, each to be opened at a specific point on the voyage. Other friends also descended with gifts, including a tin of salmon and a bottle of champagne to celebrate rounding Cape Horn.

Powles set out from Lymington on 9 July 1980 and reached the equator on 18 August, crossing the line at 10pm (UTC), and with that, he opened the first of the parcels from Rome and Annegret – tins of ham, coleslaw and fruit, a can of beer, chocolate and sweets.

Solitaire met some heavy weather south of the equator. One big worry for Powles was leakage. 'Bilges constantly filling,' he noted in the log. In Tahiti, Powles had spoken at length to Webb Chiles and learned of his dreadful ordeal with a cracked hull; he was understandably concerned.

By mid-September, worries about the heavy weather, the strain on the boat and how she would hold up preyed on Powles. *Solitaire* had sailed 10,300 kilometres (6,400 miles) in 70 days, her longest ever non-stop passage: '… so far we have been lucky and I have no reason to complain of our progress. So why do I feel so depressed?'

Powles thought a festering fear might be causing his melancholy, fear of going into the unknown – how would *Solitaire* deal with Southern Ocean conditions? His urge to round Cape Horn 'was as strong as ever', but he had a copy of Chichester's book on board, and his descriptions of the Southern Ocean and Cape Horn unnerved him. Would *Solitaire* survive a capsize? Powles reckoned the chances were pretty high that she would go over at least once – everyone else had – Chichester, Rose, Knox-Johnston, Naomi James, the lot.

Powles steered a course to pass eastwards, 480 kilometres (300 miles) south of Cape Town, to avoid the strong westward-flowing Agulhas current and stay out of the shallow waters over the continental shelf. His logic was sound but his luck was out. He sailed into the worst storm he had ever encountered. Powles handed all sails to allow *Solitaire* to lie a'hull, then retreated below to wait out the storm, soaked and freezing despite a new set of oilies. Exhausted, he wedged himself on the cabin sole between water containers and drifted into a light, fitful sleep.

About 5cm (2in) of water slopping over the floor woke Powles. He had only pumped the bilges two hours earlier. Now, at least 455 litres (100 gallons) of water had found its way in. Powles kept pumping for most of the night as massive seas swamped *Solitaire*. He could not believe the savagery of the weather, the monstrous seas and the breath-stealing wind. The spuming breaking crest of one giant wave dragged *Solitaire* along on her side for over 100 metres (325 feet) before the water released its grip. Powles had a serious problem: the winds were coming from the north. If he raised a headsail he would have to run south and he was already 480 kilometres (300 miles) south of Cape Town. If he steered, he would not be able to pump the bilges, and if he continued to lie a'hull, the boat might be rolled and dismasted. The wind was now screaming at over 100 knots – deep, deep into hurricane country. Powles decided to leave things be. By the third night of the storm, with very little sleep and no food, Powles's other enemy was the cold. The manual bilge pump located in the cockpit meant he had to be outside to keep pumping, exposed to wind and water. The boat had an electric bilge pump, but it was sitting in a locker because Powles had been unable to afford the piping to connect it up before leaving Lymington.

On the upside, Powles had traced the leak that had caused so much anxiety to the cockpit locker, where water was finding its way into the cabin through cavities and channels between the hull and the interior linings.

On the fourth day of the storm, Powles decided enough was enough and managed to get a cut-down plywood windvane onto the Hydrovane (anything bigger would have been torn away) and raise a headsail. These straightforward tasks took over an hour to complete and most of the time Powles lay spreadeagled on the foredeck while waves crashed over the boat.

Now the boat was running downwind, Powles changed into dry clothes and collapsed at the chart table, asleep within seconds. He was woken four hours later by the violence of an accidental gybe. The backed headsail was now working against the self-steering, forcing the bows back and gybing the boat once more onto her course. In his understated way, Powles recorded in the log: 'The voyage is not going too well at the moment.'

It was a miracle Powles and the boat were still in one piece. The storm lasted a full week before the winds finally backed from north to west and *Solitaire* could begin to make easting and halt the precipitous slide south into iceberg territory. Powles celebrated by opening the 'Cape of Good Hope parcel' from Rome and Annegret, and by taking to heart the lesson from the storm – 'Never again would *Solitaire* lie helpless without sails or self-steering.' As for shipping water, Powles dealt with that by fibreglassing in the cockpit locker. The test of whether *Solitaire* could stand up to Southern Ocean storms had surely been passed and, with refined and improved heavy weather tactics now learned, Powles was more confident about Cape Horn.

Rome and Annegret did not disappoint on Christmas Day when Powles, south-west of New Zealand, opened his 'Christmas Day parcel'. He found a heap of tins – one of turkey, others of sprouts and potatoes; it was Christmas dinner 'with all the trimmings'. Also included in the package were a Christmas pudding, a cake (complete with candle), a tin of salmon, a bottle of wine, chocolate, a cracker and a Christmas card. The kindness was too much for Powles and not for the first time he showed his appreciation by weeping copious tears.

With the wide South Pacific to get across before Cape Horn was reached, Powles took stock of his boat and supplies. The hull seemed in good nick, the sails too. Fibreglassing the cockpit locker seemed to have stopped the leakage. The Hydrovane was working well and the rigging was 'always a worry, but no problems so far'. Drinking water now topped the list of concerns – only 100 litres (22 gallons) remained. As for food, he took the precautionary measure of rationing. 'Rome's food parcels have been a godsend. Should be OK.'

En route towards Cape Horn, *Solitaire* experienced more gales (though nothing compared with the week-long storm off Cape Agulhas), interspersed with periods of idyllic sailing. When the yacht passed the point of no return, when it was safer to proceed east and round the Horn rather than turn and beat upwind to New Zealand, Powles felt relief, for now he was truly committed, no turning back. 'We would round it [Cape Horn], possibly without mast or instruments, food or water, but dead or alive we would pass Cape Horn.'

By 5 February, with 2,250 kilometres (1,400 miles) to Cape Horn, Powles found himself in a state. He had lost a considerable amount of weight and he worried about his fading strength. 'Very concerned in case I have to climb the mast as I just don't know how I would manage to pull myself up.' To encourage himself, Powles opened the next parcel from Rome and Annegret, the one marked: 'For cold weather sailing.' The food, chocolate and particularly a book came as a welcome relief – Powles had read everything on board twice – and yet again he wondered at the kindness of his friend.

The weather had been moderately good. *Solitaire* recorded weekly mileages in the 650 range, but any thoughts of that continuing were dashed on 8 February 1981. '*Solitaire* suffered her worst knockdown since leaving England. For the past few days I have been frightened … I will have to be more careful until past Cape Horn.' The legacy of the knockdown was a damaged storm jib – all the piston hanks had pulled out – and the halyard had parted and the cabin sole was once again submerged. *Solitaire* still had 2,025 kilometres (1,260 miles) to Cape Horn.

Powles's plan was to sail well to the south of Cape Horn, as far as the 58th parallel. With only one spare halyard left and no desire to climb the mast to rig it if there was a problem, Powles did not want to risk the shallower waters over the continental shelf. 'Chichester nearly lost his yacht by cutting in too close.' He opted instead to risk dicing with icebergs.

Symptoms of poor nutrition were now evident. Powles had bleeding salt-water sores on his back which refused to heel, bleeding gums, headaches, blurred vision and blackened toenails.

With Cape Horn 800 kilometres (500 miles) away, the westerly winds gained in strength. The air temperature was frigid. As the miles ticked by, the wind moderated. On 19 February, 465 kilometres (290 miles) from the Horn, *Solitaire* was flying along with full mainsail. 'Hard to believe we are so close to the desolate Cape Horn in such conditions, with no winds howling in the rigging and the seas flat apart from a constant high swell.' By evening, the situation had become more bizarre: *Solitaire* was becalmed overnight.

The westerlies kicked in again, blowing between force 3 and force 7 (9–30 knots), accompanied by heavy rain. A sun sight put *Solitaire* 100 kilometres (60 miles) south-west of the Diego Ramírez Islands. Powles's luck was holding. Despite the weather becoming squally, the winds only reached force 6 (24 knots) – a zephyr by Cape Horn standards.

Solitaire passed the longitude of Cape Horn at 01.00 UTC on Tuesday 24 February, a mixed bag of a day, with light breezes punctuated by squalls bringing winds gusting to storm force before fading quickly. It was a vindication of sorts. Powles's decision to voyage here allowed him a measure of forgiveness for the navigational errors that had almost cost him his boat on the reef off the Brazilian coast.

The 'Cape Horn parcel' from Rome contained more welcome food: meatballs, beans and a tin of sponge cake. The other parcel, containing salmon and champagne, came with explicit instructions penned on the label: 'Not to be opened until Cape Horn is abaft the beam: for internal use only: contents to be consumed in one sitting.' Powles was not entirely sure what 'abaft the beam' meant, but he quaffed the lot the next day, one of 'clear blue skies with a bite in the crystal air'.

Rounding Cape Horn left Powles with '… no feeling of achievement, only gratitude that the seas had allowed *Solitaire* to pass over [him] without making too many demands'. Among singlehanded sailors, Powles was not alone in feeling an anticlimax on passing Cape Horn – he was simply too modest to feel triumphant and too grateful for having survived to be exuberant. Scaling the massive psychological mountain that Cape Horn represents to any lone sailor is exhausting enough. To get down the other side is sufficient reward.

Powles's supplies were running dangerously low. About 8,000 kilometres (5,000 miles) still separated him from Lymington. His rationing became extreme – enough water to keep himself alive but with a permanent thirst, and half a cup of rice per day flavoured with curry powder or toothpaste. He did catch a large fish near the equator, which provided three meals a day for three days, but that was a one-off. He still had two of Rome's parcels left: one for Easter, one for the equator crossing. Powles opened them together at the same time, enjoying a dinner of faggots and peas followed by chocolate – unbelievable bounty among an arid landscape of rationing.

Solitaire arrived back in Lymington on 3 June 1981. The only provisions on board comprised half a cup of sugar and a quarter of a tin of condensed milk – no water, no other food, not even a teabag. Powles had used the very last one earlier that morning.

A friend, Keith Parris, who had been the last person Powles spoke to before his departure, was standing on the quayside as *Solitaire* nosed up to her mooring. Powles liked the symmetry. The first words Parris uttered were: 'Where the hell have you been?'

Much to his surprise, Powles was voted Yachtsman of the Year by the Yachting Journalists' Association.

In 1982, Powles sailed for Newport, Rhode Island. Rome had also set sail on his new boat, bound for Cape Town. The two planned to meet in Antigua for Christmas.

On 3 November, Powles was already in Antigua enjoying the warmth and looking forward to spending Christmas with his great friend. That afternoon he received a telephone call from Keith Parris in Lymington. The message was bleak. Rome had been due in at Cape Town on 25 October but had not arrived and was not responding to radio calls. He had been missing for eight days. South African rescue services had launched a search.

Two days later, on 5 November, Powles learned the rescue services had spotted wreckage from Rome's boat, but no liferaft. They had decided to call off the search. Rome's body was never recovered.

On 26 May 1988, Les Powles departed on his third circumnavigation, this time by way of the Suez Canal, stopping at Carnavon in Western Australia, Perth, Sydney, Whangarei in New Zealand, then east and around Cape Horn a second time. He arrived back in the UK on 5 July 1996.

In recognition, Lymington Yacht Haven gave Powles a free mooring for life. He lives there, on *Solitaire*.

KAY COTTEE

'Anything is possible with planning, preparation and dedication.'

Born . . . . 25 January 1954

Nationality . . . . Australian

Date of Cape Horn rounding . . . . January 1988

Boat name . . . . *Blackmore's First Lady*

Designer . . . . Lawrence Davidson

Year of build 1987

LOA . . . . 37 feet

Material . . . . Fibreglass

Rig . . . . Cutter

Where Naomi James succeeded in achieving a solo circumnavigation via Cape Horn, she failed to realise her original ambition of doing so without stopping. More than a decade later, that same motivation was fermenting in the mind of an Australian woman, Kay Cottee.

Unlike Naomi James, Kay's introduction to sailing came early, secured to the mast with a lifeline along with her three sisters on day trips in Sydney Harbour aboard their parents' boat. In 1961, her father, James McLaren, built a Tasman Seabird in the garden, launching the boat two-and-a-half years later, when Kay was nine. She was regular crew during weekend buoy racing.

Engaged at 17 and married at 18, Kay worked at her father-in-law's plumbing business – a lonely job she did not enjoy, but she kept sailing and kept dreaming of reaching beyond Sydney Harbour and all around the world without stopping. Her daydreams were more idealised contemplations rather than configured plans, her ambitions more spectral than definite, but they were persistent, taking shape in the ensuing years as Kay worked her way into her middle 20s.

In 1974, she and her husband Neville bought a 22-footer, *Jacinth*, living on board for three months while they prepared her for offshore cruising. Their first expedition, a cruise along the New South Wales coast, ended badly. Caught in a storm after leaving Crofts Harbour, tossed about on mountainous seas for three days, they cut the dinghy free from its lashings on the foredeck to prevent damaging the deck and threatening the boat. The abandoned dinghy led to fears for their safety. Kay's parents hired a spotter plane to find *Jacinth* and, sighting the boat from the air, local rescue services ordered a coal carrier bound for Newcastle to divert and take them off the boat, leaving *Jacinth* to drift. It was Christmas Eve. Kay and Neville got to Sydney for Christmas, then travelled back to Queensland. Two days later, the volunteer coastal patrol located *Jacinth*, towed her to Brisbane, and she was trucked back to Sydney.

Kay sold *Jacinth* and traded up to a Roberts 36, hiring the mould and building the boat herself. For part of the time during construction, she lived between a tent on the beach at Wollongong and her in-laws' house with her husband. They launched the boat in Sydney Harbour, but sold her 12 months later. Next came a Roberts 35, built to specifications for charter, which Kay worked on full time. The claustrophobia of living with her in-laws, coupled with the loneliness of the plumbing business and her perceptions of the narrowness of her life, combined to disillusion Kay. She took to living on the new boat, *Whimaway*, during the week and with her sister at weekends, while her marriage disintegrated.

Kay abandoned the plumbing business, moved into a flat in Newport with three friends and focused her energies on her fledgling yacht-charter and boat-management business. *Whimaway* had to go to pay off debts, but her ambition remained intact: to own another boat, one that would take her non-stop around the world via Cape Horn, alone, and become the first woman to achieve what Robin Knox-Johnston had accomplished in 1969.

To achieve her goal Kay needed money, and to earn more, she had to expand her business. Shirley King, nicknamed 'Freddo' because of her liking for chocolate frogs of the same name, joined Kay to run the charter business.

By 1985, Kay had a solid foundation in sailing, boat management, chartering, marketing and PR. The final motivation for her circumnavigation came when a friend, Mike Davidson, just returned from a two-year Pacific cruise, lent Kay his Duncanson 35 for a trip to Lord Howe Island in the Tasman Sea, 700 kilometres (440 miles) east of Sydney. Kay asked another friend, Linda Wayman (editor of *Cruising Helmsman* magazine), to join her as crew. Linda could take only a week off work, so Kay would have to sail back alone. The return leg, in 40-knot winds, took 65 hours. Kay stayed awake the entire time. When she arrived exhausted in Sydney, the singlehanded sailing bug had bitten. She sold the charter business and bought the hull and deck of a Cavalier 37 to equip and fit out herself, using an inventory of damaged kit replaced on the charter fleet.

The Trans-Tasman race, inspired by the 1968 OSTAR and first run in 1970, had quickly established itself as a quadrennial event. Kay wanted to enter the 1986 race but, with her boat just a shell, she needed sponsorship and a boat to charter. A friend introduced her to Marcus Blackmore, a keen sailor himself and chairman of Blackmore Laboratories, Australia's leading manufacturer of natural health-care products. Blackmore was keen to get involved but insisted that Kay go in her own yacht. She had three months to get the boat ready.

The Trans-Tasman ran over two legs – a two-handed race from Mooloolaba in Queensland to New Plymouth in New Zealand followed by the singlehanded return leg. Kay asked Linda Wayman to crew the two-handed race, then she would return solo. Frenetic activity followed, Kay calling in every favour she could and relying on the goodwill of family and friends to get the boat ready in time. Kay had wanted to name the boat *Jimmy Mac* after her father. Instead, sponsorship commitments took precedence, and the result was *Cinnamon Scrub*, after a Blackmore's facial-wash product. Kay launched the boat, sailable but still not finished, just in time for the race skippers' qualification passage of 800 kilometres (500 miles).

The Trans-Tasman got underway on 8 March 1986, with gales every day bar one all the way to New Plymouth. Her first real test of solo racing began on 5 April. Nervous about setting the spinnaker on her own, Kay lagged behind the other boats until, fed up with the other competitors' jeering over the radio, she forced herself to get the big sail up. During the remainder of the race, Kay raised and lowered the spinnaker five times, building her confidence, developing her self-reliance and helping her to realise that she was more capable than she had believed. Kay finished a creditable sixth out of 15 starters.

A further problem-solving test awaited on the trip from Mooloolaba back to Sydney. For this short sail, Freddo joined Kay as crew. During the passage, one of Kay's molars split. Freddo, formerly a dental nurse, had a look. The nerve was exposed. It was going to be sore. There was nothing for it but to wait until they reached Sydney and then get to a dentist immediately. Rather than endure the pain, Kay mixed up a small amount of two-part epoxy filler, applied it to the sheared surface of the tooth with a matchstick, pressed the broken piece against the stump in her mouth, then sucked mints for two hours to get rid of the taste while the epoxy set. It worked. Days later, her dentist had to drill the tooth apart so he could make a proper fix.

Short of money, jobless and with a pile of debts to pay off, Kay worked at a sailing school in Sydney for several months, devoting every spare minute to her still-unfinished boat. She landed a second job – to fit out another Cavalier 37. All through this time, her conviction to sail a solo circumnavigation never wavered. When she finally summoned the nerve to tell her parents – both very experienced offshore sailors – their support was immediate. With money still tight, Kay sold what she could – spare equipment, her car, a sailing dinghy, her windsurfer. Next – sponsorship. Marcus Blackmore had told her that his company would not sponsor any more sailing events. Disappointing as that news was, Kay put together a sponsorship proposal and then set about the soul-destroying task of asking people for money. One company in Perth expressed interest. An executive was coming to Sydney on business. If Kay could collect him from the airport and take him to his hotel they would have an opportunity to talk about her plans. Kay agreed. She borrowed a silk dress and a car, collected the executive as planned, then proceeded to get lost trying to find the hotel – prompting an unflattering comment about her navigation skills. When they finally got to the hotel, Kay's heel caught in the hem of her dress, making her stumble about like a drunk. At the lifts she dropped her bag, spilling the contents all over the floor, while the executive she was supposed to impress acted as though she was nothing to do with him. Worse still, when she looked in the mirror afterwards, the shoulder pad of her jacket (this was the 1980s) had slipped round, giving her the appearance of a hunchback. She did not get the sponsorship.

Kay had not included one of her personal objectives for the voyage – to raise funds for charity – in her sponsorship document, believing the information was not relevant. When Marcus Blackmore heard about it, though, his attitude changed. Blackmore's had provided the first corporate donations to the Life Education Program (set up to help children and young people with issues of low self-esteem and substance abuse), and if Kay agreed to direct the fundraising efforts of the voyage to this programme, then she would have her sponsorship. Rather than the sponsorship focusing on product endorsement, which some executives in the firm believed would not yield a viable return on the investment, it would centre instead on corporate identity and brand value. The boat was re-named once again. For Kay's Cape Horn circumnavigation, her Cavalier 37 became *Blackmore's First Lady*. The PR contract for the voyage, a critical aspect as far as Blackmore's was concerned, went to an outside agency, Showboat Productions, run by Peter Sutton.

A start date in mid-November would mean Kay sailing the greater part of the voyage in the austral summer and spring months, avoiding the worst of the winter weather. With a seemingly endless array of jobs to be done, Peter Sutton eased the media pressure by organising press conferences rather than myriad, time-consuming one-on-one interviews. Throughout this period Kay had to familiarise herself with the new electronic equipment installed on board and undergo a full medical examination, mainly to monitor a congenital heart defect and the pulmonary stenosis which, in extreme environments demanding high physical exertion, could leave Kay more than usually tired.

For safety and psychological reassurance, Kay took every precaution, installing two watertight crash bulkheads to mitigate damage from collision with ice or submerged sea containers. According to the Office of National Marine Sanctuaries – a department within the National Oceanic and Atmospheric Administration (NOAA), a US government agency – 5–6 million sea containers are transported annually, of which approximately 10,000 are lost over the sides of ships. These containers can float, barely submerged, for weeks or months. Estimates put floating sea containers scattered around the world's oceans at 250,000. For small boats, these drifting containers present a huge hazard akin to dancing through a minefield. Disconcerted by another statistic – an extended passage in the Southern Ocean generated a 75 per cent chance of a 360-degree rollover and a 50 per cent chance of it happening twice, with David Lewis's experiences on *Ice Bird* testifying as much – Kay ensured that her boat carried appropriate equipment for a jury rig if the boat were dismasted. In case of pirate attack, she took her father's rifle.

A host of last-minute preparations forced a postponement of the start date by two weeks, to Sunday 29 November 1987. At noon, *Blackmore's First Lady* crossed the start line. One by one the escort boats fell away until Kay was finally alone with her goal and her fears.

Kay had warning of an approaching low-pressure system before starting out, and by the evening of 2 December the wind was blowing at 45 knots with gusts to 60 knots. While Kay was below, *First Lady* was pooped, then slewed beam-on to the seas and broached. The wind generator was gone, ripped clean off the pole mounted on the transom. To lose back-up power generation so early on was not disastrous but it was inconvenient. More worrying was the evidence of how quickly and how badly *First Lady* could be damaged – winds at or over 50 knots would be routine.

Route-planning suggested Kay broadly follow the 44th and 45th parallels, to stay in the zone between the clockwise rotating lows to the south and the anti-clockwise spinning highs to the north, thus maximising the chances of westerlies. Only on approaching the Chilean coast would *First Lady* have to dive south to round Cape Horn.

As she sailed along her prescribed route contemplating the endless miles ahead and smarting from the recent damage to her boat, Kay felt acutely vulnerable about her psychological equilibrium, especially given her very sociable life ashore. Her on-board routine, designed to keep her feeling as near 'normal' as possible, included eating at the table from a plate rather than from a tin or bag, rigorous personal hygiene – a salt-water wash most days – applying make-up and perfume regularly, and keeping a clean wardrobe of clothes. Each evening, without fail, she rewarded herself with a gin and lemon (she forgot to load up any tonic) or a brandy.

First Lady was experiencing typical Southern Ocean weather – variable, storms and lulls, with winds regularly touching 50 knots gusting to 60 knots. On Christmas Day, Kay moved to her next chart, 'the first one with Cape Horn on it!'

Technological advances meant Kay's HF radio was more reliable than those of earlier lone voyagers so, unlike them, she received regular routing and weather instructions. After Christmas, the warning came of deteriorating weather and advice to go northwards to the 42nd parallel to get clear. When distance from Sydney compromised radio communications, Kay made contact with a commercial ship, *Act 7*, which continued to feed her weather information. She was also navigating with satellite GPS, avoiding the need for regular sextant sights and workings. Kay knew how to calculate her position from sun sights, but she was not practised. In 1988, GPS was still a relatively new technology on the commercial market. Originally developed by the US military for submarine tracking in the 1950s and 1960s, the concept was refined to allow vehicle tracking. In 1983, following the downing of a Korean Air Lines jet carrying 269 people, which had strayed into prohibited Russian airspace over the Kamchatka Peninsula because of navigational error, President Reagan issued a directive that would see GPS made available for civilian use. Two years later, in 1985, the US government contracted with private companies to develop the first airborne, shipboard and portable GPS receivers. Kay's on-board GPS was one of these early receivers.

After six weeks at sea and approaching Cape Horn, the boat suffered a second knockdown, causing significant damage. The boom had cracked. Kay repaired the damage with reinforcing rods cannibalised from the mainsheet track and a spare section of spinnaker pole screwed into the boom either side of the crack. A leak traced to the rudder-post gland meant constantly filling bilges, but Kay, try as she might, could not staunch the leak. She worried the rudder post might be bent, and if so, would it last the voyage? On top of that, the autohelm broke.

By 14 January, *First Lady* had tracked south to 52°. The seas were high and by midday the wind was howling at force 10 (52 knots). Cape Horn lay 940 kilometres (585 miles) east. Kay had adapted well to the conditions, feeling relief whenever the wind dropped and considering 40 knots easily manageable. This was different. She took in all sail and trailed a sea anchor. The boat still ran at speeds of up to 12 knots, surfing down steep wave faces under bare poles. Conditions deteriorated overnight. In her log of 15 January, Kay wrote: 'Wind up to force 11. First time I've felt real fear since leaving and that comes from the huge waves, and thoughts of capsizing.'

Communications with Sydney were now difficult and *Act 7* was no longer in range. An Australian yacht, *Estrellita*, cruising near New Zealand, offered to relay. The answerback from Roger Badham, her weather router in Sydney, on 16 January was: '... slow down and don't go near the Horn until after Monday night (January 18th).'

On Monday 18 January, the wind moderated to 35 knots and then died to 15 knots, but the barometer was dropping rapidly. Now approaching land, Kay tried the engine as a precaution. The engine failed to turn over. Staying calm but sensing the rush of mounting panic, she traced the problem to a blown fuse. Worrying about the boom, distracted by the problem with the engine, cold and tired, Kay had forgotten to close the saloon hatch. When she went to her bunk to rest, she found her bedding soaked.

The wind was back up to 35 knots, Cape Horn less than 160 kilometres (100 miles) away. At 11.30pm that evening, Kay sighted the Ildefonso Islands. A squall threatened. She handed the trysail and reefed the No. 4 headsail just as the wind fell away. She reset the trysail and shook out the reefs in the headsail, and *First Lady* found herself becalmed. It was an opportunity for Kay to grab some sleep.

Tuesday 19 January broke grey and squally, but the wind remained moderate. Land was close, snow-peaked mountains visible to port. After a breakfast of toast and beans, Kay grabbed another one-hour sleep. When she came on deck, Cape Horn was visible a few miles off to port, bathed in sunshine, while albatrosses wheeled overhead.

Kay had perceived Cape Horn as the single biggest obstacle on her voyage, and here she was in perfect conditions. To celebrate, she opened the bottle of vintage Penfolds Grange Hermitage which friends had given her for the occasion. Kay's mother had also put a special 'Cape Horn' present on the boat, a bottle of 'Joy' perfume. Kay sprayed herself liberally, put on some make-up and sat down to a celebratory lunch of fresh bread, crab, mayonnaise and the rest of the Hermitage.

Kay sent a message to Peter Sutton at Showboat: 'A battered but well-behaved *First Lady* and a bruised and exhausted but very elated skipper rounded Cape Horn at 1930 hours UTC on 19 January 1988. Amen!'

After crossing the South Atlantic and getting past the Cape of Good Hope, *First Lady* suffered repeated knockdowns in a force 12 storm (64+ knots) on 10 April. Flying only a storm jib, Kay recorded boat speeds topping 20 knots surfing. Going into the cockpit to stream more warps and slow the boat, she saw the lights of a ship looming close, too close. Dashing below, mountainous seas tossing the boat about violently, she switched on the radio and deck lights. No one answered her call. As a frantic last effort to avoid a collision, Kay ignited a white flare. The ship was disappearing in the wave troughs. How would anyone on the bridge see the flare? At what seemed the last minute, the ship altered course, passing 300 metres (328 yards) off *First Lady*'s starboard quarter.

As Kay watched the ship's lights fade, a boarding wave knocked *First Lady* down, sweeping Kay from the deck, over the leeward guardrails and into the sea. Two lifelines attached to her harness saved her from certain death. Exhausted by the cold and the shock, she found the physical effort to climb back on board too much. Cold can sap energy quickly. With hope fading fast, another wave gathered Kay up and dumped her in the water-filled cockpit.

Blackmore's First Lady crossed the finish line at 12.32pm on 5 June 1988. Kay remarked later: 'My experience of rounding Cape Horn alone and unassisted will forever be one of the greatest highlights of my life.'

Kay Cottee was named Australian of the Year and awarded the Order of Australia in 1989. That same year she married her PR manager, Peter Sutton. She now owns and manages Yamba Marina in New South Wales. In her free time, she paints and sculpts.

TZU HANG – GODDESS OF SEAFARERS

P ost-war Britain was a drab, unexciting place restricted by rationing,
currency control and the burgeoning bureaucracy that heralded the
National Health Service and welfare reform. Small wonder, then, that Miles
Smeeton, 39 at war's end, highly decorated and having attained the lofty
rank of brigadier general, found existence in the country unbearable, as did
his wife Beryl, who had spent the war years adventurously in India, Tibet
and Tasmania with their infant daughter, Clio. During this period, Beryl had
bought a 450-acre farm on Saltspring Island, a mile south of Vancouver in
British Columbia, as somewhere to escape to when peace eventually came.
This the Smeetons did, working the land for four years, but the venture was
not financially viable. They returned to Britain and bought a boat in Dover
with part of a small inheritance Beryl had received.

This boat was *Tzu Hang* (the Chinese goddess of seafarers), a 46-foot teak-
hulled ketch, flush-decked with a small doghouse, and built in Kowloon in
1938. Beryl spent the remainder of her inheritance on two diamond rings –
a ruse to get their money out of the country and beyond the grasp of the
socialist government.

They learned to sail with Peter Pye, another disgruntled war veteran with
escape plans, and sailed from Fowey, Cornwall in May 1951, bound for
Canada. *Tzu Hang* was effectively a floating country cottage in style and feel,
embodying all that the Smeetons felt had been lost from an earlier, gentler
way of life less fettered by regulations. They sold the Canadian farm, and
with no set itinerary but to voyage across the world, supporting themselves
on Miles's small military pension, embarked on a life of adventure and
excitement – an antidote to decaying in a stifling, reduced society.

Four years later, the Smeetons were in Melbourne for the Olympic
Games, *Tzu Hang* moored alongside the Royal Yacht *Britannia* in Port

Phillip. She had sailed from Canada to New Zealand, then across the Tasman to Sydney and finally to Melbourne. Clio, now 15, had grown up on the boat and was about to leave for boarding school in England.

Along the way, the Smeetons had come to know a young Englishman, John Guzwell, who had built his own small boat in Australia and, like them, was intent on a life at sea. The Smeetons planned to sail back to England by way of Cape Horn, on the proviso that they could find suitable crew. Guzwell volunteered his services. The Smeetons were delighted.

Tzu Hang set off from Melbourne on 22 December 1956 with a first stop in the Falkland Islands 10,780 kilometres (6,700 miles) away – but first they had to get past Cape Horn. By then only five small boats had done that – two crewed, *Pandora* and *Saoirse*, and three singlehanded, Al Hansen on *Mary-Jane* in 1934, Vito Dumas on *LEHG II* in 1943 and Marcel Bardiaux on *Les Quatre Vents* four years before them in 1952.

By the middle of February, still some 2,400 kilometres (1,500 miles) from Cape Horn and about to pass south over the 50th parallel, *Tzu Hang* was hit by strong westerly winds, building to force 9. Quickly, Miles Smeeton and Guzwell took in the twin poled-out headsails while Beryl helmed, steering to keep the boat stern-on to the seas. Next, they trailed a 110-metre-long (360-foot-long) 7.5-cm (3-in) line from the stern to act as a brake. The sea was streaked white by the wind, spindrift strafing the air. Guzwell and Beryl had retreated below to await their turn on watch while Miles stayed on watch at the helm, when a breaking wave crashed into the cockpit, bodily lifting Smeeton and depositing him on the bridge deck. Only his lifeline prevented the rushing water sweeping him from the deck.

Crawling back to the relative safety of the cockpit, Smeeton thought about streaming a second 110-metre-long (360-foot-long) line, perhaps tying the two together to create a bight. He also thought about spilling oil over the stern to quell the waves riding up behind. Beryl took over the watch, confident that she would be able to handle the boat. They discussed the oil option and whether to stream the second line. In the end, they chose to do neither. Smeeton went below, reluctant to leave Beryl on her own but equally unable to leave the hatch open. He lay down on his bunk to read.

Up on deck, Beryl constantly checked behind for the next approaching wave, helming to align the boat stern-on then correcting the slew as the wave passed by. The sequence went on with monotonous regularity until Beryl turned to look back one more time for the next wave. A wall of water much, much higher than its predecessors reared up, shear-fronted, the breaking crest spilling down its front like a waterfall and so long she could not see where it ended to either left or right. She knew instantly the boat was not going to ride over this one. The very next moment she was flying through the air and then plunging into the freezing water. As she broke the surface, there was no sign of the boat. She reached for the lifeline at her waist with the thought of pulling herself towards the boat, wherever it was, but all she felt was its frayed, broken end. A wave spun her round, and there was *Tzu Hang*, both masts gone and riding low in the water.

Below, a thunderous sound had filled Smeeton's ears. He felt himself pressed to the front and side of his bunk, then hurtling through space, enshrouded in blackness. Suddenly, he was standing again, only now waist deep in water with a riot of debris floating all over the sloshing surface. Guzwell was standing by the galley stove, uncertain how he had got there. Both men scrambled onto the deck and hauled Beryl, clinging to the broken mizzen mast, from the water just as another wave broke over the boat. The sea had splintered the bowsprit and torn away the tiller, the cockpit coaming and the entire doghouse, leaving a 1.8-square-metre (6-foot-square) hole in the deck. The deck skylights had gone too. Miles and Beryl immediately began bailing while Guzwell, a skilled carpenter, set about improvising a temporary cover for the hole. He used a broken door and battens nailed to the deck to create a framework, then a crossbeam, raised at the centre so when he nailed the folded genoa over the opening, water would run off. He covered the open skylights with the storm jib and nailed it down. Now that far less water was getting inside and the exhausting bailing was well underway, *Tzu Hang* began slowly to rise. Guzwell cobbled together a mast from the broken staysail booms and a split spinnaker pole, scarfed together, riveted through with copper rivets and whipped with wire.

A sun sight gave them a position approximately 1,450 kilometres (900 miles) from land. With the jury rig providing some power and Smeeton and Guzwell rowing using the dinghy oars, they headed tortuously for the Chilean coast – any port would do: Valparaíso, Valdivia or Talcahuano. Over the following days, Guzwell fashioned a steering oar using wood cannibalised from dismantled cupboards with a locker door for a blade. Not happy with the first mast, Guzwell then set about fashioning another, stronger version, again taking wood from the cabin. In the evenings, cold, wet and exhausted from lack of sleep while eating their sparse rations, they discussed what had happened, concluding that *Tzu Hang* must have pitchpoled.

The second mast was ready on 4 March (1957), and at 6 metres (20 feet) longer than the first, it could carry more sail. By Smeeton's reckoning, *Tzu Hang* had covered 1,200 kilometres (750 miles) with the first mast. To add to the sail area, they redeployed the shorter mast as a mizzen. More balanced under the new jury rig, *Tzu Hang* closed with the Chilean coast and on 20 March Beryl sighted land to the east. Creeping forwards slowly, often blighted by fog, *Tzu Hang* made landfall at Cronel in the Bay of Arauco two days later.

Here, the British Consul, Leslie Poutney, helped organise matters with the local Chilean authorities, including a tow for *Tzu Hang* to the better facilities at Talcahuano. Guzwell agreed to stay on to rebuild the doghouse and oversee other repairs before returning to his own boat, *Trekka*, in New Zealand.

The safest passage to England – north with the wind behind and involving a transit of the Panama Canal – would be an acknowledgement of failure as far as the Smeetons were concerned, something they would not countenance. In order to make the Horn before the southerly winds set in, the Chilean admiral stationed at Talcahuano advised the Smeetons to leave during October. It was a moot point in the end. The extensive repairs took so long that *Tzu Hang* did not depart Talcahuano until 9 December 1957, almost a year since leaving Melbourne.

The Smeetons modified their plan, opting for the Strait of Magellan rather than Cape Horn, propelled by the need to expunge the sediment of fear deposited when *Tzu Hang* had pitchpoled. It would be enough to head south into the high latitudes and through the canals to wipe clean the muddied surface of contentedness. *Tzu Hang* sailed close-hauled heading south-west against the southerly wind and the northerly set of the current, the idea being to get sufficiently far south to pick up the westerlies, come onto the starboard tack while still some 320 kilometres (200 miles) offshore, then head east for the entrance to the strait.

On 21 December, *Tzu Hang* was at 45° south when the barometer began to slide. The wind blew to force 8 (37 knots) and then calmed, then accelerated again. This oscillating pattern continued for the next five days while the barometer continued its ominous decline. By four o'clock in the afternoon of Boxing Day 1957, a full gale had been blowing for 10 hours. Smeeton decided to make tea, and while he was below in the comfortable snug of the cabin, *Tzu Hang* went over. Water burst in through the companionway hatch, half-filling the cabin. The light disappeared as the boat inverted. Then came the muted sound of submerged wood tearing as the masts broke. *Tzu Hang* came through the rollover. Grey light filtered in through the portholes, a weak spotlight on the chaos. The new doghouse, so lovingly made by Guzwell – and he had ensured it was much more robust than the previous version – was still *in situ* but badly staved in. The hatch had gone, as had one of the new skylights. To his dismay when he peered up at the deck, Miles Smeeton saw the mainmast snapped at its base, the mizzen at the spreaders. It was a near repeat of their previous catastrophe. As Guzwell had done previously, the Smeetons nailed the genoa over the doghouse to staunch the water spilling inside. The location of the rollover was very close to where *Tzu Hang* had suffered the pitchpole.

Again, amid the raging wind, Miles and Beryl Smeeton set up a jury rig and nursed the boat back northwards, limping into the harbour at Valparaíso at the end of January.

The Smeetons subsequently freighted *Tzu Hang* back to England on the deck of a cargo ship, offloaded her in London and, with the little jury mast and under engine power (which the ship's engineers had worked on during the passage), took the boat to Burnham-on-Crouch.

It was now the end of March 1958. They had not seen Clio for 15 months. Soon after their reunion, '… at one of those meals which astound parents all over the world, Clio said, "Are you going to have another shot at Cape Horn?"'

Miles Smeeton baulked at the idea. 'I think once is probably enough,' he said.

'As for twice, that really is too much,' Beryl added.

From within the perimeters of a fearsome reputation there emanates a challenge, like a silent broadcast, that will be heard by those whose instinct is to hunt for such a challenge and then set themselves against it. For those who seek their release or find their peace at sea, Cape Horn transmits such a signal. Despite being twice defeated, neither Miles nor Beryl Smeeton could accept failure to attain something they truly desired, their attitudes honed by their background and wartime experiences.

Miles and Beryl Smeeton repaired and refitted *Tzu Hang* once again. Years later, in 1968, they finally rounded Cape Horn the hard way, westabout against wind and current.

MIKE GOLDING

'Though you strive towards one goal, you achieve others along the way.'

Born . . . . 27 August 1960
Nationality . . . . British
Date of Cape Horn rounding . . . . January 1994
Boat name . . . . *Group 4*
Designer . . . . David Thomas
Year of build 1990
LOA . . . . 67 feet
Material . . . . Steel
Rig . . . . Bermudan cutter

C hay Blyth's disastrous introduction to sailing during the Golden Globe Race of 1968 does not reflect the influence he would come to have on future generations of yachtsmen and women. His successful westward circumnavigation in 1971 was followed by two Whitbread round-the-world races – the first in 1973–1974 on *Great Britain II*, the second in 1981–1982 on *United Friendly* – but his most ambitious endeavour came later. In 1989, he set up the Challenge Business, a round-the-world yacht race in a fleet of one-design steel yachts, each manned by a paying crew of ordinary men and women led by a professional skipper. The planned route, mimicking his own circumnavigation, was westabout via Cape Horn, and if the race proved commercially viable, it would be run every four years.

One of the skippers recruited for the inaugural race in 1992 was Mike Golding. The boats, 67 feet in length, could carry a crew of 14 and each had a title sponsor. Blyth put Golding, then aged 32, in charge of the yacht *Group 4*, sponsored by Group 4 Securitas, a private company headed by Swede Jørgen Philip-Sørensen.

Golding started sailing as a boy in the gravel pits around London. He attended Lowestoft College, venturing as far as Icelandic waters on commercial fishing trawlers before joining the Royal Berkshire Fire and Rescue Service. During his time in the fire service he founded the National Fire Service Sailing Association and competed in the Azores Race, the Single-Handed Transatlantic Race and the Round Britain and Ireland Race.

Philip-Sørensen had agreed to the sponsorship of a Challenge yacht for two reasons. He admired Chay Blyth, well remembering his 1971 triumph, and the round-the-world race Blyth proposed exactly fitted the marketing strategy Philip-Sørensen envisaged to emphasise his company's international growth. At the same time, the challenge race offered the advantage 'of being an exciting adventure in which Group 4, as a company, could participate', with an employee joining the yacht on each of the four legs that made up the circumnavigation route.

The two aspects of the race Philip-Sørensen had no control over were the weather and the skipper. So when *Group 4*, after planned race stopovers in Hobart, Cape Town and Rio de Janeiro, crossed the finish line on 23 May 1993 after 48,300 kilometres (30,000 miles) in overall second place, only

70 minutes behind the race winner – having won two of the four legs – Philip-Sørensen was delighted. As far as he was concerned, Golding had demonstrated 'superb leadership qualities', and those were precisely the type of qualities he was looking to bring into his business.

After the success of the race, Philip-Sørensen did two things: his company bought the boat from the Challenge Business; and he invited Golding to join his organisation to run a new division, Group 4 PromOcean, to run outward-bound-type management training, personal development and team skills courses centred on the yacht. Golding accepted immediately.

During the following months, Golding took the yacht to Sweden, Holland and Belgium on promotional visits, while developing ideas for the courses the new training company could offer. It was on the return trip from Belgium to England, alone at the helm while the crew slept, that an altogether different idea began to take shape in Golding's mind. With more time needed to research and develop the training courses and winter looming, it was unlikely that PromOcean would become active before the spring of 1994, which meant a slack period of six to nine months. Golding wanted to sail singlehanded around the world, going westwards via Cape Horn – just as Chay Blyth had done 22 years before – but faster, much faster, and set a new record. The slack period presented a perfect opportunity – and the company had the boat.

At a meeting in September 1993 at *Group 4* headquarters to discuss PromOcean's progress, and remembering something Chay Blyth had once said to him – 'Always have a hidden agenda' – Golding tentatively broached the idea with two senior managers. They suggested he put together a more detailed proposal and take it directly to the boss.

A singlehanded venture is a very different proposition to a multi-participant race scenario as a promotional platform for corporate sponsorship. The risks, should anything go wrong, are enormous, attracting the full glare of the media. There would be no dilution effect. As he considered Golding's proposal, Philip-Sørensen had to balance that risk against his belief in Golding and the potential marketing rewards of success. He took two days to mull it over. When he spoke to Golding, the decision was unequivocal. *Group 4* would back the project.

The immediate task for Golding was to call Blyth – it was he after all who had built the boat and introduced Golding to *Group 4*. Blyth, like Philip-Sørensen, backed Golding and offered to put the Challenge Race support team at his disposal.

The next stage was to modify the boat to make her manageable for a singlehander. Work had to conform to a tight deadline. Golding had just six weeks to make the necessary modifications to the boat, run trials and provision the yacht for the 180 days at sea Golding anticipated. Blyth had made the voyage westwards in 1971 in 292 days. Golding planned a departure date in November to round Cape Horn and make the transit of the Southern Ocean during the austral summer. Storm frequency in the Southern Ocean is lower at this time of year so Golding could expect fewer headwinds. He also had a bigger, faster boat compared with Blyth's *British Steel*.

Extensive changes to the boat would take too long, be too costly and not leave sufficient time for trialling. Moreover, the cost of reversing the work for the boat's entry in the next fully crewed Challenge Race in 1996 – already agreed between Chay Blyth and Jørgen Philip-Sørensen – meant that Golding had to keep the changes simple. He focused on the sail plan. The boat would need a fully battened mainsail and furlers for the headsail and staysail in addition to the installation of autopilots and the boosting of on-board power generation via a new diesel generator.

During a very brief period of trials, Golding never actually took the boat out alone and made only two tacks, handling the manoeuvres and sail changes alone. With time pressing, Golding began his venture from Southampton on Sunday 21 November 1993.

On the second day, the autopilot glitched, cutting out and not re-engaging – a major concern because at 67 feet and weighing 38 tons (laden), the boat was far too big to be guided by a more traditional wind-driven self-steering system, and as it was singlehanded and therefore it was not possible for the helm to be manned at all times, the autopilot was essential. A broken autopilot was a showstopper. To troubleshoot problems more efficiently, engineers at the Autohelm factory had mirrored the on-board system with an identical set-up to replicate problems and identify solutions without a lengthy interchange of emails and telephone calls. The engineers solved the autopilot's cutting-out issue by instructing Golding to use the full-function remote controls, one mounted below decks, the other at the mast, instead of the central controls.

The two-week run to the Canary Islands effectively served as a shakedown voyage, giving Golding the opportunity to play with the sail plan to find optimum performance in different wind conditions and to develop an on-board routine.

Running south off the coast of Brazil, Golding received a telex from two friends who were sailing east across the South Pacific in an ultra-light 60-foot yacht, *Cardiff Discovery*, delivering the boat to a new owner in the USA. It was possible, given relative distances and speeds, that their paths might cross at Cape Horn. It was an interesting thought, but an unlikely prospect in view of the vagaries of wind and weather, so Golding soon forgot about the idea.

Golding had worked out a definitive sail plan to suit different conditions, which required less effort struggling with the massive sails while getting the best out of the boat. The speed record was always at the front of his mind, and although he had set out to run the boat 'one gear' below maximum, his natural competitiveness propelled him to work the boat at close to its maximum.

The test of his sail plan came on day 32 of the voyage, 22 December. A gale had sprung up the previous evening and in the early hours Golding collapsed exhausted on the bench in the saloon. He was instantly asleep. When he woke, the autopilot had switched itself off but the boat, because of the correct balance of the sails, was still on course. That was enough to tell Golding that the variations to the sail plan he had figured out were working well.

As Golding drove the boat hard further south, his main concern became the threat of icebergs and, worse, growlers – chunks of ice that barely break the surface and are not detectable on radar. Growlers are difficult to see even with a crew standing round-the-clock watches and are impossible for a singlehander to spot. Southern Ocean weather was also adding to his anxiety. 'I prayed that the Horn itself would be in a good mood. I was convinced we had all got past too easily last year [during the Challenge Race] – the Horn could be a terrible place to do battle around alone.'

Group 4 experienced the first 'full blown gale' of the voyage on Christmas Day. Exhausted but satisfied with the way the boat was handling the weather, Golding slept. Waking to more moderate conditions, it was time to open the Christmas presents family and friends had organised at departure. One, a blow-up doll, whom Golding named Griselder, was duly inflated and left hanging from the ceiling while Golding got on with the task of unwrapping the rest of the presents and calling home. A dash up to the deck to make sail changes distracted him so completely that he totally forgot about Griselder. Returning to the cabin, 'I frightened myself to death as I turned into the saloon. I had forgotten I had left Griselder swinging from the ceiling. She was immediately deflated and returned to her box, my heart still pounding from the shock of seeing another body, even an inflatable one, on board.'

With 11,250 kilometres (7,000 miles) now under *Group 4*'s keel, and three gales testing both the boat's systems and her skipper's ability to handle her, Golding was confident about going into the Cape Horn area. With the practical aspect under control, Golding began to suffer mood swings as he tried 'coming to terms with being alone for so long'. Although only little more than a month had passed since the start, this was the first time Golding had sailed solo. The sustained effort of handling such a large boat was exhausting him physically and mentally. Fearing a creeping downward spiral, a loss of motivation and a descent into morbid introspection, Golding set himself many small goals, reducing the scale of the voyage from the months stretching ahead to the moments within immediate reach. He also put much of this mental fatigue down to the 'tenseness' he was feeling approaching the Horn.

Like Chay Blyth's 22 years earlier, Golding's plan was to pass through Le Maire Strait, shortcutting his route to Cape Horn by 160 kilometres (100 miles). The forecast was not favourable, with gales threatening from the south-west, forcing the boat to bash to windward if he went into the strait. The boat had proved herself rugged and capable of taking the pounding, but the real danger would come when the tide turned and ripped along, up to 6 knots directly against the wind. Wind against tide can produce a horrible sea-state of very short wavelength, extremely steep-faced wave sets – as Marcel Bardiaux had discovered to his cost and almost at the cost of his life. The boat, driving into the onrushing water, would burst through a wave, the bow airborne momentarily, then crash into the wave trough as the wave swept past. The constant physical pummelling would stress the rig, and Golding, who would not be able to trust to the autopilots with land in close proximity either side, would have to man the helm for the entire transit.

By Boxing Day, the barometer had plunged, wind had built to 40 knots and the temperature had plummeted to near freezing. All the signs were ominous.

The traditional tactics of either lying a'hull or running before the wind streaming sea anchors to slow the boat did not appeal to Golding on a big boat with good windward sailing characteristics. He was much more of the school pioneered by Vito Dumas and enthusiastically embraced by Bernard Moitessier – sail fast directly into the weather. Golding's rule was: 'There must be enough power in the sail plan to climb the next wave.'

Sticking to that philosophy, as the wind eased, Golding went to shake out more sail, easing the headsail sheet. Satisfied, he began to make turns around the winch, at which point a gust punched the sail. The sail snatched the sheet and pulled his left hand into the winch and self-tailer, and the rope turns over his middle and index fingers went bar tight with the pull of the sail. The leather sailing glove protecting his hand from rope burn was split, his two trapped fingers crushed and copious amounts of wind-blown blood sprayed all around the cockpit.

Dangerously close to land and with a serious injury, a decision was needed – go through Le Maire Strait or take the longer route east around Staten Island?

The fact that his hand was swollen and throbbing, the wounds not healing and stinging viciously each time seawater found its way into the lacerations, forced Golding to decide to stay in the lee of Tierra del Fuego and wait for a suitable weather window to get through the strait.

He woke from a brief nap to waves crashing over the boat. The temperamental autopilot appeared to be working but the wheel was not responding. He clambered on deck and saw damage to the mainsail. Foul weather, breakages and an agonising injury seemed to be conspiring to stop him from going any further. 'Physically and mentally I was becoming exhausted, by all the hours spent nervously watching wind speeds or directions, looking for the time to reef or tack, asking myself should I or shouldn't I?'

In calmer weather on New Year's Day, despite a huge swell generated by a storm passing further south, Golding fixed the autopilot. Weather reports suggested the wind would stay moderate and shift to the north – a perfect window to get through Le Maire Strait. By afternoon, nature confounded the forecasts with 35-knot winds funnelling up through the strait from the south-west. If he chose to take the shortcut, it would mean a beat into wind. Golding calculated the tides – he would not arrive in time for a favourable current. As well as having the wind against him, *Group 4* would be fighting a 6-knot rip and if he waited for the tide to turn, streaming against the wind, he would be faced with fierce seas. The decision was made – he would have to go east around Staten Island just as Blyth had done.

By the morning of 3 January, *Group 4* was past the eastern end of Staten Island and clear of the treacherous overfalls that extend 16 kilometres (10 miles) east of land's end. The boat's log showed boat speed of 10 knots. The GPS indicated speed over the ground of 5 knots. They were fighting a northerly trending Cape Horn current easily powerful enough to carry an unwary crew onto the jagged rocks of Staten Island's southern coast.

Visibility was poor, obscured by a fine mist, but the air was 'thick with the scent of heather from Tierra del Fuego'. As Golding guided *Group 4* south-west, away from land, and into deeper water at the edge of the continental shelf, the current eased, the mist lifted like a curtain, revealing the snow-wrapped mountains of Staten Island, the sun shone warmly, and a pod of pilot whales gambolled around the boat. *Group 4* was becalmed.

The following day, a light north-westerly breeze kicked in. Golding read the signs and knew what to expect – spinning clockwise in the southern hemisphere, a depression to the south of the boat's position would announce itself with a north-westerly wind, backing to west then south-west as the system passed eastwards.

Group 4, sailing close-hauled, made good ground, passing only a few miles south of Cape Horn. Amazingly, *Cardiff Discovery* was passing Cape Horn from the opposite direction. The two yachts met west of Cape Horn that afternoon. Golding stopped his boat by heaving-to and greeted his two friends aboard *Cardiff Discovery* with a hastily compiled Christmas hamper of ready meals, Scotch, champagne, chocolate and, of all things, a bottle of 'Fireman Sam' bubble bath (lending weight to the view that sometimes unwanted Christmas presents come in useful) packed into a watertight container and slung over the stern on a heaving line. The rules of solo circumnavigating for record-breaking purposes forbade Golding receiving anything in return. The rendezvous lasted four minutes.

The forecast indicated deteriorating weather. Golding headed south-west, to get off the continental shelf and into deeper water, passing close to the Diego Ramírez Islands. Here, a chartered Chilean aircraft carrying a film crew approached from the north. Golding could not see the plane but could hear the pilot on his radio insisting he had spotted the boat. In fact, the boat the pilot could see was *Cardiff Discovery*. Golding recounts what he describes as an inane conversation with the pilot:

Pilot: 'Okay, I see you ahead, I see you. Over.'
Golding: 'It's not me. Over.'
Pilot: 'But yes, I see you. Over.'
Golding: 'No, you don't. Over.'

Then Golding's VHF radio batteries gave out. Meanwhile, the two men on *Cardiff Discovery*, toasting Golding with their newly acquired champagne, were frantically signalling to the plane by pointing west. In response, the pilot waved frantically back. Golding plugged his radio into the charger and after five minutes managed to persuade the pilot that he was indeed looking at the wrong boat, suspecting that maybe the pilot had already figured that out seeing as there was only supposed to be one man on the boat he had come to find.

In the relative safety of deeper water, Cape Horn now passed, Golding's mood recovered from the slump of the past week. 'I felt ten feet tall and grinned maniacally from ear to ear. I was on my way and surely nothing could stop me now.'

These words may have tempted fate. A weather depression moved in the following day, engulfing *Group 4* in a gale, 50-knot winds and huge seas, conditions 'as rough as I had ever seen', Golding later wrote. The wind had forced *Group 4* down to the 58th parallel and into the iceberg danger zone. Golding desperately wanted to make more northing, but the storm raged for two days, creating seas of 'staggering proportions'. The boat was now crashing into waves head-on, thumping down into the troughs with keel-shuddering impacts. If he damaged the rig with this continued windward bashing there would be little he could do in the ferocious conditions. He thought about heaving-to and riding out the storm. Even now, he had to crawl about on deck. His injured hand had become pus-filled and excruciating, limiting his capabilities if an emergency developed. Fortunately, on 7 January, the wind backed to south-west as the storm passed over. Golding put the boat gratefully onto the port tack and started to make northing, away from the iceberg zone, away from danger.

The worst was now over, although Golding suffered plenty more uncomfortable encounters on his passage across the Southern Ocean, including being almost swept from the deck and over the side on one occasion. His hand eventually healed.

Group 4 arrived back in Southampton on 7 May 1994. According to the records of the World Sailing Speed Record Council (WSSRC), the official arbiter of such things, Golding's voyage had taken a mere 161 days 16 hours 35 minutes and 42 seconds, beating Chay Blyth's record of 292 days by a huge margin. Golding was delighted. It was not only his larger, faster boat that had made the difference, it was perhaps more to do with the manner in which he had sailed her. Perceptions had changed from 1971 when Blyth made his voyage. Stopping and heaving-to in big weather was routine back then – to do otherwise would have been considered unseamanlike. Golding, reared in a more competitive, race-oriented environment, pushed the boat hard, every day, relentlessly, along a route which, before Blyth set off, was considered impossible, and on which Blyth had exercised caution and restraint. When Golding shattered the record, the route was by then a well-understood quantity, and as a veteran of the 1992 British Steel Challenge race, he took with him invaluable experience on a proven, familiar boat. Above all else though, Golding's drive, determination and tenacity won through.

In 1997, Golding won the BT Global Challenge race in *Group 4* at the second time of asking, winning five of the six legs. He went on to enjoy a successful professional yacht-racing career.

LISA CLAYTON

'There isn't much that is easy on a boat in bad weather.'

Born . . . . 30 December 1958

Nationality . . . . British

Date of Cape Horn rounding . . . . March 1995

Boat name . . . . *Spirit of Birmingham*

Designer . . . . ER Barnes

Year of build 1994

LOA . . . . 38 feet

Material . . . . Steel

Rig . . . . Cutter

Like Les Powles, Lisa Clayton was born in Birmingham, on 30 December 1958, and, like him, came to sailing as an adult, and then only as a reluctant participant more through being eager to please her boss than from any intuitive desire or love of the sea.

A privileged upbringing with an elder brother and a younger sister, private education and a reliable choice of accountancy as a career might have pointed to a safe, unremarkable passage through life negotiated primarily to avoid risk but for a maverick streak that found early expression. Lisa was married at 19 and divorced at 23. The idea, too, that chartered accountancy would hold any long-term appeal waned when she went to work as the financial controller of a travel company, Horizon Holidays, although it was through this work that she first experienced boating, when the managing director, Ken Franklin, a keen yachtsman, invited her sailing one weekend.

Leaving Dartmouth to visit the Channel Islands, the weather was miserable, a state reflected by the mood of the crew, who abandoned the cross-Channel trip and instead sailed to Brixham in Devon for an overnight stop. Despite the lousy weather, her complete inexperience and a nagging worry that she would be bored stiff, Lisa came away from that weekend surprising herself – she had actually enjoyed sailing and found herself looking forward to the next time.

In his capacity as chairman of the Tour Operators' Council, Ken Franklin invited Lisa to accompany him on an extravagant six-week, all-expenses-paid promotional tour. She leaped at the chance and during the time away became enmeshed in his plans to sail his boat first to the Mediterranean and then further afield. In due course they both resigned from their jobs and set off in March 1987 to spend the first season chartering in the Mediterranean before venturing to more distant horizons. That first season turned into two, then three, then four, with winter trips home to the UK to visit family and friends. One sunny afternoon during that fourth season of chartering, with no paying clients on board and some time to herself, Lisa picked up a book, bought second-hand to add to the boat's ever-revolving library, and began to read. Speed-reading was her norm, but on this occasion, Lisa found herself reading more slowly, and re-reading some sections, totally immersed. The story that gripped her was Naomi James's account of her circumnavigation. Originally intended as a non-stop voyage, Naomi had been forced to halt twice, in Cape Town and near Tasmania, to make repairs to her boat and pick up supplies and spare parts. A question began to evolve in Lisa's mind. Had another woman completed a non-stop solo circumnavigation since Naomi James had tried? If not, could she become the first woman to sail non-stop around the world?

Lisa's researches quickly identified Kay Cottee's voyage in 1988. She was devastated, but on closer examination, reading Cottee's book, *Blackmore's First Lady*, Lisa was encouraged. Cottee's route, bar a brief excursion above the equator in the Atlantic (to satisfy the WSSRC's requirement for an equator crossing to qualify the voyage as a circumnavigation) had not been antipodal. No two points on Cottee's track were diametrically opposed to one another on the earth's surface, which, bizarrely, is not a WSSRC requirement. Chichester always maintained that an antipodal route was necessary to shape a boat's track as closely as possible to a Great Circle – a line around the diameter of the earth. A pure Great Circle route is not possible because of interference by landmasses, but Chichester insisted it should conform as closely as possible. Lisa therefore discounted Kay Cottee's voyage and, newly encouraged, set her mind to putting together her own project. 'What Kay had done was fantastic, but I was glad she had still left something for me to achieve. I was elated and filled with renewed excitement.'

As Lisa pondered, one thing concerned her – her psychological resilience. 'There would obviously be times when I would feel depressed. But how depressed would I get? The pressures on the mind are appalling.' Another concern was her total lack of singlehanded sailing experience. Ken Franklin agreed, albeit reluctantly, to let her sail his boat from Spain back to the UK on her own. He was particularly worried about the engine, which was out of action due to a cracked oil sump. A stop at Gibraltar confirmed the extent of the problem. The fix required removal of the engine, incurring a costly time delay Lisa could ill afford. She therefore persuaded Franklin that the lack of an engine should not be a deterrent, since WSSRC rules forbade the use of an engine to make way – a dubious line of logic given that an engine is necessary in case of emergency, for battery-charging to power the ship's navigation and communication systems, and for close manoeuvring. The trial voyage did not go smoothly. The weather was atrocious, the boat slamming into big seas.

The engine seized completely, spilling oil into the bilges and blocking the bilge pumps, and some of the standing rigging failed. Nevertheless, Lisa felt she coped well with the circumstances.

In 1992, she began the dispiriting hunt for sponsors to finance a boat. Eight months later, she was no further forward. To add to her woes, a female Japanese sailor, Kyoko Imakiire, was nearing the end of a non-stop round-the-world voyage following an antipodal route. Lisa waited anxiously to see whether Imakiire would succeed. Then news came that Imakiire had been forced to take assistance. The record was still up for grabs.

With sponsorship looking unlikely, Lisa found a steel hull and deck for sale in Cumbria. She could just about afford the cost, but the boat still needed fitting out. The University of Birmingham agreed to let her use a shed to house the boat during the fit-out and Birmingham City Council became interested in supporting the project. As publicity grew, some local companies offered support, mainly in the form of materials.

The fit-out of the boat, now named *Spirit of Birmingham*, lurched from one crisis to another, with promises of major sponsorship failing to materialise, well-intentioned but misleading advice, and severe financial interruptions forcing a succession of delays. By April 1993, progress had ground to a halt and a planned departure date in September became unlikely. Lisa re-examined her options. She would have to postpone the project for 12 months.

In spite of the additional year, constant financial dramas, various people joining the team then leaving on bad terms, confusion and further delays meant the boat was barely ready for the rescheduled departure date and there was no time to run any sea trials; Lisa had the boat transported from Birmingham to Dartmouth and launched before stepping the mast. One of the more reliable people Lisa did speak to was Mike Golding, recently returned from his round-the-world voyage, who advised her about communications systems.

Lisa set sail on 4 September 1994 and immediately ran into a battery of problems – numerous leakages, serious chafing of the running rigging and issues with the communications systems. The most discouraging aspect was her complete lack of familiarity with the boat and, consequently, she felt no empathy with *Spirit of Birmingham*. 'Of course, I know how she was put together and where nearly everything is, but I don't have the feel of her. Instead of feeling at one with her she feels as hostile as she had been the day she went in the water.'

Depressed, disillusioned and angry, Lisa turned round and sailed to Plymouth. Too many issues needed sorting out. Stores were unpacked, streamlined and re-stowed. With the checklist complete, she sailed back to Dartmouth for the restart. *Spirit of Birmingham* set sail again on 17 September.

Lisa spent the first month of the voyage coming to terms with the boat – effectively a shakedown, much like Golding on *Group 4*, having run out of time before any meaningful sea trials could be undertaken.

Lisa's concerns about psychological equilibrium were well founded. She bounced between moods, up one day and down the next, bemoaning her lack of 'luck' with the wind and feeling apathetic more often than was healthy. To gauge her progress, she compared it against Naomi James's and Robin Knox-Johnston's previous voyages. She was ahead in relative terms, '… but even though I am doing better than them it doesn't seem to help.'

In early December, *Spirit of Birmingham* arrived near Cape Town for a prearranged rendezvous to hand over documentary film to Peter Harding, the project manager, who had flown from England.

Peter Harding had become involved while working as promotions manager for Birmingham City Council's education department. Hearing of Lisa's upcoming voyage, he had wanted to explore the concept, involving local schools. In the end, the idea came to nothing. Harding had since left Birmingham City Council to start his own company, but had become so embroiled with Lisa Clayton's venture that he was effectively working as a full-time, unpaid expedition manager even though he knew 'absolutely nothing about sailing'.

Spirit of Birmingham headed south and west after the rendezvous before turning back east to avoid sailing over the 'frightening and notorious' Agulhas Bank where Chay Blyth had almost come to grief during the Golden Globe Race.

Clayton's mood did not improve after the rendezvous, in terms of either herself or her boat, recording in her log of 10 December: 'I don't feel that I like Spirit today', and: 'I don't think I like myself when I look too deeply into my rather confused mind.' A few days later, on 16 December, in response to fickle wind, she wrote: 'Oh God, this is awful. I'm finding it all quite stressful ... never have I felt so low. I wondered before I set off how I would cope with these sort of negative feelings ... I've never experienced this sort of despair before and for the first time can understand why people just step off the side.' The very next day, she noted down a completely contrary mood: 'I haven't felt so exhilarated for ages.'

Clayton was missing the routine of normal life. Her mood swings surprised her and she questioned her ability to cope. This psychological volatility was to plague her for the duration of the voyage.

On Christmas day, Lisa woke up 'feeling wonderful', had a shower, opened a sack of presents and tried to make the boat 'christmassy' while the wind built to 50 knots. She spoke to her parents and Peter Harding on the radio and then learned from her sister in California that no one at home had been able to enjoy Christmas lunch because of worry. She quickly plunged into another grim mood 'and just couldn't wait for the day to end'.

The weather deteriorated. The seas were huge. Waves crashed over the deck. On 28 December, *Spirit of Birmingham* suffered a knockdown. She righted quickly. It was to be the first of many.

Celebrating her 36th birthday on 30 December was marred because she could not get through to her parents by radio but, on New Year's Day, Lisa felt uplifted because she could now say to herself, 'I shall be home this summer.' It was a tremendous psychological fillip to be thinking in terms of *this* year not *next* year. By the following day, though, Lisa was back to '... really hating every minute at the moment.' The self-steering system was failing and either the rudder or the autopilot to which it was connected had developed a problem – she could not tell which one. The heating system had also failed. It was freezing below decks.

On 3 January, Lisa, writing in her log, touched on the real reason behind the apparent volatility of her moods. 'I feel as though I am a bit of a failure. I've felt like this at various stages over the past few years, I guess now it might be caused by the fact that *Spirit* is a bit of a lump and we are making embarrassingly slow time. It makes me feel very second rate somehow.'

Far from being the fillip she needed, the New Year was beginning as a very emotionally turbulent period. On 4 January Lisa noted in her log: 'I feel depressed. I need to be with people. I've had enough of being on my own. What on earth am I doing out here?' After a night of reflection, she wrote the next day, 'God, what on earth is the matter with me? One minute I'm fine and then for absolutely no reason and without warning I can feel panic welling up inside me and it's taking all my control not to flip … I just don't feel in control of my inner self and it's a frightening experience … I've got to be more rational and in control.' She resorted to taking Prozac, a powerful anti-depressant, to try to regain a measure of consistency.

Lisa was helped by reading Chichester's book *The Lonely Sea and the Sky*, in which he acknowledged his own unpredictable mood swings and his vulnerability to fear, followed by his realisation that he had pursued flying in his younger days and sailing in later life not because he particularly enjoyed either, but rather because they gave him cause for satisfaction.

Spirit of Birmingham was experiencing the full gamut of Southern Ocean weather and on 7 January force 10 winds (52 knots) were hammering the boat. Lisa estimated wave heights at 15 metres (50 feet).

On 17 February, now closing with Cape Horn, Lisa experienced the worst weather of the voyage so far, winds screaming at 65 knots and big, powerful seas. She was undecided whether to heave-to, lie a'hull or run before the wind. The problem with running came as waves swept beneath the boat, neutralising the rudder and then slewing the boat beam-on to the weather. 'It's never been this bad before, it's almost unreal. I'm scared to death … I feel like a sitting duck.'

Uncertain about which tactic to deploy, Lisa hove-to, went below, strapped herself into the chair at the chart table and hoped. Almost immediately a wave knocked the boat flat onto its side.

As the miles ticked by, the weather stayed bad with only intermittent lulls between a succession of storm systems streaming west and delivering regular force 10 winds. On 2 March, Lisa went on deck to sheet in the storm jib to find that a sail stowed on deck had come free and was trailing in the water.

As she attempted to drag it back on board, part of the sail inflated, pulling her over the side and then flipping her back onto the deck. Wave action had also snapped the self-steering gear.

Shocked by the trauma and the damage to the self-steering, she went below to recover. Then the boat capsized. No sooner had the boat come upright than she capsized again. Forty minutes later, the boat capsized a third time, at which point Lisa fired off a message to Peter Harding: 'God this is frightening.'

Fifteen minutes later, the boat went over again. Not trusting herself to go on deck, her boat floundered helplessly, beam-on to the massive seas, naked and exposed with no defence strategy – *Spirit of Birmingham* was taking a thrashing. By now, Lisa believed she was not going to come through the storm, and the prospect of worse to come at Cape Horn eroded her frayed resilience.

Harding repeatedly asked if he should activate a rescue, but the gesture was pointless – she was too far from any viable rescue and the conditions would have prevented any rescue attempt even if another vessel or aircraft were in the vicinity. At 8.20pm, the boat went over once more, the fifth capsize of the day, rolling a complete 360 degrees.

Peter Harding stayed on the Inmarsat fax through the night to support Lisa. He received a message from the boat at 3.20am, then nothing for nine hours. Assuming the worst, he notified Falmouth Maritime Rescue Coordination Centre (MRCC). At 1.45pm, Falmouth sent a message to the boat asking if Lisa needed help. She responded to Harding at 2.45pm (nine hours since her last transmission, taking account of the time difference between the UK and *Spirit of Birmingham*'s position). The boat had capsized again and she reckoned she had been unconscious, which accounted for her delayed response, Lisa explained to Peter Harding.

The 1994–1995 BOC Challenge race (now rebranded the Velux 5 Oceans race), a singlehanded round-the-world event held every four years, had started from Charleston, South Carolina in September with stopovers in Cape Town, Sydney and Punta del Este in Uruguay before finishing back in Charleston. By now the tail-enders of the race fleet were a few hundred miles east of Lisa Clayton's position, approaching Cape Horn and taking a battering in the same vicious storm that had repeatedly capsized *Spirit of Birmingham*. Falmouth MRCC had received Emergency Position Indicating Radio Beacon (EPIRB) distress signals from two of the race fleet: one from a British boat, *Henry Hornblower*, skippered by 70-year-old Harry Mitchell, and the other from a Japanese boat, *Shuten dohji II*, with Minoru Saitō on board. Falmouth MRCC had tried contacting both. Saitō had responded, Harry Mitchell had not. The Chilean Navy was organising a rescue. At 3pm, Falmouth MRCC sent a message to Lisa, requesting her exact position, estimating that she was 480 kilometres (300 miles) from *Henry Hornblower*. What, they wanted to know, were the conditions and sea-state like, and was she in any fit state to be able to render assistance to the apparently stricken British racing yacht? The exchange of messages between Lisa, Peter Harding and Falmouth MRCC continued over the next two hours, until Falmouth eventually suggested that *Spirit of Birmingham* was not in the best position to help and that Lisa should carry on her route. By this time the wind had eased to 50 knots but the seas were still enormous.

Harry Mitchell was the oldest competitor in the BOC Challenge race. His dream was not to win – a highly improbable outcome given his older, slower boat – but to round Cape Horn singlehanded and to earn the right to wear the gold earring, that singular badge of honour among those who sail. It had been his dream from childhood, since he had watched the last of the Cape Horner square-riggers arriving at Portsmouth docks from Australia.

He had taken up sailing in his mid-40s, and entered the 1986–1987 BOC Challenge race but retired after running aground in New Zealand. Four years later, he had damaged his boat crossing the Atlantic for the race start. The 1994–1995 BOC race was his third. Just before the start, Harry Mitchell had told the assembled press: 'If I don't sail around the Horn before I'm 100, then it will be too late.'

Harry Mitchell never responded to the emergency calls that night and no wreckage from Harry's boat was ever found nor was his body. Cape Horn had claimed one more.

Fate looked more kindly on Lisa Clayton. In total, *Spirit of Birmingham* suffered seven capsizes, two of them complete rollovers. Moreover, quite amazingly, her mast remained standing. The self-steering rudder suffered the only appreciable physical damage, although below there was a chaos of littered items, spilt food and sloshing bilge water. The heater had packed up after being repaired, the engine too, but that was traced to a blocked fuel line and quickly cleared. Water damage to the computer had rendered it temperamental.

The minor problem with the engine continued with a leaking bleed screw – nothing too serious. Lisa tried fixing it with thread seal (PTFE) tape and chewing gum to no avail and then joked to Harding that she had fixed it with superglue. Peter Harding, exhausted trying to summon help from engineers, computer specialists, mechanics and a host of other technicians, wrote back to tell her he was aghast; if superglue got into the injectors, the engine would probably seize permanently. She told him she was kidding. He replied that he was not amused, whereupon she lost her temper with him.

A lull on 10 March provided an opportunity to fix the self-steering gear in time to pass Cape Horn. Weather warnings were coming through: force 10 winds expected. By 13 March, 320 kilometres (200 miles) from Cape Horn, the catalogue of equipment failure continued – the heater went on the blink again, the radar was no longer working and the self-steering was broken once more.

Spirit of Birmingham had now dropped south to 56°, the latitude of the Horn, and at 5.30am on 17 March passed south of the Diego Ramírez Islands. The barometer started to fall. In line with the forecast, winds gathered strength to force 9 (44 knots) and a heavy swell was still running from the storm.

Spirit of Birmingham was now close to Cape Horn but in severely reduced visibility. A sudden snow blizzard descended. As the last flurries thinned and died, the dense blanket of cloud overhead broke, revealing strips of blue sky spilling shafts of sunlight. The black pyramid of Cape Horn stood defiant in the cold grey sea. Lisa was overcome. 'I suddenly felt tears running down my face. I'd made it; God, I'd made it.'

Ken Franklin had given her a parcel to open at Cape Horn. Inside was brandy, shortcake, a banner and a CD. The CD player was broken, the banner would just add to the mess below, but Lisa did swig some brandy and polish off the shortcake.

Once clear of the Cape Horn area and heading north towards home, *Spirit of Birmingham* was dogged by headwinds and calms although, overall, the boat forged decent progress. Lisa, frustrated, continued to gyrate from one bad mood to another, complaining about her 'bad luck'. On 25 April, she recorded in the log: 'I feel totally demoralised today ... I really feel God has deserted me ... I had a screaming fit on deck today. It really frightens me that I can react in such a wild way.' The following day, she wrote: 'I made up my mind during the night to give up.' Two days later on 28 April, with the arrival of some wind, her mood had swung back to optimism: 'I feel totally at peace with myself.'

The sense of ease most sailors experience after a Cape Horn rounding seems not to have had any moderating effect on Lisa Clayton. The isolation – an attraction to many who choose long-distance singlehanded sailing – continued to generate terrible mood swings in her. On 15 May, after yet another loss of temper, she wrote: 'I quite frightened myself after I had calmed down.'

Lisa Clayton's impatience to get home turned the final phase of her voyage into a torment. Within sight of the English coast, she recorded:

I'm sure I should feel something about this momentous part of my voyage but I don't, I just feel tired. God, I am just 40 miles away – so close but still ages away. With the right wind I could be there in a few hours but I just don't seem to be getting much closer. Spirit is sailing like a pig.

Spirit of Birmingham arrived back at Dartmouth on 29 June 1995.

After weeks of speculation in the media amid insinuations of cheating, the WSSRC eventually ratified Lisa Clayton's voyage as an antipodal circumnavigation, making her the first woman to have achieved an 'unassisted single-handed women's circumnavigation under sail'.

The next year, Lisa was made an Honorary Freeman of the City of Birmingham.

MINORU SAITŌ

'I hate sports played in the confines of a stadium. I can be free at sea.
You are no longer just a cog in the machine.'

Born	7 January 1934
Nationality	Japanese
Date of Cape Horn rounding	April 2009
Boat name	*Nicole BMW Shuten-dohji III*
Year of build	1989
LOA	56 feet
Material	Steel
Rig	Cutter

Veteran ocean racer Minoru Saitō has participated in three singlehanded around-the-world BOC Challenge races. He has completed eight solo circumnavigations, one of them non-stop in 2004–2005. By some margin, Saitō is the most experienced blue-water yachtsman from Japan, with transoceanic voyages totalling more than 426,500 kilometres (265,000 nautical miles) – further than the distance to the moon.

Saitō, a diminutive, softly spoken and avuncular man, was awarded the 2006 Blue Water Medal. Part of the award's citation read: 'His dogged persistence, cheerful attitude and indomitable spirit have been praised in yachting circles worldwide.'

Not bad for a boy born into a humble family in Asakusa, Tokyo on 7 January 1934. An early test of that dogged persistence and indomitable spirit came when he contracted tuberculosis as a child, spending a year in a TB sanatorium run by a Catholic mission. He emerged from that experience with a hybrid belief in Buddhism, Shintoism and Christianity, a rudimentary command of English, and a conviction in the benefits of vigorous physical exercise.

His trials continued with the advent of World War II, when Allied bombing destroyed Saitō's childhood home. Aged 10, he was evacuated with his family to the countryside, and began to gain a feel for the environment and an interest in climbing, which he pursued in earnest as a teenager. 'Climbing gear was very expensive at that time. I had only three second-hand wool blankets I bought from the U.S. occupation army base.' With time, his skills and equipment improved and he became the first Japanese mountaineer to summit the 1,977-metre (6,450-foot) Mount Tanigawa.

When he wasn't climbing, Saitō earned his living managing the family garage in Asakusa. By the early 1970s, though, his love of mountaineering began to pall. 'Amateurs climb mountains without serious preparation and leave garbage all over the place. These people make me upset.' In 1973, now aged 39, Saitō tried his hand at sailing, entering the 290-kilometre (180-mile) Toba Pearl race. He continued to gain more experience, and then in 1988, aged 55, he tried his hand at something more ambitious: the Around Australia singlehanded race. However, a serious angina attack forced him out of contention – he has been on heart medication ever since.

A persistent medical condition would normally persuade most people to desist from strenuous physical exertion, particularly if that exertion meant being alone hundreds, possibly thousands, of miles from the nearest hospital. Not Saitō. He was determined to enter the top flight of yacht racing, bought a yacht he named *Shuten-dohji* after a popular figure from 10th-century Japanese folklore, and sailed 19,300 kilometres (12,000 miles) alone from Sydney to Newport, Rhode Island to qualify for entry in the 1990–1991 BOC Challenge race.

Fellow competitor Australian Don McIntyre – who would later be instrumental in Jessica Watson's round-the-world preparations – became a friend. Among Saitō's fellow racers, *Shuten-dohji*, which also translates as 'drunkard's son', was known affectionately as *shoot your doggy*.

Saitō finished third in his class. He was also in love, with Hisako, a Japanese yachtswoman whom he hoped to marry 'when I stop racing'. His life seemed complete. Sadly, within minutes of stepping ashore in Charleston, South Carolina at the BOC race finish, Saitō learned that Hisako had died, killed in a sail-training accident in Hawaii.

In the face of disaster, Saitō knew only one way to respond: keep going. He entered the next BOC challenge race four years later, upgrading his boat to an aluminium 50-foot blue-water cruiser, which he modified for singlehanded racing. During this period, another tragedy was to strike when his good friend and race competitor Harry Mitchell was lost at Cape Horn in the same storm through which Lisa Clayton was struggling.

Saitō's own experience at Cape Horn, positioned close to Mitchell, had been unnerving – *Shuten-dohji II* had rolled through 360 degrees. However, the trauma of the rollover did nothing to quash Saitō's enthusiasm. He once said: 'Japanese young people are often too weak and don't do enough. They need to challenge themselves to really try hard. You only have one life to lead so must always do your very best.'

At 65, when most men of his age are retiring, Saitō entered the Around Alone race – a rebranding of the original BOC race – in 1998. Mike Golding was on the start line, someone with whom Saitō would strike up a lasting friendship.

Although Saitō had now completed three recognised solo circumnavigations, his singlehanded voyages to and from the start lines equated to a further three round-the-world voyages.

Still not satisfied, Saitō embarked on his seventh circumnavigation on 16 October 2004, now aged 71. This time he wanted to get all the way around the world without stopping, to mirror the epic voyage of his other great friend, Sir Robin Knox-Johnston. He succeeded, arriving home in Japan 233 days later.

Only at sea has Saitō found solace and freedom from a strife-torn world. At 73, he could have hung up his oilskins and sought other, less strenuous ways to while away his days. But what's the point in stopping? Far from just keeping going, Saitō decided to do something that would stretch even his lofty ambitions – to take on another singlehanded circumnavigation, only this time westwards around Cape Horn. He thus put together a shore team headed by an American, Hunter Brumfield, a former Tennessee newspaper editor. A veteran sailor himself, Brumfield had moved to Japan in 1983 and set up a technical publishing company with his Japanese wife, Eiko. 'I knew Saitō through our boating group, the Tokyo Sail & Power Squadron. I guess I've known him about 25 years going back to his BOC Challenge days. I threw a party for him when he got the Guinness record as the oldest non-stop circumnavigator. At the party, he asked me to help him on his next effort. I agreed.'

Six months previously, at the age of only 56, Brumfield had suffered a stroke. 'I retired after that so I had the time to devote to his campaign. All volunteer effort, of course.' Brumfield's medical misfortune was Saitō's gain. His support would go far beyond anything the two of them might have imagined.

Their first task was to find a suitable boat. The search led to Honolulu and *Peregrine*, a 56-foot steel-hulled cutter-rigged sloop with fuel tankage of 5,500 litres (1,200 gallons), designed and built in Hawaii in 1989 and weighing a colossal 43 tons. This boat was no racehorse with upwind sailing agility. She was a tank, but that promised greater security at sea.

Finding sponsorship was another matter. Saitō reckons there is a different perception of yachting in Japan compared with elsewhere. 'In the west, a yachtsman is seen as a sort of hero. They sail the oceans not for money but honour or adventure. In Japan, sailing a yacht is just a hobby for the rich.' In such an environment, who was going to risk money on a septuagenarian in a floating fortress?

In the perpetual scramble for sponsorship dollars among today's sailors, the hope is to find someone with a bit more vision than his neighbours. Brumfield and his team contacted the Nicole group of companies in Yokohama, a car dealership. Chief executive and former racing driver Nico Roreke saw plenty of opportunity. 'Merely succeeding means finishing a race, but only by exceeding do you win a race and you win by communication and cooperation with your partners.'

Brumfield had found a kindred spirit. The boat was renamed *Nicole BMW Shuten-dohji III*, and she sailed to Auckland for an extensive 12-month refit, including all-new navigation equipment, a more powerful diesel engine, a new drive train and new rigging and sails, with the mast stepped to the keel and the running rigging modified for singlehanded sailing. A solar-panel array complemented a new generator, and communications equipment was installed comprising an Iridium Satellite Phone System, an Inmarsat satellite phone and a single sideband radio. New plumbing with a manual-flush toilet, new batteries, replacement wiring, reinforced hatches and hydraulic pumps for the steering system completed the equipment check.

The checklist may have sported plenty of ticks, but having singlehanded command of so big a vessel crammed with electronic and mechanical gadgetry, all of which requires routine and frequent maintenance, brings with it a very long list of potential failures. Anyone taking on that responsibility, no matter what their previous experience, is perhaps asking for trouble. Given the trials to come, it is a wonder Saitō did not want to shoot this particular doggy.

To mitigate the risks, Saitō pinned a picture of Hisako to the navigation station bulkhead and resorted to superstition, carrying the tail of a rattlesnake, which he says brings him good luck.

Departure was set for 2 October 2008 with a start at the Kenzaki lighthouse, near Yokohama. Asked about his upcoming voyage, Saitō replied: 'I'm not confident at all, but I'll give it my best.'

Saitō's proposed route would take him south around Australia's eastern seaboard then west across the Southern Ocean, passing south of the Cape of Good Hope, across the South Atlantic and westwards around Cape Horn. Once back in the South Pacific, the track would aim at Hawaii and into the Northern Pacific, where Saitō would cross his outward track and head for home. The intention was to complete the voyage non-stop. This being Saitō's attempt at an eighth circumnavigation, the challenge was branded *Saitō-8*.

The shore team reckoned on a stupendously ambitious 184–240 days until Minoru Saitō was back in Yokohama. At departure, Saitō was 74 years and nine months old. It would be 1,080 days before he saw Yokohama again and he'd be just shy of his 78th birthday. Saitō crossed the start line at 11.54am and almost immediately began to feel seasick.

In addition to the 5,500 litres (1,200 gallons) of diesel in the tanks, Saitō also carried an additional 600 litres (130 gallons) in thirty 20-litre (4.4-gallon) jerry cans. According to the shore team, the reason for all this fuel was to power the generator, which 'is expected to be used two or three times a day, several hours each time, to keep the batteries charged and permit electrical generation for AC devices'. They estimated fuel consumption of 24 litres (5 gallons) a day and based their calculation for the on-board supply for 250 days accordingly.

The extensive refit had omitted a fuel gauge, so estimations of fuel consumption were based on the number of generator hours multiplied by the *assumed* hourly consumption. However, this rate of consumption did not take into account motoring under light or windless conditions or any extension of the ambitious target they had set.

Early in the voyage, at 7am Japan standard time (JST) on 18 October, the shore team reported: 'Saitō-san has spent the past 24 hours mostly motoring to get through and past the numerous atolls and small islands of the Federated States of Micronesia.'

Use of the engine seems not to have been a concern for either Saitō or the shore team despite WSSRC rules specifying engine use only in an emergency. The WSSRC, affiliated to the International Sailing Federation (ISAF), is the only adjudicating body for these types of sailing events.

Two days later, Saitō encountered the most difficult conditions of the voyage so far with winds at 35 knots. Saitō described the night as 'completely black', so he could only guess wave heights at up to 2.5 metres (8 feet). 'The boat is really rolling … good practice for the Southern Ocean.'

That same night, biting into a hard biscuit, Saitō broke three front teeth on an upper bridge. He called the shore team. 'It's really bad,' he said.

'Good thing you have lots of rice!'

'Yes, I guess so,' Saitō laughed.

The matter of damaged dental work was not too much of a hardship in the end, since Saitō's favourite food is rice and boiled cabbage.

Aside from his years of experience, Saitō is blessed with the most valuable weapons in the armoury of any long-distance lone sailor – good humour, the ability not to take himself too seriously and, as the Cruising Club of America recognised, an indomitable spirit. He would need all of these for the fight ahead.

Any long-distance voyager always welcomes free food to vary the diet. On 3 November, the 32nd day of his voyage, Saitō happily reported that: '… a large flying fish about 30cm length, about a foot, jumped on to the deck. Soon I caught it, cut it up, and enjoyed it for lunch.'

As a man with so much time at sea, in the raw cradle of the natural world, Saitō was environmentally aware. Off the eastern coast of Australia he observed: 'I think there used to be more flying fish and so dozens of birds around here, the Coral Sea east of Cairns. Strangely, I have only seen two birds this time. Something must have been changed to reduce the number of fish and the birds that live off them.'

Less than a week later, Saitō experienced the first in a sequence of mechanical failures that were to dog the entire voyage. The pump on the hydraulic steering system failed. He could still steer manually, but the autopilot could not operate. While *Shuten-dohji III* drifted southwards on the East Australian Current, Saitō replaced the faulty unit with a spare pump delivered the day before he left Yokohama.

Further along the coast and approaching the latitude of Brisbane, *Shuten-dohji III* was caught in a gale. 'This is the first time I have seen a gale last this long in this area,' Saitō told his shore team, recalling that on earlier voyages in the Coral Sea stormy conditions typically lasted only 20 hours.

During four days of punishment – headwinds of up to 37 knots and steep seas of 3–4 metres (10–13 feet) – Saitō had the engine and generator each running for a combined 40 hours. On 12 November, the generator packed up. In addition, water was finding its way into the electrical panel and the boat had sprung a leak. The shore team, concerned about 'much heavier weather conditions he will face in the Indian Ocean, and then later in the Southern Ocean at Cape Horn', decided he should stop in Sydney to make repairs.

Saitō's friend Don McIntyre, who had since founded the Shorthanded Sailing Association of Australia (SSAA), sent a message to his contacts in Sydney asking for volunteers to help Saitō:

You will remember Minoru Saitō for sure and hopefully you are following his latest crazy voyage … amazing stuff for a pensioner!!! … and his support guys have asked me for some advice … when Margie and I started the SSAA back in 1983 we always envisioned the camaraderie of shorthanded sailors as being all part of the fun … and Minoru was the official Special Guest at our first function awarding prizes … now 25 years later he needs some help. He needs advice, opinions on where best to go … he would like sympathetic tradesmen who may consider a discount labour rate and I am sure he would love to see many volunteers giving him a hand when he arrives so he feels like he is with friends. This is a great chance for all the SSAA members to meet a crazy guy with too many stories and a real hero out there having a go. If anyone can help him it will make a huge difference.

Volunteers answered McIntyre's call, one even flying in from Auckland to lend a hand and take charge of the repairs. Another found a berth at the Rozelle super-yacht marina. Engineers serviced the generator, deck leaks were isolated and sealed, the Inmarsat fixed, the bilge pumps mended and the entire hydraulic steering system overhauled.

Saitō resumed his voyage on Sunday 24 November. Within 48 hours, the generator had failed again. Saitō was back in port a week later, this time in

Hobart, Tasmania. A persistent leak had Saitō wondering whether the boat had developed a hull fracture. However, with *Shuten-dohji III* hauled out of the water, a marine surveyor pronounced the hull sound. Saitō and his helpers subsequently traced the leak to a through-deck fitting for an antenna concealed behind diesel jerry cans and covered with a tarp. The fitting was re-caulked. While in port, Saitō replaced a cracked backstay turnbuckle, had the engine-room door modified, secured the batteries with steel bars, and topped up the fuel tanks. Engineers traced the cause of the generator failure to an air bleed in the fuel line and rectified the problem by replacing the ring seals.

Saitō slipped his lines on Sunday 7 December into 35-knot winds, the tail swipe of a storm system 115 kilometres (70 miles) to the south, but not on a trajectory that would cause him further difficulty. On Christmas Day, a broken steering rod and a malfunctioning Iridium phone forced Saitō into port, this time Fremantle, Australia. By coincidence, Mike Golding had arrived just three hours earlier after dismasting his boat, *Ecover 3*, deep in the Southern Ocean, forcing him out of the Vendée Globe race.

Saitō got underway again on 28 December. Most men turning 75 might reasonably be tending their roses or enjoying a drink with friends. On Saitō's birthday, 7 January, *he* had the desolate wastes of the Southern Ocean stretching thousands of miles ahead and, at its end, Cape Horn to look forward to. He did, however, celebrate the day with a telephone hook-up with his friends and shore team who had gathered at the Hokkaido Restaurant in Ningyōchō.

Two days later, Saitō's observations reminded him once again of the fragility of the planet over whose surface he had spent so much time sailing.

There are few fish around this area although there used to be lots of fish, including the famous tuna from this part of the world. Now they seem to be gone. This is quite a change. I once saw dolphins line dance around here. It was more than 10 years ago, about 30 dolphins formed a line jumping and dancing. It was really fun to watch. However, I cannot see anything like that now. No birds as well, perhaps because they cannot find fish. You know? The global climate change.

Returning to the vexed question of using the engine versus strictly sailing, Saitō wrote to his shore team: 'I must use diesel sometimes or there would be no progress possible against the wind.' His intention was to employ the engine sparingly except at the Cape of Good Hope and then at Cape Horn. 'After that, with improved relative wind direction, it should be no problem to go faster.'

With the three unscheduled delays in Australia, the shore team wondered whether Saitō would make it back to Yokohama in time for the week-long 150th-anniversary Yokohama port celebrations starting on 31 May. Those celebrations were 129 days away. The shore team calculated Saitō's return in 144 days, provided that he could maintain the current boat speed of 4.55 knots. He still had 25,270 kilometres (15,700 miles) to go. They were hopeful, setting a target date of 1 April to reach Cape Horn even if, as they put it, '…that requires increased motoring to keep up the pace.' If Saitō could achieve that, they were back in the game. While the shore team agitated about a party, Saitō was worrying about the steering system, which had started leaking hydraulic fluid.

Rather than risk the headwinds and big seas of the Southern Ocean, Saitō followed a course along the 31st parallel, prime motoring country. He reported back to Tokyo: 'There are no waves at all – nothing at all!'

Heavy use of the engine and generator had taken its toll and on Friday 13 February, Saitō stopped at Cape Town, a guest of the Royal Cape Yacht Club. During the six-day layover, both the engine and the generator were serviced and the hydraulic steering system given a once-over. The Inmarsat and Iridium phones needed maintenance and more fuel and replacement filters were taken on board.

By 1 March, Saitō's track towards Cape Horn, almost 1,600 kilometres (1,000 miles) further south than his present latitude, compelled him to drop into the Roaring Forties. Winds of 50 knots and a 4-metre (13-foot) swell greeted *Shuten-dohji III*. By 19 March, Saitō was down at 47° south with 2,250 kilometres (1,400 miles) still to go to Cape Horn. A depression was passing eastwards. He telephoned the shore team. 'I'm okay, the boat's okay – but it's rough!'

The schedule to make Cape Horn by 1 April looked doubtful. Estimates put *Shuten-dohji III* 20 days away. To buy some time, Saitō made frequent use of the engine. For 12 days between 19 and 31 March, *Shuten-dohji III* logged 129 engine hours – nearly 11 hours a day. On 1 April, Saitō was still 800 kilometres (500 miles) short of Cape Horn and at the latitude of the Falkland Islands, which lay to his west. The shore team, who had always recognised rounding Cape Horn as the most treacherous part of the voyage, contacted the Argentine coastguard as a precaution to advise them of Saitō's approach.

A passing depression lashed *Shuten-dohji III* with 40-knot winds, kicking the seas into 6-metre (20-foot) monsters. Over a crackling Iridium connection, Saitō informed his shore team: 'No good sleep, but I'm fine and I think the boat is okay.'

Very close to Saitō's present position exactly one year previously, in April 2008, Canadian singlehander Glenn Wakefield – a 57-year-old carpenter attempting a westward circumnavigation aboard his fibreglass Cheoy Lee Offshore 40 *Kim Chow* – had run out of luck in these treacherous waters. A boarding sea had rolled the boat, flinging Wakefield about below decks to such an extent that he had lost consciousness. When he had regained his senses and inspected the deck, he had found a deck hatch ripped off, the solar array and wind generator swept away, and the liferaft gone. The Argentine coastguard had mounted a rescue bid, plucking Wakefield to safety on 27 April. To avoid *Kim Chow* drifting as a navigation hazard, they had scuttled the yacht and with that the five years Wakefield had spent meticulously reconditioning her.

As if he needed a reminder of just how treacherous the Cape Horn area can be, a massive storm to the west was heading Saitō's way, its centre on a track north of his position. To avoid a frontal assault, he dropped further south, to 54°. This was not only an evasive manoeuvre, it was clever tactics too, as it meant that Saitō could harness the easterly winds.

Another depression followed hard on the heels of the one before. Again, the storm system's centre was well north of Cape Horn, meaning the south side of the depression would feed Saitō yet more easterly winds. *Shuten-dohji III*, however, had another problem. The lower cars of the mainsail had pulled out of the track. Saitō insists that he could not deploy the mainsail even reduced to the third reef without risking substantial damage. Instead, he supplemented the genoa by having the engine on constantly.

Shuten-dohji III had now dropped even further south, to 56° (the latitude of Cape Horn), and was due south of the Falkland Islands. Saitō was now truly in Cape Horn country, and with easterly winds driving him forwards from astern, the weather scenario could not have been better.

With a storm frequency of at least 10 per cent at Cape Horn in April and a minimum of 1,125 kilometres (700 miles) to travel before *Shuten-dohji III* could get clear of the Chilean coast and begin to head north into the South Pacific, the chances of Saitō encountering a big blow were a near certainty. With his heavy reliance on the engine, it was likely he would be running on vapour to clear Cape Horn's maws. But, for the moment, the low-pressure system to the north-east and a high-pressure system centred south-west of his position were conspiring to provide *Shuten-dohji III* with a perfect weather window to get west quickly.

It was *Shuten-dohji III* herself who seemed reluctant to cooperate. In tandem with the damaged mainsail, the hydraulic steering system was playing up, forcing Saitō to man the helm for long, draining stretches. To mitigate this, he angled his heading south-west to put the boat on a port tack, bringing the winds over her port side. The compromise – he was slowing his progress west.

The problem of the mainsail cars pulling out of the track was still a major concern, so Saitō urged his shore team to consult Don McIntyre in Hobart. McIntyre's advice: put into Ushuaia. The dilemma played on Saitō's mind. The weather window was simply too good to miss. He therefore pushed on, piling on the miles towards Cape Horn.

Some 645 kilometres (400 miles) to the west, another depression was building, but this one was centred on a latitude well to the south of *Shuten-dohji III*'s position. If it stayed on that track and continued to deepen, Saitō would get a battering from strong westerly winds screaming in straight over the bow. The shore team reckoned he had three days, maybe four, before conditions deteriorated: time enough to get west of Cape Horn, create some sea room, and then head north and out of danger. The longitude of Cape Horn was within touching distance, only 80 kilometres (50 miles) west.

At 8.10am local time on Monday 6 April, *Shuten-dohji III* crossed the longitude of Cape Horn. It was a momentous occasion: the fifth time Saitō had bisected this line of longitude and the first going west. He celebrated with a half-bottle of champagne, pouring a portion into the sea in thanks. 'I'm really happy,' he exclaimed, as he *kanpai*'ed with the shore team back in Tokyo over the satellite phone.

Whatever gods Saitō thought he might have placated, they rejected the champagne offering. The winds backed from the east to north-west, forcing Saitō to head south-west and maintain a starboard tack. The forecast for the next 38 hours predicted winds rising to 30 knots from the north-west quadrant, bringing with them 5-metre (16-foot) seas. Saitō cranked on the power, running the engine for almost 17 hours.

Saitō contacted his shore team. 'I see an island, no, three islands, but they're not on my chart. I think they are about 12 miles away.'

The shore team, bemused, consulted Google Earth. No islands. Next, they had a look at their weather forecasting charts. Still no islands.

It seems extraordinary that Minoru Saitō, having sailed eastwards around Cape Horn four times previously, would not be aware of these islands. Yet *Shuten-dohji III* was carrying paper charts for the entire route. According to Hunter Brumfield, 'Yes, he had most or all the charts, some new, many from his previous circumnavigations.'

Perhaps even more alarming is that the shore team should consult a non-navigation source like Google Earth for confirmation. They finally resolved the issue with a posting on their daily blog on 8 April: 'Then, almost as an afterthought we looked at the detailed chart specially ordered for Drake Passage, and there they were: Islas Diego Ramírez, consisting of 3 tiny islands that were now less than 10 miles off … in the gathering light of dawn a full 45 miles south of the cape. Yikes!'

By 9 April, the winds were coming from the west as forecast. The mainsail was out of action and fuel was running low. Saitō rationed use of the engine to a few hours a day and found himself losing ground, pushed back by the relentless onslaught of wind. 'I'm going back to Cape Horn!' he reported to his shore team on 10 April. Another depression was gathering strength in the west. He described conditions as 'very difficult' with large seas and winds he estimated at 'over 40 knots, probably 40 to 45 knots'. He thought the seas were 'at least 5 meters, maybe 6'. By now *Shuten-dohji III* had almost reached latitude 57°. To Saitō's horror, he saw a 'bergy bit' of ice drifting passed.

Any hope of a relatively pain-free passage round Cape Horn vanished as the massive depression swept east, filling the entire expanse of the Drake Passage, its centre 400 kilometres (250 miles) south of Saitō's position, and delivering survival conditions. He handed all sail, secured all hatches and set *Shuten-dojhi III* to lie a'hull. She drifted eastwards in 45-knot winds, pummelled by 10-metre (33-foot) seas. The liferaft dislodged from its mountings. Saitō did not dare go on deck to re-secure it. He would just have to wait until conditions calmed and the severe rolling ceased. 'I can't go out on deck at all until then,' he explained to the shore team.

On Sunday 12 April, disaster struck. A halyard, torn loose by the violent motion of the boat, became tangled around the rudder and then caught in the spinning propeller. The rope, wrenched bar tight around the rudder, bent the rudder post twenty degrees out of alignment, disabling the boat.

Saitō called the shore team, who contacted the Chilean Navy, which judged the situation an emergency. A Chilean fish-processing factory ship, the closest vessel large enough to negotiate the violent seas, was given *Shuten-dohji III*'s position with a request that they render immediate assistance.

In frantic discussion between the Chilean Navy and Saitō's shore team, the naval officer at the rescue coordination centre in Puerto Williams warned, 'We can save the skipper, but not the ship.' The instruction to the captain of the factory ship was clear: get Saitō off his boat and leave *Shuten-dohji III* to her fate.

Saitō had no Spanish and the captain could not speak English, much less Japanese. Whatever the desperate exchanges were over the heaving waves and screaming winds, Saitō refused to abandon his vessel. Eventually, the captain relented and took *Shuten-dohji III* in tow for the 645-kilometre (400-mile passage) to Punta Arenas.

Three days later, on Wednesday 15 April, *Shuten-dohji III* was safely moored in Punta Arenas, the same port where the square-rigger *County of Peebles*, which did battle with Cape Horn many decades previously, now makes her home. Able to take stock, Saitō acknowledged that he had never before experienced such dangerous sea conditions, 'even in the biggest typhoon'.

Pesca Chile SA, the owners of the factory fishing ship, dashed any hope Saitō might have had for a quick turnaround in Punta Arenas and any notion the shore team had of Saitō returning to Yokohama in time for the 150th-anniversary port celebrations because the company lodged a salvage claim. The matter consumed months of arbitration. Finally, with a settlement reached in court, the port authorities released *Shuten-dohji III* to Saitō on Friday 3 July.

The list of repairs needed to prepare the boat for sea was extensive, not least because of considerable damage incurred during the tow itself. Happily for Saitō, a local businessman, Hitoshi Hanaoka – owner of a commercial fishing business employing 60 people and fluent in Japanese, Spanish and English – was on hand to navigate the labyrinthine bureaucracy and mediate in the repairs to *Shuten-dohji III*.

Saitō stayed on board *Shuten-dohji III* most of the time at her allocated mooring rafted in among the local fishing fleet, concerned about her security and with only a borrowed heater to make the cabin bearable. Saitō recounts this period as the darkest of the voyage. 'I had these big steel fishing boats hitting me on both sides and if my boat had not been made of steel, it would have been crushed and sunk. I was really worried I might die from stress and the cold but I could not leave the boat unprotected.'

In August, with repairs underway, the shore team anticipated a departure from Punta Arenas sometime in September, but Saitō himself was in dire need of repair. He had severe abdominal pain. Doctors diagnosed a hernia; the only treatment option – surgery.

Post-operatively, recovery was slow. 'I'm getting old, so I don't heal as quickly as I used to,' Saitō said during a call to Tokyo. 'But I'll be all right if I take it easy.' The shore team re-scheduled departure for Saturday 10 October.

Despite his setbacks, Saitō had lucked out when it came to Hitoshi Hanaoka, a fact that was duly acknowledged by Hunter Brumfield. 'Not only has Hanaoka-san provided his home, shower, meals, and friendship, but has eased some of the payment matters as we have accrued expenses there. His tri-lingual assistance dealing with port authorities, medical staff, boat repairs, delivery and other matters has placed us in eternal debt to him, not to mention reimbursing him for Saitō-san's hospital fees!'

Saitō's exit strategy was to sail eastwards along the Strait of Magellan to its Atlantic entrance, then, staying close to land to minimise the risk of ice, follow the coast round Cape Horn to the position where he had been rescued and continue on from there. All good on paper, but sea trials threw up more problems. Worse still, Saitō's Chilean visa had expired, further delaying the re-start.

The visa issue became a classic bureaucratic bungle. The only way to sort it out was to travel by car into Argentina then return to Chile on a temporary tourist visa. That done on 18 October, persistent depressions funnelling in from the west bringing 50-knot winds with them continued to thwart departure. Saitō and *Shuten-dohji III* finally slipped their lines on Saturday 24 October.

Two days later Saitō passed east of Staten Island. Twenty-four hours from there, *Shuten-dohji III* found herself 61 kilometres (38 miles) east and slightly north of Cape Horn. She passed west over the longitude of Cape Horn just after midday local time on Tuesday 27 October. Saitō decided to hold off on any celebration until he was heading north up Chile's west coast. He had good reason for caution; the engine had been running constantly since departing Punta Arenas and the fuel filters were clogging.

Saitō continued to motor, heading north-west, 56 kilometres (35 miles) off the coast. By Saturday 31 October, *Shuten-dohji III* was at latitude 52°25' south – right opposite the western entrance to the Strait of Magellan. Barometric pressure stood at 1005mb and rising. Winds from the west were blowing at a comfortable 20 knots. Everything looked rosy. Calmer seas and the warmth of the lower latitudes beckoned.

At 2.30pm the engine and generator died. The batteries could not recharge and without battery power, the autopilot was out of commission.

Saitō called Tokyo. Tokyo called the Chilean coastguard. The coastguard dispatched a vessel. He had to come in. Saitō manoeuvred his boat under sail into the Strait of Magellan and picked up a tow from the coastguard vessel

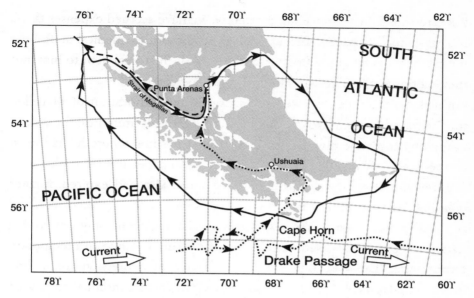

Minoru Saitō's Cape Horn transits – the dotted line shows the route of his first attempt, the solid line his second and the dashed line his final departure

at 4.35am on Monday 2 November. He was back in Punta Arenas two days later, with the faithful Hitoshi Hanaoka pressed into service once more.

As well as sorting out the dirty fuel problem, the forward sail furling gear had damaged the staysail and genoa very badly. The nearest sail loft in Buenos Aires did not have the right Dacron thickness. Rather than send the sail back to the manufacturer in Auckland for repair, the simplest solution would be to order a new sail. By the turn of the year, Saitō was still in Punta Arenas and celebrated his 76th birthday there on 7 January.

With the new genoa from Auckland rigged, myriad other repairs made, and the boat loaded with what Saitō hoped was clean fuel, he was ready to leave Punta Arenas for the second time on Saturday 30 January. The plan was straightforward – motor westwards along the Strait of Magellan this time and reconnect with his track beyond its western entrance.

The Strait of Magellan is essentially a tidal river between two oceans with plenty of difficult twists and turns along the way. It is only 2 kilometres (1.25 miles) wide at its narrowest point. Currents in some places run at 4 knots. Huge tidal ranges on the Atlantic side vary from 7.1 metres (23.3 feet) to

9 metres (29.5 feet), moderating to between 1.1 metres (3.6 feet) and 1.2 metres (6.6 feet) on the Pacific side. As a shortcut, the strait has obvious merits. Approximately 600 Chilean ships and 1,700 foreign vessels transit the strait annually. The navigation dangers are also obvious, especially for skippers lacking local knowledge. Pilotage is compulsory. Saitō got round this by travelling in convoy with a local fishing vessel named *Lucky Dream*, though by this time he must have been wondering about both his dream and his luck.

Saitō was under an additional pressure. The Chilean coastguard operates a 'three strikes rule'. Saitō had this one last chance to leave. A third rescue, whether he called for one or not, would mean that the Chilean coastguard would get him to safety but would not contemplate trying to save the boat.

By Thursday 4 February, Saitō had reached the Pacific. *Lucky Dream* would hold station at the mouth of the Strait of Magellan for three hours in case she had to take Saitō off his boat. If not, she would turn for home.

Shuten-dohji III rejoined her original track without mishap, hitching a ride on the northwards-moving Humboldt Current. She was, at last, on her way. However, if the boat and her weary skipper were relieved by every mile they put between themselves and their Cape Horn nemesis, that relief soon evaporated.

Within one week, the boat had developed engine problems, again because of dirty fuel. Saitō had to put into port. He had a choice – either Valdivia, approximately halfway along the Chilean coast, or Concepción, 320 kilometres (200 miles) further north. Prudence won over and on 11 February *Shuten-dojhi III* put into Valdivia. Although Saitō may have cursed his luck, putting into Valdivia was a stroke of good fortune.

At 3.34am on Wednesday 27 February a devastating earthquake measuring 8.8 magnitude rocked Chile. Its epicentre was very near Concepción, and the death toll reached 800 in the capital Santiago, Concepción and the outlying areas. Michelle Bachelet, then president of Chile, declared a 'state of catastrophe'.

Another stark reminder of his vulnerability (and perhaps of the fact that his rattlesnake tail was earning its keep) came shortly after Saitō departed

Valdivia on Friday 26 March. The family of another Japanese singlehanded sailor had contacted the Saitō-8 shore team concerned about 62-year-old Keiichi Chinami, sailing his 35-foot ketch *Kifu*. He had last made contact on 11 March, giving his position at latitude 51° south, 87° west, which put him 690 kilometres (430 miles) west of the entrance to the Strait of Magellan and very close to where Miles and Beryl Smeeton had capsized, twice. Hunter Brumfield publicised the missing yachtsman on the Saitō-8 blog, appealing for information. None was forthcoming. Neither Keiichi Chinami nor his boat *Kifu* were ever found.

Saitō continued north-west before making another unscheduled stop on 28 April in Puerto Ayora on Santa Cruz in the Galápagos islands to replace hydraulic cylinders on the steering system.

By 21 June, Saitō was in Honolulu. The mainsail needed repairs, the engine needed overhauling and cracks had appeared in the mast. He left on 10 July, but only days later found himself having to pump out the bilges for 20 minutes every two hours because of corrosion in the engine's heat exchanger.

With the onset of the typhoon season, the engine was essential, so Saitō turned back for Honolulu. Repairs would take a while and Saitō decided to remain in Hawaii and see out the typhoon season.

Shuten-dohji III was in shocking condition, suffering from the accumulation of excess punishment. Saitō was not in a much better state – thin and harrowed and suffering with a sore back. To make matters worse, a car hit him as he was crossing a road, damaging his knee. Shortly after celebrating his 77th birthday with friends and volunteer helpers at the Honolulu Yacht Club on 7 January 2011, he underwent knee surgery.

Saitō was still recovering in Honolulu on 11 March when the devastating Tōhoku earthquake shook Japan, taking out the Fukushima Daiichi Nuclear Power Plant. The resultant tsunami hit Hawaii. Two of Saitō's helpers sought the relative safety of deep water in their own boats. A third found his boat, which was also his home, drifting in the bay with a finger pier still attached after a 1.8-metre (6-foot) surge swamped the marina. *Shuten-dohji III*, tied to a floating dock, survived intact. Saitō was not on board at the time, instead sheltering in a friend's home.

Saitō finally left Honolulu on Thursday 26 May 2011. He had been in Hawaii for almost one year. A departure in May was not without risk – *Shuten-dohji III* would be approaching Japan during the typhoon season.

On 26 June, the generator's cooling water pump failed, leaving Saitō with the now familiar difficulty of being unable to charge the batteries to power the autopilot. Faced with this new situation, he headed for Ogasawara, a small port on Chichijima Island, 1,035 kilometres (643 miles) distant and 800 kilometres (500 miles) south of Yokohama.

Nearly a fortnight after arriving, Saitō left Ogasawara only to be forced back into port with a failed gearbox. As with his stop at Valdivia, it was to prove serendipitous. It was late July, the height of the typhoon season. A series of depressions developing to the east like pearls on a string were threatening Japan. Four passed by Chichijima without incident, but the fifth, Typhoon Talas, slammed into the island. In anticipation, Saitō had moved *Shuten-dohji III* onto a ship's mooring buoy in the harbour to ride out the storm, insisting to the local coastguard commander that he stay on board his vessel. 'He's the talk of the island, and many of the fishermen here are concerned about him,' a senior coastguard officer told Saitō's shore team in Tokyo. The coastguard kept an eye on the boat from the safety of their shoreside facility.

Shuten-dohji III motored out of Ogasawara harbour on Wednesday 7 September for the 800-kilometre (500-mile) passage home. *Nicole BMW Shuten-dohji III* and her beaming skipper eased into Yokohama Harbour on Saturday morning, 17 September.

Cheering crowds and the media greeted *Shuten-dohji III* as Saitō tied up alongside the Minato-Mirai Pukari pier. The sea had almost erased the boat's name from her bows, rust stains streaked the once-pristine white paint and tangles of weathered ropes lay piled in the stern.

'I'm very, very happy to be back but it was difficult,' Saitō said with characteristic understatement. 'It was my longest trip. It went on for months and months and years and years, I had so many problems. But it's great to be back. I missed a lot of things, mostly cherry blossoms and Japanese food. But I feel very young in both mind and body and I feel I'm in great shape.'

Saitō was 77 years 8 months and 10 days old. With apt irony, Saitō's arrival home coincided with a national holiday, Respect for the Elderly Day.

Minoru Saitō lives on his boat at the Yokohama Yacht Club and is busy writing the third volume of his autobiography, *Fighting Alone*. He never married and he still has his rattlesnake tail.

JESSICA WATSON

'You are only as big as the dreams you dare to live.'

Born .... 18 May 1993
Nationality .... Australian
Date of Cape Horn rounding .... January 2010
Boat name .... *Ella's Pink Lady*
Designer .... Sparkman & Stephens
Year of build 1984
LOA.............................. 34 feet
Material .... Fibreglass
Rig .... Cutter

Jessica Watson spent her childhood by the sea, growing up on Queensland's Gold Coast and learning the nuts and bolts of sailing most weekends at the Southport Yacht Club. She was shy and retiring as a child, but sailing brought out her competitive instincts, and with her burgeoning skills on the water came a blossoming self-confidence.

Jessica was born in 1993, the second of four children, and the Watson siblings experienced an unusual upbringing. Originally from New Zealand, Jessica's parents, Julie and Roger, decided that television was undesirable, so the children had to be more creative when it came to amusing themselves. When Roger sold his estate agency, the family bought a bus and a 52-foot motorboat, the idea being to explore both the interior of Australia and the coast. What began as a family-centred adventure morphed into a lifestyle. The boat, *Home Abroad*, became the family home for the next five-and-a-half years, with Julie homeschooling the children.

The initial thought of sailing around the world and taking on the challenge of Cape Horn came while still living on board the family's floating home. Julie read *Lionheart* to Jessica; it was the story of fellow Australian Jesse Martin's circumnavigation via Cape Horn aged 18, leaving from Sydney on 7 December 1998 and returning on 31 October 1999.

Jessica had already overcome one big obstacle in her life by beating dyslexia, an early sign of her determination. She loved sailing, and the question for her became: could she face a challenge like this by minimising risk, preparing as thoroughly as possible, relying on her problem-solving capabilities and ultimately testing herself to exceed expectations?

After much reflection, she decided she could. The first stage of her mental preparation was to visualise the voyage by plastering her small berth space on *Home Abroad* with pictures of Southern Ocean waves, and reading books on previous circumnavigations, among them that by Kay Cottee's *First Lady*. As to the fact that she was still a child with a diminutive stature, Jessica concluded that 'sailing is not about strength, it is about knowledge'. Talking over the idea with her sister, she then had to steel herself to tell her parents. Remarkably, Jessica was only 12 years old at the time. It is likely that most people would put such expression from one so young down to youthful exuberance, naivety perhaps or childish fantasy. With Jessica, none of that applied. She meant what she said because she knew it in her heart.

Julie quickly got behind her daughter, while Jessica's father was more circumspect. To demonstrate her seriousness, Jessica took a job washing dishes at a restaurant while still doing schoolwork to pay for anything that might be required as the project took root. After nearly three years of researching, learning, talking to whoever would listen, scouring marinas and yards, searching for grants (unsuccessfully) and writing to newspapers in the hope of attracting sponsors, Jessica was introduced to Bruce Arms through mutual friends of her parents. Bruce had a lifetime's experience on the water. He was a previous winner of the Tasman singlehanded race and an experienced boat-builder. Jessica had found the perfect mentor. Bruce took Jessica on some trial voyages aboard his 46-foot catamaran, telling her parents afterwards: 'She has a talent for sailing and is a quick learner.'

Despite this, Jessica needed more offshore experience. Other friends of her parents were looking for crew to sail a 42-foot yacht from Vanuatu back to Australia. Jessica volunteered and flew to Vanuatu to join the boat, paying for the airfare with funds saved from her job as a *dishy*. After an uneventful 1,600-kilometre (1,000-mile) passage, she enrolled at a sailing school to gain her coastal skipper ticket. Jessica's aunt, Wendy, who had worked for the New Zealand Meteorological Service, then organised a crew position for her on *Evohe*, an 82-foot steel yacht specifically designed for the harsh environments of the Arctic and Antarctic. Jessica joined the crew on *Evohe* for a passage from Bluff on New Zealand's southern tip to the Campbell Island group. It would be an opportunity for Jessica to gain invaluable experience of the Southern Ocean.

Bruce then introduced Jessica to Don McIntyre, a one-time BOC singlehanded round-the-world race participant. He drilled down to the central issue immediately: 'You can't do this without a boat ... and you don't have a boat.' Still only 14, Jessica had secured promises of support from several would-be sponsors willing to supply equipment, but each would only commit to the project once Jessica had a boat.

As the media became more alive to Jessica's plans, which she encouraged in her ongoing search for sponsorship, the inevitable backlash – criticism of her parents given that she was still a minor – added to the difficulties of getting the project launched. She still did not have a boat or any idea of how to get one.

Unbeknown to her, however, Don McIntyre, impressed by her determination and the support she had garnered so far, and satisfied that she was not being pressured by 'fame-seeking' parents, decided he would purchase an appropriate boat that Jessica could sail on her circumnavigation. In March 2009, he found a Sparkman & Stephens 34, built in 1984, named *Shanty*. He checked her over, negotiated on price and purchased the boat. Jessica was ecstatic. Quite suddenly, her dream had become a tangible reality.

Jessica upgraded her sailing qualification to Yachtmaster Ocean, learning celestial navigation as a course component. She renamed the boat *Youngestround*, and after trial sails with Bruce Arms to get a feel of the boat's sailing characteristics, a date was set for departure: September 2009, only four months away. The boat required a major refit and no sponsor had yet come forward.

The project was officially launched to the media on 9 May 2009, resulting in a flood of interviews – radio, TV and print – but as a counterpoint to the many positive and encouraging comments came a tide of hostility aimed at her parents. Jessica turned 16 a few days later, on 18 May. Now that she was of legal age, with a licence to skipper a boat and a boat ready for refit, the criticism was an unwelcome distraction at a time when preparations for an extended expedition demand total attention.

At the Sanctuary Cove Boat Show a few days later, Jessica met Andrew Fraser of 5 Oceans Media, a media-management company specialising in sports. He agreed to take Jessica on as a client, escalating the chances of landing a sponsorship deal. After Don McIntyre advertised for volunteers, a small army descended on the shed in Brisbane to help with the refit. 5 Oceans Media devised a creative way to raise awareness and possibly attract a sponsor by organising a 'name Jessica's boat' competition through the *Sunshine Coast Daily* newspaper and a fundraising dinner to announce the winning entry. The marketing approach worked and the boat was renamed *Pink Lady*.

With the refit complete and the boat en route to Sydney, the low-loader hit cables hanging from a road bridge, badly damaging a tubular frame structure mounted on the boat's stern deck that supported the solar panels, the wind generator, the GPS aerials and the satellite communications dome. The implications were serious – more cost, more delay, but, even worse, the damage was a psychological setback disturbing the delicate balance between keeping upbeat and maintaining focus and the all-too-easy slide into despondency. Jessica was deeply upset.

During her time in Sydney, Jessica went to the National Maritime Museum to have a look at Kay Cottee's *First Lady*, taking some ideas that Cottee had implemented, such as safety lines on the coach-house roof. Private donations covered the costs of the extensive refit but still no sponsor had emerged despite an avalanche of publicity generated at the Sydney Boat Show.

Final fittings of electronic equipment, sea trials and victualling burned through the remaining time before the September departure date. By late August, with the boat back on the Sunshine Coast, Jessica finally managed to get out of Mooloolaba for her first solo trial sail on *Pink Lady*. The next day, she received the news that Ella Baché, a skincare company, had agreed to join the team as title sponsor. For the third time, the boat's name changed, to *Ella's Pink Lady*.

The delivery trip from Mooloolaba to Sydney for the official launch provided a last opportunity to test the boat. Jessica set out on 8 September, cheered on by large crowds lining the riverbanks. Two press helicopters buzzed overhead. By evening, feeling a little seasick and worried that she might be too close inshore and near a fishing fleet, Jessica switched on the radar and Automatic Identification System (AIS) alarms before turning in for a short sleep, still wearing her lifejacket and harness.

A 'horrible bone-shuddering explosion of noise' woke Jessica. *Ella's Pink Lady* had collided with a ship, its towering steel sides sliding by in the darkness, scraping and screeching against the small, vulnerable yacht. The rigging caught against the ship, ripping a chain plate from the yacht's deck and causing a cupboard below to disintegrate.

Safe but deeply shocked, Jessica cleared and lashed the broken rigging, handed sail, started the engine and got underway, limping the six hours back to Mooloolaba, occasionally leaning over the side to throw up. Investigations by Maritime Safety Queensland and the Australian Transport Safety Board later identified the ship as the 63,000-tonne *Silver Yang*.

The media descended in a scrum, some commentators braying about the inevitable stupidity of allowing a young girl to undertake such a venture. Local marine businesses, however, remained positive and offered to repair the boat free of charge.

Ella's Pink Lady re-launched on Monday 28 September and, despite a persistent note of pessimism in some sections of the media, sailed safely to Sydney. One of those with a more positive frame of mind who also offered help was Andrew Short – a successful boat dealer and marina operator in Sydney – who gave *Ella's Pink Lady* a berth at his marina at The Spit. Only days later, Jessica's mindset, now resettled after the collision, was thrown into turmoil when on 10 October she learned that Andrew Short had been killed at sea, thrown overboard when his 80-foot maxi yacht *Shockwave* had hit rocks off Flinders Islet during a race. It was a shattering reminder of the dangers Jessica would face.

Ella's Pink Lady finally departed on her odyssey on 18 October 2009.

To qualify for a circumnavigation, Jessica first headed north to cross the equator near Kiritimati (Christmas Island), experiencing no more than occasional 30-knot winds, enjoying fair sailing and, the opportunity of establishing a shipboard routine, and giving the boat a proper shakedown.

Heading south-east after rounding Kiritimati and with more than 6,450 kilometres (4,000 miles) to Cape Horn, on 9 December Jessica wrote: 'Chances are that things are going to get pretty bumpy for me tomorrow. Call me crazy but hearing that *Ella's Pink Lady* and I are finally going to get some rough stuff was in one way a big relief, as it's been keeping me in suspense waiting.'

By 17 December, the air temperature now much cooler, Jessica began to think more and more about Cape Horn, recalling Chichester's words about the sea-state he had experienced through the Drake Passage, the 'helplessness' he felt before the 'remorseless power' of the waves.

On Boxing Day, Jessica slipped south past the 50th parallel and had yet to experience any really severe weather – the Roaring Forties for once had been hoarse. The Furious Fifties welcomed *Ella's Pink Lady* with a burst of sunshine and light winds. Bob Davitt of the New Zealand Meteorological Service, part of the shoreside team, was doing an excellent job guiding Jessica around the worst of the conditions.

The following day, still nothing! Almost apologetically, Jessica wrote: 'It's been a bit of a slow day with only a little wind. You wouldn't guess that this is the Southern Ocean.'

Jessica was also in contact with 42-year-old Dilip Donde – a commander in the Indian Navy attempting to become the first Indian to complete a circumnavigation – positioned to the west of her in his faster 47-foot yacht, *Mhadei*. He was also heading eastwards around Cape Horn, having set out from Mumbai on 19 August.

On 30 December Jessica experienced her first Southern Ocean gale: 44-knot winds and 15-metre (49-foot) waves. The self-steering gear held the boat on course. A dolphin swam alongside for six hours. Cape Horn lay 2,400 kilometres (1,500 miles) away to the east.

By Friday 8 January, a threatening storm had not materialised, winds only reaching 30 knots before dying and leaving Jessica becalmed for periods. Cape Horn was now 725 kilometres (450 miles) east. A newspaper had flown her parents to Punta Arenas for a planned flyover as *Ella's Pink Lady* passed Cape Horn, but the persistently still conditions meant that Jessica was not making any meaningful progress eastwards.

On 11 January, Jessica wrote: 'I'm not really having the most exciting time down here at the moment. We've still got very, very little wind.' With only 435 kilometres (270 miles) to Cape Horn, the wind finally picked up to 12 knots, slowly building to 30 knots as *Ella's Pink Lady* approached Cape Horn, now just 130 kilometres (80 miles) away. The conditions were not what Jessica had been expecting as she sighted the Diego Ramírez Islands. At dawn on Thursday 14 January and after a sleepless night, Jessica sighted Cape Horn itself, grey and brooding through the misty air. 'Against the grey sky and with albatross flying in the foreground, it was just as I'd imagined for so long. Mythical and striking just about sums it up.'

After a few failed attempts because of adverse flying conditions, the chartered plane carrying her parents eventually spotted the boat and spent 45 minutes circling around, speaking with Jessica on VHF radio.

'For me, the power of sailing around Cape Horn was the combination of the area's fierce and demanding reputation, the years I spent dreaming about doing it and the weeks of build-up as we edged closer and closer ... it really was a dream come true.'

Jessica called Don McIntyre. 'I wanted to share my excitement with someone who really understood what it felt like.' He was on board a small ship, *Orion*, returning from an expedition to Antarctica. He patched her call through to the PA system so that his fellow passengers could listen in. It came as a huge and pleasant surprise to Jessica when Don told her that Kay Cottee was among those on board.

It was a perfect window to get past the Horn and two days later, *Ella's Pink Lady* was already close to the Falkland Islands.

It might have been something of a reprieve to get past Cape Horn in moderate conditions, but on 24 January, 65-knot winds and huge seas buffeted *Ella's Pink Lady*. Running under a storm jib, the main lashed tight to the boom, surrounded by gigantic walls of rushing water, there was nothing more she could achieve on deck, and by now suffering from cold after hand steering for hours, Jessica went below to strap herself in and wait out the storm. 'With everything battened down and conditions far too dangerous to be on deck, there wasn't anything I could do but belt myself in and hold on ... With one eye on the instruments, all I could do was settle in and let whatever was going to happen, happen.'

The first knockdown was quick, the boat righting itself immediately. In the ensuing hours, Jessica called her parents and Bruce Arms. The second knockdown caused lockers to burst open and spill their contents all over the cabin.

The third knockdown was the worst, preceded by the thunderous roar of the approaching wave. 'The only thing I can compare it to is an aeroplane engine, only throatier and scarier.' When the boat finally came up, a quick glance through the companionway revealed the stern deck frame staved in. The self-steering gear looked bent out of shape and the liferaft had broken free of its lashings in the cockpit. With difficulty, Jessica managed to get it below.

Bob Davitt was on hand round the clock to advise Jessica. The news was not good. The storm was set to worsen. The advice from the shore team was to gybe onto a course that might help her avoid the worst of the storm to come. Once she had set the boat onto its new heading, a wave knocked the boat over for a fourth time.

One of the EPIRBs, mounted under the spray canopy, had turned itself on during one of the knockdowns. The signal gave the boat's position to the nearest MRCC, which passed the information on to the Australian RCC. The ARCC then called Jessica's mother. By coincidence, Jessica radioed her team only a few minutes later and was able to reassure everyone the EPIRB relay was accidental.

Jessica endured more knockdowns near Tasmania towards the end of April 2010 but without serious damage to the masts or rigging. She arrived in Sydney on 15 May. She was only 17 years old. This time, the press gave her all the credit she deserved and the country honoured her with the 2011 Young Australian of the Year award.

A few days after her arrival in Sydney, Dilip Donde completed his circumnavigation, becoming the first Indian singlehander to do so, putting into Mumbai harbour on 22 May after 276 days at sea.

On 31 May, Jessica took *Ella's Pink Lady* out of Sydney harbour, accompanied by another yacht, for the final journey home to Mooloolaba. En route she put in at Yamba Marina where, finally, she met Kay Cottee, whose warmth and welcome quickly dispelled any trepidation Jessica felt at coming face to face with her heroine.

CAPE HORNER TRADITIONS

In 1936, 28 French Master Mariners, all of whom had either commanded or crewed square-riggers around Cape Horn, gathered for a dinner at Hotel de l'Univers in Saint-Malo to honour their former teacher, Georges Delarney, professor of navigation at the Saint-Malo nautical college. With the demise of the commercial Cape Horn route and the encroaching domination of steam power over sail, this group formed the *Amicale Internationale des Capitaines au Long Cours Cap Horniers* (AICH). Qualification for membership was very specific – applicants must have 'sailed round Cape Horn in square rigged sailing ships'.

The purpose of the AICH was equally clear:

> To promote and strengthen the ties of comradeship which bind together
> a unique body of men and women who embody the distinction of
> having sailed round Cape Horn in a commercial sailing vessel, and to
> keep alive in various ways memories of the stout ships that regularly
> sailed on voyages of exceptional difficulty and peril, and of the
> endurance, courage and skill of the sailors who manned them.

Excitement permeated subsequent meetings as the captains sought to draft a constitution and elect their first president. He would need a title, something befitting the history the new organisation was trying to preserve, and a suitably nautical sobriquet. They decided on '*Grand Mât*', or 'Main Mast'.

The honour of being the first president fell to Captain Louis Allaire, and various classes of membership were agreed: Albatross – a Master Mariner who had commanded a sailing ship around Cape Horn; Mollyhawk – anyone who had served in a sailing ship going around Cape Horn; and Cape Pigeon – for those who had formed part of the ship's company but not been directly involved in handling the vessel – cooks, stewards, stewardesses, tutors, passengers and any members of a captain's family who sailed with him.

The inaugural meeting of the AICH was held in May 1937 at the Hôtel des Ajoncs d'Or. The organisation's emblem, designed with input from all the founding members and showing an albatross biting down on a traditional lure, was approved.

As its membership declined with the natural passing away of many of the original square-rigger men and women, the AICH created a new class of membership in response to the first staging of the Whitbread round-the-world race in 1973: Yacht Member, both to recognise the achievements of these sailors and to maintain the original purpose of the association.

The AICH spawned various international chapters. Commander Claude Woollard RN, himself a member of the French section, formed the British section in 1957, the same year *Pamir* was lost in mid-Atlantic. Henceforth, it would be known as the International Association of Cape Horners UK Section (IACH UK).

In 1996, the IACH took the decision to drop the 'UK' part of the title. The AICH met for the final time in May 2003, but the IACH continues today, both to maintain the heritage of the original fellowship and to embrace the present and the future through the exploits of yachtsmen and women from around the world.

The dreadful price exacted from the ships that sailed the Cape Horn route and the sailors who manned those ships compounded the Horn's reputation as a fearsome place. Those who survived were perceived by others as having somehow reached a loftier status as men of the sea. Something was needed that marked these men out as a breed apart. Most notably, Cape Horners could wear a gold loop earring, which tradition demands be worn on the side nearest the Horn when they passed – the left ear for a downwind eastward passage, the right ear for an upwind westward rounding. Or, as a recognisable badge of honour, sailors could be tattooed with the image of a square-rigger flying all sail. Being a Cape Horner also conferred certain rights – including the right to have one foot on the table while eating on any ship, and the magical ability to piss to windward, in a literal sense pissing on the west wind.

If I could, I would set a wager. Gather everyone who has been round Cape Horn, from Captain Willem Schouten in 1616 to the modern-day sailor in a hi-tech boat bedecked with electronic gizmos, atop that high pinnacle of black rock, and invite each to defile that place in the way tradition allows. Who would break rank? Who would wish to desecrate a geographical masterpiece the power of which is so much greater than our own, whose beauty is infinitely more radiant, whose history is written in crevice of rock and crack of bone, where 10,000 lay claim to eternal rest, where forces of nature conspire to torment or relent at their own command, where we are merely inconspicuous, privileged, grateful and temporary spectators? My wager would be this: not a man or woman would step forward.

Cape Horn lies within Chilean territorial waters. The Chilean Navy maintains a station on Horn Island, consisting of a residence, a utility building, a chapel and a lighthouse. Such is the toll in human life in these waters that a memorial to those lost was inaugurated on 5 December 1992 by the Chilean section of the Cape Horn Captains' International Brotherhood.

The memorial, commissioned from Chilean sculptor José Balcells Eyquem, depicts the silhouette of an albatross on the wing, pressed from 10 steel plates each 6mm (¼in) in thickness, the albatross being both the emblem of the Brotherhood and, according to myth, the embodiment of the soul of a sailor lost at sea. The monument stands 7 metres (23 feet) high, perched

Cape Horn monument on Horn Island

50 metres (164 feet) above the sea at the southern end of Cape Horn itself and built to withstand wind gusts of 200kph (125mph). Flanking it is a marble plaque bearing a poem by the Chilean author Sara Vial:

I, the albatross that awaits you at the end of the world...

I, the forgotten soul of the sailors lost that crossed Cape Horn from all the seas of the world.

But die they did not in the fierce waves, for today towards eternity in my wings they soar in the last crevice of the Antarctic winds.

Sara Vial, 1992

EPILOGUE

I believe that Captain Warwick M Tompkins was right when he described a Cape Horn transit as the 'ultimate test' for any mariner. He was also right in saying it was 'given to very few to know', much less those choosing to go alone. By 1936, when *Wander Bird* doubled Cape Horn westwards, only one had tried it singlehanded: Alfon Hansen, two years previously in 1934. Since then, not many sailors in small boats have tried because there is neither the need nor the desire to do so. To take to the oceans in a small boat is one thing, but to try going round Cape Horn alone without some comprehensible or necessary rationale is arguably – or to many, inarguably – bordering on lunacy. Outside the commercial imperative of the bygone age of sail, why then *do* sailors pit themselves against so fearsome a challenge? Some may be a bit wild, overtaken by a devil-may-care attitude, but most are perfectly sane, sensible, logical men and women. If you met them, most would seem unremarkable and some quite forgettable. So, what is it within these people that fosters that urge to risk all in a pursuit that has little if any practical application or value?

These questions can be applied equally to mountaineers, polar explorers, anyone placing themselves in dire jeopardy for no apparently useful purpose. It is not enough to suppose the inspiration is a quest for fame or gold – there are easier and frankly better ways to do that. Perhaps it is to live life at the extreme, in the present moment, with no margin for error, on the knife-edge, to breathe that heady elixir of meticulously planned abandon. If so, then why not go down a black run or parachute from 10,000 feet? That would be short, sharp, to the point, and then afterwards they could relax with friends over a beer. Indeed, this is what many prefer. Why is it necessary to have death lurk in the gloaming for long periods? Ask anyone who has taken on a great endeavour, be it on land, by sea or in the air, and they would be hard pushed to come up with a satisfactory answer.

In his book *The Ulysses Factor: The Exploring Instinct in Man*, published in 1970, author JRL Anderson sought the rationale behind the compunction to risk all in the pursuit of some unknown, deriving his title from the mythical character of Homer's *Ulysses*. Personality traits of courage, selfishness, self-discipline, endurance, cunning, unscrupulousness, imagination and self-reliance, a certain social inadequacy or intolerance and dissatisfaction with convention combine to create a thirst to know what lies beyond the predictable horizons of a regular life. He suggested that a genetic trait in all of us – though more highly expressed in some – was necessary for our early survival, an overwhelming instinct to venture forth and seek. Anderson's theory suggests these self-contained Ulysses types, propelled by curiosity, led the way, wandering from the cradle of man's evolution in Africa in search of more or better.

This common if largely vestigial instinct to explore is what allows the many to identify with the deeds of the few, if only on a subliminal, subconscious level. People understand in some unknowing way that particular compunction to set forth into the unknown and discover there something of ourselves.

In 1924, just before his ill-fated attempt on Everest, George Mallory answered the question of *Why?* by simply stating, 'Because it is there.' Some might think it an obtuse response. Others might opt for flippant. Most would probably agree that it just about sums up the Ulysses factor – because it is there, I can't ignore it, I need to go to the top to find out if I can and discover what is there, what I might see, how I'll feel, and when I've done that I can come back down again and be satisfied.

Does this mean that these endurance adventurers, Drake, Burton, Peary, Scott, Amundsen, Shackleton, Amy Johnson, Amelia Earhart, Fiennes and a host of others before, since and yet to come, are all lumpen social misfits, heavy of muscle and light on conversation, loners who can only survive adequately by absenting themselves from normalcy?

The gender and nationality mix, wide age variation, multiplicity of backgrounds sufficient to paint the entire socio-economic spectrum, and differing educations suggest otherwise. Whether these characters camouflaged their adventuring with the pursuit of scientific knowledge or the hunt for treasure, they were all – if Anderson's theory has any validity – intent on expression of the Ulysses factor, whether they knew it or not. If this type of behaviour is the consequence of a genetic throwback, then it no more defines a person than having blue eyes might. They were doing what instinct drove them to do.

For mariners, Cape Horn has come to epitomise that distant horizon where geography and weather combine to produce an environment so frequently savage as to be lethal. It is now 400 years since the discovery of Cape Horn in 1616 by men capable of navigating over vast distances in ships that, if skilfully handled, might stand a chance of surviving the passage. Although the Yaghan people had colonised the Cape Horn area many centuries before then, the discovery of the Cape Horn route linking the Atlantic to the Pacific heralded a new era in global trade. The history of the place since then – the thousands of lives lost and ships destroyed – makes this place the Holy Grail for modern-day mariners imbued with that Ulysses trait that makes them reach beyond the known limits of their own realms of personality, spirit and desire. It is the last horizon beyond which they may yet find that ethereal thing they seek.

APPENDIX:
SINGLEHANDED, NON-RACING
ROUNDINGS OF CAPE HORN

There is no official register of singlehanded sailors who have been round Cape Horn. The International Association of Cape Horners (IACH) keeps a register of Yacht Members who apply for membership. The World Sailing Speed Record Council (WSSRC) maintains a list of records and voyages in exchange for a fee. If sailors do not apply to the IACH or the WSSRC, however, then no record of their voyages or achievements will be kept unless details are published in books or appear in print media. Organisations such as the Vendée Globe Race and the Velux 5 Oceans Race maintain registers of participants in isolation.

The following list of singlehanded sailors who have successfully rounded Cape Horn may, therefore, not be complete. Aside from participants in the Golden Globe Race (included here because participants set off on different dates, but principally because far greater emotion and desire was invested by competitors in being the first to achieve a non-stop circumnavigation than in being the fastest finisher), the list does not include participants from other later races.

Singlehanded, Non-Racing Westward Roundings of Cape Horn

Name	Nationality	Boat	Date
Al Hansen	Norwegian	*Mary-Jane*	1934
Marcel Bardiaux	French	*Les Quatre Vents*	1952
Chay Blyth	British	*British Steel*	1970
Edward Allcard	British	*Sea Wanderer*	1973
Kenichi Horie	Japanese	*Mermaid III*	1974
Eilco Kasemier	Dutch	*Bylgia*	1977
David Scott-Cowper	British	*Ocean Bound*	1982
Jonathan Sanders	Australian	*Parry Endeavour*	1986
Mike Golding	British	*Group 4*	1994
Samantha Brewster	British	*Heath Assured II*	1996
Philippe Monnet	French	*Uunet*	2000
Wilfried Erdmann	German	*Kathena Nui*	2000
Jean-Luc van den Heede	French	*Adrien*	2004
Dee Caffari	British	*Aviva*	2006
Adrian Flanagan	British	*Barrabas*	2006
Minoru Saitō	Japanese	*Shuten-dohji III*	2009

Singlehanded, Non-Racing Eastward Roundings of Cape Horn

Name	Nationality	Boat	Date
Vito Dumas	Argentinian	*Lehg II*	1943
William Nance	Australian	*Cardinal Vertue*	1965
Francis Chichester	British	*Gipsy Moth IV*	1967
Alec Rose	British	*Lively Lady*	1968
Bernard Moitessier	French	*Joshua*	1969
Robin Knox-Johnston	British	*Suhaili*	1969
Nigel Tetley	British	*Victress*	1969
William King	Irish	*Galway Blazer*	1973

Name	Nationality	Boat	Date
Kris Baranowski	Polish	*Polonez*	1973
David Lewis	New Zealand	*Ice Bird*	1973
Hiroshi Aoki	Japanese	*Ahodori*	1973
Ryusuke Ushijima	Japanese	*Cingitsune*	1974
Ambrogio Fogar	Italian	*Surprise*	1974
Alain Colas	French	*Manureva*	1974
Webb Chiles	American	*Egregious*	1975
Loïck Fougeron	French	*Captain Browne II*	1976
Gedaliah Shtirmer	Israeli	*New Penny*	1977
Naomi James	New Zealand	*Express Crusader*	1978
Brigitte Oudry	French	*Gea*	1978
Kees Den Hartoog	Dutch	*Sentign*	1979
David Scott-Cowper	British	*Ocean Bound*	1980
Horst Timreck	German	*Brigitte*	1980
Henryk Jaskula	Polish	*Dar Przemyśla*	1980
Leslie Powles	British	*Solitaire*	1981
Jan Swertz	Belgian	*Peti*	1981
Jonathan Sanders	Australian	*Perie Banou*	1981
Jonathan Sanders	Australian	*Perie Banou*	1982
Pleun van der Lugt	Dutch	*De Zeeuwse Stromen*	1982
Paul Rogers	British	*Spirit of Pentax*	1982
Yves Gélinas	Canadian	*Jean du Sud*	1983
Mark Schrader	American	*Resourceful*	1983
Nikolai Dzhambazov	Bulgarian	*Tangra*	1985
Wilfried Erdmann	German	*Kathena Nui*	1985
Dodge Morgan	American	*American Promise*	1986
Jonathan Sanders	Australian	*Parry Endeavour*	1987
Jonathan Sanders	Australian	*Parry Endeavour*	1988
Philippe Monnet	French	*Kriter*	1987
Doncho Papazov	Bulgarian	*Tivia*	1988

Name	Nationality	Boat	Date
Kay Cottee	Australian	*Blackmore's First Lady*	1988
Hafsteinn Johansson	Icelandic	*Elding*	1991
Istvan Kopar	Hungarian	*Salammbo*	1991
Kyoko Imakiire	Japanese	*Kairen*	1992
William Pinkney	American	*Commitment*	1992
Jan Wit	Dutch	*Bastaert van Campen*	1992
Peter Keig	Irish	*Zeal*	1993
Lisa Clayton	British	*Spirit of Birmingham*	1995
Leslie Powles	British	*Solitaire*	1996
David Dicks	Australian	*Seaflight*	1996
Jan Wit	Dutch	*Bastaert van Campen*	1996
Karen Thorndike	American	*Amelia*	1997
Jesse Martin	Australian	*Lionheart*	1999
Azhar Mansor	Malaysian	*Jalur Gemilang*	1999
Peter Keig	Irish	*Zeal*	1999
Vincent Lauwers	Australian	*Vision Quest*	2000
Tony Mowbray	Australian	*Solo Globe Challenger*	2001
Edwin Arnold	American	*Nomad*	2002
Uwe Röttgering	German	*FanFan*	2003
Anthony Gooch	Canadian	*Taonui*	2004
Francis Joyon	French	*IDEC*	2004
Minoru Saitō	Japanese	*Shuten-dohji II*	2005
Ellen MacArthur	British	*B&Q*	2005
Ken Gourlay	Australian	*Spirit Silver Edition*	2007
Alain Maignan	French	*Sun Rise*	2007
Francis Joyon	French	*IDEC II*	2008
Jessica Watson	Australian	*Ella's Pink Lady*	2010
Dilip Donde	Indian	*Mhadei*	2010
Alessandro Di Benedetto	Italian	*Findomestic*	2010
Abigail Sunderland	American	*Wild Eyes*	2010

Name	Nationality	Boat	Date
Patrick Macklin	British	*Tessa*	2011
Matthew Rutherford	American	*Saint Brendan*	2012
Jeanne Socrates	British	*Nereida*	2013
Christian Liebergreen	Danish	*Jonna*	2013
Abhilash Tomy	Indian	*Mhadei*	2013
Gerry Hughes	British	*Quest III*	2013
Guo Chuan	Chinese	*Quingdao*	2013

ACKNOWLEDGEMENTS

My thanks to the team at Bloomsbury – Janet Murphy for her immediate and unstinting enthusiasm, Liz Multon for her insightful and sensitive editing, Dave Saunders for his detailed illustrations, John Plumer for his instructive maps and Clara Jump for her unfailing efficiency in bringing the whole project to fruition. Most especially, I owe a debt to the sailors and their families who allowed me to tell their stories.

I gratefully acknowledge the authors and publishers of the following copyrighted works from which excerpts have been reproduced:

© Sir Francis Chichester, 1967, *Gipsy Moth Circles the World*, Hodder & Stoughton, London. Reproduced with permission of Curtis Brown Limited, London

© Robin Knox-Johnston, 1969, *A World of My Own*, Cassell, London

© Nigel Tetley, 1970, *Trimaran Solo*, The Nautical Publishing Company, Lymington

© Chay Blyth, 1971, *The Impossible Voyage*, Hodder & Stoughton, London. Reproduced by permission of Hodder and Stoughton Limited

© Dr David Lewis, 1975, *Ice Bird*, William Collins & Sons, London. Excerpts from the edition published by Sheridan House, New York, 2002. By arrangement with the Licensor, The David Lewis Estate, c/o Curtis Brown (Aust) Pty Ltd

© Webb Chiles, 1977, *Storm Passage*, The New York Times Book Company, New York

© Alain Colas, 1978, *Around the World Alone*, Barron's Educational Series Inc, New York. Reproduced with permission of Teura Colas

© Naomi James, 1979, *At One with the Sea*, Hutchinson, London

I also acknowledge the helpfulness of the following titles:

Anderson, JRL, *The Ulysses Factor* (London: Hodder & Stoughton, 1970)

Bardiaux, Marcel, *4 Winds of Adventure* (London: Adlard Coles Limited, 1961)

Barker, James P, *Log of a Limejuicer* (New York: Macmillan, 1936)

Clarke, DH, *An Evolution of Singlehanders* (London: Stanford Maritime, 1976)

Coloane, Francisco, *Cape Horn and Other Stories from the End of the World* (Pittsburg: The Latin American Literary Review Press, 1990)

Dumas, Vito, *Alone through the Roaring Forties* (London: Adlard Coles Limited, 1960)

Hough, Richard, *The Blind Horn's Hate* (London: Hutchinson, 1971)

Knox-Johnston, Robin, *Cape Horn – A Maritime History* (London: Hodder & Stoughton, 1994)

Lansing, Alfred, *Endurance* (London: Wiedenfeld & Nicolson, 2000)

Murphy, Dallas, *Rounding the Horn* (New York: Basic Books, 2004)

Nichols, Peter, *A Voyage for Madmen* (London: Profile Books, 2001)

Riesenberg, Felix, *Cape Horn* (London: Robert Hale Limited, 1941)

Rose, Alec, *My Lively Lady* (Lymington: The Nautical Publishing Company, 1968)

Smeeton, Miles, *Once is Enough* (London: Hart-Davis, 1959)

Tompkins, Warren M, *Fifty South to Fifty South* (Woodbridge: Ox Bow Press, 1938)

Vairo, Carlos, *Shipwrecks in Cape Horn* (Ushuaia: Zagier & Urruty Publications, 2000)

Villiers, Alan, *The War with Cape Horn* (London: Hodder & Stoughton, 1971)

PICTURE CREDITS

pvii © Allan White, Getty Images; p7 and p8 © Louise Flanagan; p32 © PPL; p42 © Keystone-France, Getty Images; p63 © Keystone/Stringer, Getty Images; p71 © Chichester Archive/PPL; p78 © Sunday Times/Chichester Archive/PPL; p83 © Keystone/Stringer, Getty Images; p93 © Bettmann, Getty Images; p95 © Fine Art, Getty Images; p96 © Rob Tuytel, WFM; p104 © Bill Rowntree/PPL; p112 © McCarthy/Stringer, Getty Images; p123 © Central Press, Stringer, Getty Images; p144 © Eileen Ramsay, PPL; p156 © Francis Apesteguy, Getty Images; p171 from State Library of Victoria, via Wikicommons; p173 © Webb Chiles; p183 © Evening Standard, Stringer, Getty Images; p201 © Les Powles; p213 © Bob Ross, PPL; p229 © AFP, Stringer, Getty Images; p240 © Nigel Bennetts/PPL; p251 © AFP, Stringer, Getty Images; p272 © Brendon Thorne, Stringer, Getty Images; p283 © Jonathan Irish, Getty Images

Around Cape Horn

Around Cape Horn we've got to go,
To me way, hay, o-hio!
Around Cape Horn to Calleao
A long time ago!

Round Cape Horn where the stiff winds blow,
To me way, hay, o-hio!
Round Cape Horn where there's sleet and snow.
A long time ago!

I wish to God I'd never been born
To me way, hay, o-hio!
To drag my carcass around Cape Horn.
A long time ago!